OUR LIFE IN THE SWISS HIGHLANDS

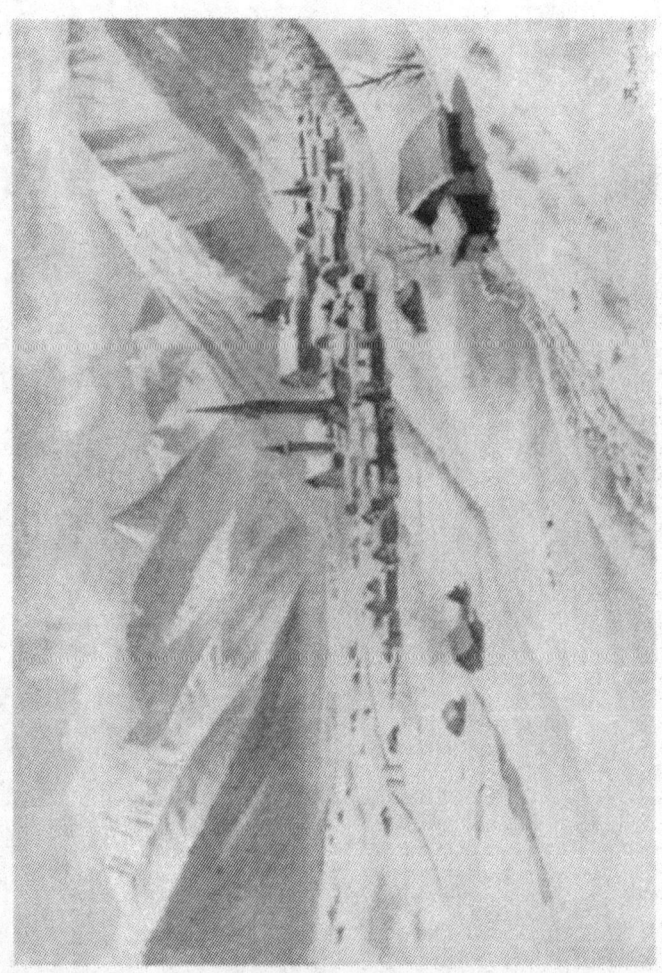

DAVOS IN WINTER.

OUR LIFE IN
THE SWISS HIGHLANDS

JOHN ADDINGTON SYMONDS
AND HIS DAUGHTER MARGARET

Fredonia Books
Amsterdam, The Netherlands

Our Life in the Swiss Highlands

by
John Addington Symonds
Margaret Symonds

ISBN: 1-58963-786-0

Reprinted from the 1907 edition

Fredonia Books
Amsterdam, The Netherlands
http://www.fredoniabooks.com

In order to make original editions of historical works
available to scholars at an economical price, this
facsimile of the original edition of 1907 is
reproduced from the best available copy and has
been digitally enhanced to improve legibility, but the
text remains unaltered to retain historical
authenticity.

To Mother

PREFACE TO SECOND EDITION

It would be difficult to imagine a change more complete than that which has come over the little Alpine village of Davos since the end of the nineteenth century. Davos was the centre of a very old civilisation, and one of the important political meeting-grounds of the Grey League from the thirteenth, and on into the middle of the seventeenth, century. But in spite of her prominent position, it seems that her inhabitants were contented with a very simple mode of life. However fine their costumes may have been at foreign Courts, it is certain that they did not wear their pomps upon their sleeve at home as far as architecture was concerned, and very little in the shape of building was left at Davos to mark the period of historic prosperity at the period when the first visitors began to creep up into the valley, save the fine old parish church, the Rathaus, and one or two solid stone houses and big barns.

From that first group of ancient buildings an immense heterogeneous mass of stone and mortar has arisen like mushrooms in the night. The old church is there, but almost smothered. A massive Catholic church stands on the hill. Vast hotels, fine Kursaals, great barrack-like lodging-houses, restaurants, rinks, toboggan-runs and roads—all these things have spread themselves in every direction from the original centre. The river, which

Preface to Second Edition

formerly wound in and out of meadows, has been canalised, and huge sanatoriums stand up from the pine-forests on the mountain-side above.*

This is no place in which to form vague estimates of results in the whole great fabric which has gradually been built up out of what at first was a mere experiment—namely, the attempt to cure a certain form of human ill by carrying the patient out of the miasmas of the plains and the fog of cities into the stronger sunlight and the rarefied air of mountains. An account of the system which effected the first cures, and of the men who made them, and the conditions under which the patients lived, is given by my father in the first chapter of this book. It will be enough to say here that, thanks to the knowledge learned by treatment in air as nearly perfect as that of the High Alps, doctors and patients are now able to carry their practice into what would formerly have been considered quite unsuitable surroundings. The age of heavy carpets, closed windows, respirators, and general warding-off of air is passed. Fresh and wild winds rush in at the sick man's window, the sunlight scorches his skin. But the young generation can barely realise what a novelty all this is, and Davos, St. Moritz, and one or two other places, have been, as it were, the schoolroom of what is now an accepted doctrine in the life of many nations.

After a long struggle with ill-health and excessive brainwork in England, my father finally had a severe breakdown in the summer of 1877, and it was decreed that he

* Recent statistics show that the present permanent population of Davos is about 5,000, and in the height of the season—namely, in December and January—about 4,000 visitors are added to this. Some 19,000 visitors pass annually through Davos. There are about twenty large hotels and twenty smaller pensions in Davos and Davos Dorf, thirteen sanatoriums, and many flats and villas.

THE DAVOS VALLEY AND HAY-MAKING IN THE SUMMER OF 1877

From a pencil sketch by John Addington Symonds

Preface to Second Edition

must make experiment of some long cure abroad. A sea voyage was recommended, but presented many disadvantages, and a winter in Egypt was at last decided upon, and all the elaborate paraphernalia required for this purpose were hastily gathered together. Pith helmet-hats, long green veils, a Union Jack to hoist upon our dahabieh, books of Egyptian birds—how well do I remember all these unfamiliar and, to a child, delightful objects ! But it was too early in the year to think of the Nile—some half-way house had to be chosen, and it was a mere chance of circumstance which made this stage the Valley of Davos. It happened that my father's sister, Mrs. T. H. Green, and her husband were spending some weeks there. Their account of the place was pleasant, and a rapid start for it was made. How well do I remember the journey, and how my father, weary and ill as he was, roused my sister and me as we crossed the plains at dawn to look out on our first view of the Alps. I had drawn many imaginary ranges, and I remember that the reality depressed me, and, being a very long way off, clashed with the mighty visions which had arisen round our carved wooden bears and Mürren photographs in the nurseries at Clifton !

A variety of accidents delayed us on our journey. Our large party became divided, and it must have been several days later that my cousin, Mrs. Robert Otter, and I arrived late one night at Davos. In those days the journey from Landquart was all done by road. The diligence, and its stream of extra carriages, stopped to deposit the passengers at their various destinations, and I remember the sort of confusion of postilions' whips, barking dogs, lanterns, and unknown tongues into which I tumbled in the dark, and whence I was rescued and bundled into bed in the peasant's cottage where we had taken rooms. My first memory of the Davos Valley is a

Preface to Second Edition

vivid one. I woke to find myself in a little low room entirely panelled with wood. A great pink-and-white feather-bed encumbered me, but the window was just at my head, and I could peep straight out at the valley. The sun had risen. Everything looked green and rather flat. In the centre of the valley was a big white church, and the river took wide curves through the meadows. My aunt, Mrs. T. H. Green, and her husband were coming down the path below our window, accompanied by a huge St. Bernard dog, and she carried in her hands a bunch of meadow-pinks, which I have always since connected with that vision.

We never went up the Nile, and some four years later the Union Jack which was to have floated from our Nile boat streamed from the flagstaff of the delightful new house which my parents built in the Swiss valley when they found that my father could no longer hope for a permanent return to England.

Davos society in the winter of 1877 consisted chiefly of Germans and other foreign people; but there was a small circle of English people collected in the Hôtel Belvedere (this hotel, now an immense building with accommodation for some two hundred people, was then a small four-storied house with a pent-roof). There were only three or four other hotels, all in miniature. Our sports were of a sober sort, and we were quite contented to toboggan on the slight incline which led from the hotel to the post-road. Ice-runs and American toboggans were objects undreamed of. There was, of course, no railway, and shops were of the most primitive order. Society was small, and we soon became acquainted with its leading figures. There was a fascinating young Polish Prince Czartoriski, who inhabited a pension in the village. He used to call upon my mother

in the most correct French clothes, and to kiss her hand
before he romped with her children. Late one snowy
night he rang us all up from sleep. His father was dying
in Poland, and he had come to say good-bye in a beautiful
astrachan coat and a flood of tears ; then he drove out
into the darkness, and we never saw him again. There
was a Frenchman, who studied art with an Abbé. The
Abbé taught us to skate, and I can remember holding
on to his flying skirts as he shot rapidly over the surface
of the village mill-pool which served us for rink in those
prehistoric times. On Christmas Eve our hotel gave a
party, to which the " society " flocked. It was a fancy-
dress dance, and a German gentleman appeared as a
Highland chief. He wore a kilt which was made of a
transparent rose-coloured tarlatan. At about eleven the
doctor, who was then a perfect Pope in the place, arrived
and sent every one off to their beds.

We went into our new house in the summer of 1881.
Then began a wonderful and delightful life, full of interests, and work, and happiness. Looking at the lives
of the ordinary, and even of the most happily circum-
stanced young English families, I invariably feel that
my own childhood compares with theirs extremely
favourably. We had freedom, but a good deal of hard
mental work and stimulus besides. The mountains, with
all their wonders, stood outside our doors ; within was a
world of books, and study, and good friends. On the
rare occasions when I was sent to pay a round of English
visits in what my father called the " hedgerow scheme of
existence," I used to feel in some ways smothered. In
answer to some letters of mine describing this sensation,
my father writes : ". . . After all, I quite feel with you
that I want the friendship stern and wild, yet close and
tranquillising, of mountains. Of course, they coop one

up more than hedges and copses, but they do not coop the spirit up. There is no fatness in them."

Of the thousands of people who now annually winter at Davos, and of the large number of permanent residents, it is probable that few realise, even dimly, the actual life of the valley to which they are driven by the necessity of illness. Yet the stern enduring peasant life goes on with its toils, its pleasures, and its pains. It is totally uninfluenced—except, perhaps, in some merely mercenary manner, or through an occasional tobogganing competition—by the fluctuating crowd of foreigners and their luxurious ways. To my father it would have been impossible to live in any place without possessing himself of every side of its life. It was this power of grasping a complete situation which made life so interesting to him and to those who lived with him. That a man so physically frail, bred in cities, cultivated with all the accumulated culture of the ages, should be able to throw himself heart and soul, not only into the mixed life of a foreign colony, but also into that far more impenetrable one of an old and reticent mountain race, is, indeed, extraordinary. He did this, however, with the whole of his heart, and at the same time he continued to work as few men can or do work even under the most favourable conditions. "The only way out," he writes to me in one letter—"the only way out . . . is to work!" His was hard physical and mental labour, no dream of a dreamer. "If ever you come to the real pains of authorship," he says in another letter—"to printing and publishing what you have written in your chamber, I wish you more joy of it than ever I have got. It is a dreadful toil. Masses of proofs and manuscripts. Perpetual correction of details, alterations of plan. . . . The technical work wears down the free birth of your spirit to a dead dumb level, and yet you have always to keep spurring yourself on to final effort of pure style and sharp delineation. . . . I have bored holes in my lungs in old days by the process, and bored so many that I was at last sent to strand here. . . ."

Yet never for one instant would my father have been without his work, for to him it was the very key of his life. The actual wages for labour of this sort are small indeed, but they meant a great deal to my father, for he always regarded these earnings as his " pin money." And the pin money was invariably spent, not upon himself, but upon objects which perhaps are finer and more enduring than ordinary " charities "—namely, on the intelligent help given to individuals of his acquaintance, whose private needs he, with judgment and with patience, learned to know. What fine new cart-horses were purchased out of the proceeds of some written life of a man of letters, or Italian despot ! What barges and gondolas, what barns and bits of family furniture redeemed from pawn, by the written results of long research in archives ! His Graubünden and Italian peasant friends could tell curious, and to them impressive, tales of the good which thus came to them through their intercourse with my father. Of the source of this bounty they had only a dim, probably a half - contemptuous inkling ; for the peasant has little of the reverence for the scholar's work, such as the scholar himself feels for the healthy work of the fields.

Once, I remember how a clever Englishman was left alone in my father's study with a certain young peasant. They smoked in silence. At length the peasant spoke. He waved his pipe round the book-cases with which the room was lined, and which contained the works of the English dramatists and poets, and of many Italian,

Preface to Second Edition

French, and German poets and historians. " Yes, yes," he volunteered, "Herr Symonds has not only read all these books, but has written the greater part of them !"

* * * * *

We look through the mists of the Past. We try to push aside the curtain, not of forgetfulness, but of a certain unavoidable sadness which falls about our memory with the advance of time. My father had suffered grievously throughout his life. Yet to his children his presence spelt simply Joy; and this I fancy was in some part owing to the renewed buoyancy which the life of the Alps brought to him, and greatly also to his contact with the hard-working, healthy race of men bred up in it. Summoning some memory of his living presence, I see him best on a sunny afternoon running headlong down an Alpine meadow, his Venetian boat-dog barking behind him, and jumping the path or the stream at the bottom, then kneeling upon the ground to gather a certain scented vetch which had a peculiar attraction for him. I see him in the grey homespun made by his peasant friends, the big straw hat with the Magdalen lilies covering his eyes till he looked up to smile at his children. . . . Our life in the Swiss Highlands, with whatever wreckage of the past it had been bought, was certainly one of health and happiness to my father and to all who shared it with him.

MARGARET VAUGHAN.

GIGGLESWICK SCHOOL,
YORKSHIRE,
July 26, 1907.

xvi

PREFACE TO FIRST EDITION

THE Essays which compose this volume were written partly by myself and partly by my daughter Margaret. Mine are signed " J. A. S.," hers " M. S."

Some of them have not been printed. Others are republished from the *Fortnightly Review*, the *Cornhill Magazine*, the *Pall Mall Gazette*, and the *St. Moritz Post*.

I ought to add that two of the series were included in a former book of mine, called *Italian Byways*, which appeared in 1883. But they are so obviously appropriate to this volume that I felt myself justified in not omitting them from the collection.

JOHN ADDINGTON SYMONDS.

AM HOF, DAVOS-PLATZ.

CONTENTS

Contents

LIST OF ILLUSTRATIONS IN COLOUR

BY J. HARDWICKE LEWIS

List of Illustrations in Colour

JOHN ADDINGTON SYMONDS

OUR LIFE IN THE SWISS HIGHLANDS

DAVOS IN WINTER (1878)

It has long been acknowledged that high Alpine air in summer is beneficial to people suffering from lung troubles, but only of late years, and in one locality, has the experiment of a winter residence at a considerable elevation above the sea been made. The general results of that experiment are so satisfactory that the conditions of life in winter at Davos, and the advantages it offers to invalids, ought to be fairly set before the English public. My own experience of eight months spent at Davos, between August, 1877, and April, 1878, enables me to speak with some confidence ; while a long previous familiarity with the health-stations of the Riviera—Cannes, Bordighera, Nice, Mentone, and San Remo—furnishes a standard of comparison between two methods of cure at first sight radically opposite.

Accustomed as we are to think that warmth is essential to the satisfactory treatment of pulmonary complaints, it requires no little courage to face the severity of winter in an Alpine valley, where the snow lies for seven months, and where the thermometer frequently falls to 10° or 15° Fahrenheit below Zero. Nor is it easy, by any stretch of the imagination, to realise the fact that, in spite of

A

Our Life in the Swiss Highlands

this intense cold, the most sensitive invalids can drive in open sledges with impunity, expose themselves without risk to falling snow through hours of exercise, or sit upon their bedroom balconies, basking in a hot sun, with the world all white around them, and a spiky row of icicles above their heads. Yet such is a state of things which a few months spent in Davos renders quite familiar ; and perhaps the best way of making it intelligible is to describe diffusely, without any scientific pretence or display of theory, what sort of place Davos is, and what manner of life sick people may lead there.

Davos is the name given to a district, the principal village of which is Davos-am-Platz, situated at an elevation of 5,200 feet above the sea. It is an open and tolerably broad valley, lying almost exactly south and north, and so placed as, roughly speaking, to be parallel with the Upper Engadine, on the one side, and the Rheinthal, between Chur and Landquart, on the other. The mountains which enclose it are of no commanding altitude ; only one insignificant glacier can be seen from any point in the valley : but the position of great rocky masses both to south and north is such that the most disagreeable winds, whether the keen north wind or the relaxing south-wester, known by the dreaded name of *föhn*, are fairly excluded. Comparative stillness is, indeed, a great merit of Davos ; the best nights and days of winter present a cloudless sky, clear frost, and absolutely unstirred atmosphere. At the same time it would be ridiculous to say that there is no wind in this happy valley. March there, as elsewhere, is apt to be disturbed and stormy ; and during the summer months the valley-wind, which rises regularly every morning and blows for several hours, will cause discomfort to chilly people who have not learned how to avoid it by taking refuge in the pine-

2

woods or frequenting sheltered promenades. All travellers in Switzerland are well aware that where there is a broad valley lying north and south they will meet with a *thalwind*. At Davos it is not nearly so strong as in the Upper Engadine or the Rhonthal ; nor is it at all dreaded for their patients by the physicians. Colds, strange to say, are rarely caught at Davos, and, if caught, are easily got rid of under prudent observance of ordinary rules. For my own part, I can say with certainty that no wind there ever plagued me or imperilled my recovery so much as a mistral at San Remo or a sirocco at Palermo.

Davos was settled in the middle of the thirteenth century by vassals of the Empire, who held it till the people freed themselves in the fifteenth century, and, together with the population of the neighbouring valleys, formed the independent state of the Graubünden. The mountaineers are a hardy, sober, frugal race of peasants, owning their own land, and sending the superfluous members of each family, for whom no work can be found at home, forth into the world. In old days the Davosers preferred military service. I have before me the pedigree of one family, called Buol, who now own a large hotel at Davos. I find from it that between the years 1400 and 1800, thirty-eight of its members held various offices in the French, Austrian, Venetian, Dutch, Milanese, Spanish, English, and Neapolitan armies, varying from the rank of Field-Marshal down to that of private soldier. Nearly as many served their country as governors of districts, captains, generals, and ambassadors. A curious history might be written of this family's vicissitudes, and a strange list of its honours might be drawn up ; for it claims one earldom of the Empire, and two German baronies, as well as a French title of nobility, dating from the reign of Henry IV. Nor is this a solitary instance. Several

Our Life in the Swiss Highlands

Grisons families have old historic names ; and, were they not republican, would bear titles as ancient as any but a select few of the English peerage. Many of these people are, however, simple peasants now, and, instead of seeking glory in foreign service, they content themselves with trades and commerce. Until the year 1865 Davos remained in the hands of its own people, who lived substantially and soberly, each family in its great farmhouse of stone or fir-wood, at a discreet distance from their neighbours. Platz was the capital of the district, where the church with its tall sharp spire stands, where the public business of the Landschaft is transacted in the ancient Rathhaus, and where in those old days there was but one primitive little inn. In that year a German physician of repute and experience, Dr. Unger, determined to try whether high Alpine air was really a cure for serious lung disease. The district physician of that epoch, Dr. Spengler, who is now one of the most popular *Kur-aerzte* of Davos, had previously observed, first, that phthisis was unknown among the inhabitants of the valley ; and secondly, that those Davosers who had contracted pulmonary complaints in foreign countries made rapid and easy cures on their return. He published the results of his observations in the *Deutsche Klinik* for 1862, and the reading of his paper impelled Dr. Unger to test the truth of his opinion by personal experience. Fortunately for the future of Davos, Dr. Unger was himself far gone in consumption, and he was accompanied by a young friend in the same plight. In spite of having to rough it more than invalids find safe or pleasant, both Dr. Unger and his friend, Herr Hugo Richter, derived so much benefit from their first visit that they persevered and ultimately recovered their health. The result was that Dr. Unger and his fellow-workers have transformed Davos during the last thirteen years from a mere mountain village into a health-station, frequented by nearly one thousand invalids, who pass the winter with every comfort of good accommodation, excellent food, and not a few amusements. The large majority of these visitors are Germans; but Poles, Belgians, Russians, Danes, and a good many English and Americans, may now be found in the colony. It speaks volumes for the place, and for the genuine nature of the cures effected there, that it has grown up gradually in this short space of time, without the attraction of mineral waters or fascinating specialities of treatment; without the intervention of speculative capitalists, intent on floating a new watering-place; without the charms of a luxurious climate, and without the patronage of royal or illustrious names. Until quite recently it has been known to few but middle-class Germans; and, if its fame is now spreading more widely, every step it makes is made through its own merits. There is absolutely nothing in the place—no social advantages, no distinguished beauty of scenery, no delightful southern air—nothing but the fact that if you go there ill, it very often happens that you come away better, after a sufficient time spent in the cure process—to recommend a residence in the austere monotony of this frost-bound, snow-clad valley.

The method of cure is very simple. After a minute personal examination of the ordinary kind, your physician tells you to give up medicines, and to sit warmly clothed in the sun as long as it is shining, to eat as much as possible, to drink a fair quantity of Valtelline wine, and not to take any exercise. He comes at first to see you every day, and soon forms a more definite opinion of your capacity and constitution. Then, little by little, he allows you to walk; at first upon the level, next up-hill, until the daily walks begin to occupy from four to five

Our Life in the Swiss Highlands

hours. The one thing relied upon is air. To inhale the maximum quantity of the pure mountain air, and to imbibe the maximum quantity of the keen mountain sunlight, is the *sine quâ non*. Everything else—milk-drinking, douches, baths, friction, counter-irritant applications, and so forth—is subsidiary. Medicine is very rarely used : and yet the physicians are not pedantic in their dislike of drugs. They only find by long experience that they can get on better without medicine. Therefore they do not use it except in cases where their observation shows that it is needed. And certainly they are justified by the result. The worst symptoms of pulmonary sickness—fever, restless nights, cough, blood-spitting, and expectoration—gradually subside by merely living and breathing. The appetite returns, and the power of taking exercise is wonderfully increased. When I came to Davos, for example, at the beginning of last August, I could not climb two pairs of stairs without the greatest discomfort. At the end of September I was able to walk 1,000 feet uphill without pain and without fear of hæmorrhage. This progress was maintained throughout the winter ; and when I left Davos in April the physician could confirm my own sensation that the lung, which had been seriously injured, was comparatively sound again, and that its wound had been healed. Of course, I do not mean that the impossible had been achieved, or, in other words, that what had ceased to be organic had been recomposed for me, but that the disease had been arrested by a natural process of contraction. For such personal details I hope I may receive indulgence. It is only by translating general into particular statements that a layman can express himself in these matters to his brother-laymen.

The fact, however theorised, that colds are rarely

Davos in Winter

caught in this keen Alpine climate, and that recurrent fever tends to disappear, enables the patient to inhale a far greater amount of air than is possible under almost any other conditions, and renders him much freer in the indulgence of his appetite. He need not be afraid of eating and drinking what he chooses, while the bracing of his system makes him very ready indeed to eat. The result is that he speedily increases in weight; and if he has the strength to take exercise, his whole body loses the atony of wasting sickness. Davos does indeed seem to offer the advantages of almost unlimited air and general invigoration which we seek in a long sea-voyage or a journey up the Nile, without the confinement of the former or the many drawbacks which the latter presents to one who is seriously ill. It has, besides, its own quality of bracing dryness and the stimulus that only comes from rarified cold air. Those who are enthusiastic for this new Alpine method assert that it alone offers a radical cure. Sick folk, they say, may have their lives prolonged, their sufferings mitigated, on the Riviera; they may live with happiness in Madeira, or may enjoy existence above the first Cataract; but they can only return from the brink of the grave to an active home-life after passing through the summers and winters of the high Alps. Whether this proud claim be really justified must be left to experts and prolonged experience to decide. To the same tribunal must be referred the question whether, if the case be established, the result is obtained by checking and obliterating the germs of a disease that tends to reproduce itself in the affected organ; or by fortifying the constitution and rendering it less liable to the attacks of cold; or by the diminished pressure of the atmosphere on debilitated organs of respiration; or by the perfect purity of air that travels over boundless fields of snow,

Our Life in the Swiss Highlands

untainted by exhalations, charged neither with dust nor gases, nor yet with Professor Tyndall's redoubtable bacteria ; or else by the tension of the nervous system that reanimates and rallies the last sparks of life in an exhausted organism. I am myself inclined to believe that somewhat too much is claimed for Davos by its devotees, and that instances of quite as complete a cure can also be adduced by rival methods—by the long sea-voyage, the Dahabeeyah, and the residence in tropic or subtropic climates. But this at least seems proved, that a large percentage of almost hopeless cases attain rapidly and without relapse at Davos to the condition of ordinary health, and that this desirable result is effected at a very small pecuniary outlay, with no collateral risk, and with no sacrifice of the common conveniences of civilised life. Not only the cases recorded in technical treatises, but the testimony of many persons with whom I have conversed upon the details of their cure, together with my own experience, based upon a comparison of Davos with Italy and the Riviera, convince me that it is the soundest, surest, and most radical system as yet discovered.

It is a great injury to any new system to describe it in too roseate colours, or to withhold the drawbacks which it shares with all things that are merely ours and mortal. No candid advocate can conceal the fact that there are serious deductions to be made from the great advantages offered by Davos. First and foremost stands the fact that life in a confined Alpine valley during winter is monotonous. It is true that the post comes regularly every day, and that the Swiss post for letters, books, and parcels is so admirably managed that almost anything a man desires can be had within forty-eight hours from London. It is true that the Alps, in their winter robe of

Davos in Winter

snow, offer a spectacle which for novelty and splendour is not surpassed by anything the fancy can imagine. It is true that sledging is an excellent amusement, and that a fair amount of skating can be reckoned on. It is also true that the climate enables weak people to enjoy all opportunities of rational amusement without stint or hindrance. But, in spite of this, life is monotonous. The mechanic pacings to and fro, which are a condition of the cure, become irksome ; and the discontented invalid is apt to sigh for the blue Mediterranean and the skies he remembers on a sunny Riviera shore. Then it cannot be denied that a great deal of snow falls in the winter. The peasants concur in telling me that it is rare to have four fine weeks together, and my own experience of one winter, not exceptionally bad, leads me to expect two snowy days to three fine ones. Snowfall is, however, no interruption to exercise, and I never found that my health suffered from bad weather. On the contrary, I had the exhilarating consciousness that I could bear it, harden myself against it, and advance steadily under conditions which in England would have been hopeless. Another drawback to the system is the stern and strict rule of health which the invalid must observe if he wishes to secure its advantages. He must be content to rise early in order to enjoy the first gleams of sunshine, and to retire to bed early in order to get the prescribed quantity of sleep. He must not shirk his daily exercise upon the same frost-hardened roads, varied by nothing better than sledge exercise in favourable weather, or by the Canadian amusement of " tobogganing." Many who have not moral energy enough to live the ascetic life for several months together, neutralise the good of the climate by lounging in cafés and billiard-rooms, by smoking and drinking, by sitting up late at night, and by

9

trading on the stimulus of the air to pass a lazy, good-for-nothing existence, which leaves them where it found them. Still, it might be argued that, in this respect at any rate, Davos does not differ from other health-stations. It is well known that people who spend the winter at Cannes or Mentone often disobey the directions of their doctors, and suffer in consequence ; while Davos offers less enticements to imprudent living than places where nature and society are more alluring. Another disadvantage, shared in common with the Riviera, is the problem, where to pass the spring ? It is pretty generally conceded by the doctors that to stay on in Davos after the second week in April is unadvisable. The great mass of winter snow is then melting, the roads are almost impassable by walkers, and the sun has acquired great power. Chills, almost unknown in the winter or the summer, may now be taken, and the irksomeness of the protracted residence in one place is beginning to tell on nerves and spirits. Therefore the colony breaks up. Some go to German baths, some to Montreux on the Lake of Geneva, some to the Italian lakes. But wherever the invalids may go, they feel the transition from the bracing mountain air to a lower climate very trying. Strange to say, they now suffer cold for the first time for many months. They have borne 42° of frost with only an increased sense of exhilaration during February and March ; they have driven in open sledges over the Splügen with only a delightful consciousness of freedom and security ; they have been half buried in avalanches and snowstorms on the Fluela and Maloja : but they settle at Bellagio, and shiver in a temperature of 60°. Accustomed to the most perfect dryness, they resent the tepid moisture of the plains. Having been indulged all through the winter with double windows and warm rooms, they hate the draughts and

Davos in Winter

stagnant chilliness of an Italian residence. Nothing can
make up to them for the loss of the subtle, all-pervasive
stimulus to which they are habituated. After a while,
indeed, the disagreeable sensation passes away, and they
recognise that they are only returning with an immensely
increased vital force to the ordinary conditions of their
old existence. But it requires some self-restraint and
much observance of hygienic rules to effect the transition
without injury. I think they would do well to use sub-
Alpine situations, like Glion, on the Lake of Geneva, or
Monte Generoso, above Como, as intermediate stations
between the Grisons and the plains of Europe. Mere dry
cold they need not dread. Davos has surrounded them
with triple brass to brave it. But they have to fear
dampness, heat, and all those elements which go to make
up what is called a relaxing climate. After all, no one
who has once benefited by a Davos winter would shrink
from another season there because of this slight drawback,
when his own sensations and the verdict of his medical
adviser assure him that he is far more capable of bearing
adverse influences than he was six months ago.

So much of the cure at Davos depends on exercise that
it is wise for those who are very weak to seek it tolerably
early in the autumn, not later than the middle of August
perhaps, in order that they may acclimatise themselves
while the season is yet warm, and get upon their legs before
the snow has fallen. The first snow generally comes
in the middle of November; and if an invalid arrives at
that time, he may be debarred from the benefit of the
winter by not being able to leave his room. That some
occupation is desirable during the winter months need
hardly be stated. Those only suffer from the monotony
of the place to any extent who are absolutely without
resources in themselves; but anyone who is able to amuse

11

himself with reading will find to his delight that he can study with increased facility, all his faculties, both mental and physical, being quickened ; and his only regret will be that so little time is left after the prescribed hours of exercise and rest have been observed.

There are many excellent hotels at Davos, all of which have grown up under the inspection of the medical authorities, and are therefore above the average in sanitary arrangements. All fear of typhoid or malarious fevers, those too real bugbears of many southern watering-places, may at present, at least, be dismissed from the mind at Davos. The water supplied is first-rate in quality, and the food is both abundant and well-served. The houses are solidly built of stone, with double windows for the winter months. All are warmed throughout, but not on the same principle. Some of the hotels have a system of steam-heating which may, I think, be fairly criticised. Stoves of brick and china are used in the other houses ; and these work so admirably that one never suffers from closeness or overheating. Before I tried it, I confess that I dreaded a winter at Davos on account of these stoves and double windows, which I knew were necessary in a climate of such rigour. But I never suffered the least inconvenience from them. It may here be incidentally remarked that in ordinary weather one lighting of the stove a day suffices. A temperature of 56° in a sitting-room, and of 45° in a bedroom, is quite agreeable to an invalid who feels chilly in England with his room below 65° by day and 60° by night. This I know to be the fact ; for I am at present shivering on Monte Generoso, with my thermometer at 62°, to an extent I never knew at Davos-Platz. There was not a single day in the whole winter on which I was debarred from taking a moderate amount of exercise, and on a large majority of

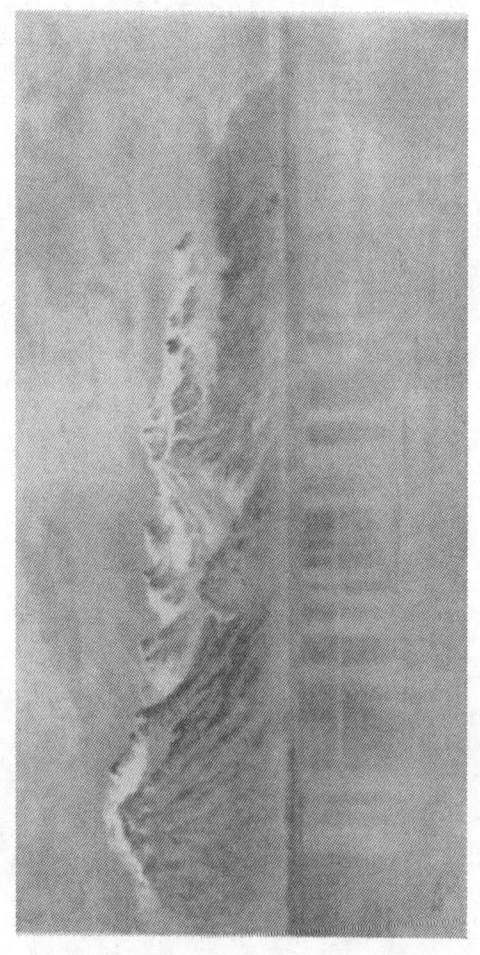

THE VIEW FROM GLION—THE SAVOY
ALPS AND LAKE OF GENEVA.

Davos in Winter

days I spent from 9 a.m. to 5 p.m. in the open air, partly walking and partly sitting when I was not driving, often adding a walk at night before bedtime. At sunset there is no appreciable chill, though it is then advisable to supplement the loss of sun-heat by exercise. That delicate people should sit in the middle of the snow for hours together, under conditions of temperature described above, and that the snow itself should not rapidly begin to melt around them, may seem incredible ; but such is the ordinary practice at Davos, and neither the extreme of solar heat nor the intensity of frost presents the slightest inconvenience.

The gradual approach of winter is very lovely at Davos. The valley itself is not beautiful, as Alpine valleys go, though it has scenery both picturesque and grand within easy reach. But when summer is passing into autumn, even the bare slopes of the least romantic glen are glorified. Golden lights and crimson are cast over the grey-green world by the fading of innumerable plants. Then the larches begin to put on sallow tints that deepen into orange, burning against the solid blue sky like amber. The frosts are severe at night, and the meadow grass turns dry and wan. The last lilac crocuses die upon the fields. Icicles, hanging from water-course or mill-wheel, glitter in the noonday sunlight. The wind blows keenly from the north, and now the snow begins to fall and thaw, and freeze, and fall and thaw again. The seasons are confused ; wonderful days of flawless purity are intermingled with storm and gloom. At last the time comes when a great snowfall has to be expected. There is hard frost in the early morning, and at nine o'clock the thermometer stands at 2°. The sky is clear, but it clouds rapidly with films of cirrus and of stratus in the south and west. Soon it is covered over with grey vapour in a level sheet,

13

Our Life in the Swiss Highlands

all the hill-tops standing hard against the steely heavens.
The cold wind from the west freezes the moustache to
one's pipe-stem. By noon the air is thick with a congealed mist; the temperature meanwhile has risen, and
a little snow falls at intervals. The valleys are filled with
a curious opaque blue, from which the peaks rise, phan-
tom-like and pallid, into the grey air, scarcely distinguishable from their background. The pine-forests on
the mountain-side are of darkest indigo. There is an
indescribable stillness and a sense of incubation. The
wind has fallen. Later on, the snowflakes flutter silently
and sparely through the lifeless air. The most distant
landscape is quite blotted out. After sunset the clouds
have settled down upon the hills, and the snow comes in
thick, impenetrable fleeces. At night our hair crackles
and sparkles when we brush it. Next morning there is
a foot and a half of finely-powdered snow, and still the
snow is falling. Strangely loom the châlets through the
semi-solid whiteness. Yet the air is now dry and singularly soothing. The pines are heavy with their wadded
coverings; now and again one shakes himself in silence,
and his burden falls in a white cloud, to leave a black-
green patch upon the hillside, whitening again as the imperturbable fall continues. The stakes by the roadside
are almost buried. No sound is audible. Nothing is
seen but the snow-plough, a long raft of planks with a
heavy stone at its stern and a sharp prow, drawn by four
strong horses and driven by a young man erect upon the
stem. So we live through two days and nights, and on the
third a north wind blows. The snow-clouds break and
hang upon the hills in scattered fleeces, glimpses of blue
sky shine through, and sunlight glints along the heavy
masses. The blues of the shadows are everywhere
intense. As the clouds disperse, they form in moulded

14

Davos in Winter

domes, tawny like sun-burned marble in the distant south lands. Every châlet is a miracle of fantastic curves, built by the heavy hanging snow. Snow lies mounded on the roads and fields, writhed into loveliest wreaths, or outspread in the softest undulations. All the irregularities of the hills are softened into swelling billows like the mouldings of Titanic statuary. It happened once or twice last winter that such a clearing after snowfall took place at full moon. Then the moon rose in a swirl of fleecy vapour—clouds above, beneath, and all around. The sky was blue as steel, and infinitely deep with mist-entangled stars. The horn above which she first appeared stood carved of solid black, and through the valley's length from end to end yawned chasms and clefts of liquid darkness. As the moon rose, the clouds were conquered and massed into rolling waves upon the ridges of the hills. The spaces of open sky grew still more blue. At last the silver light comes flooding over all, and here and there the fresh snow glistens on the crags. There 's movement, palpitation, life of light through earth and sky. To walk out on such a night, when the perturbation of storm is over and the heavens are free, is one of the greatest pleasures offered by this winter life. It is so light that you can read the smallest print with ease. The upper sky looks quite black, shading by violet and sapphire into turquoise upon the horizon. There is the colour of ivory upon the nearest snow-fields, and the distant peaks sparkle like silver ; crystals glitter in all directions on the surface of the snow, white, yellow, and pale blue. The stars are exceedingly keen, but only a few can shine in the intensity of moonlight. The air is perfectly still, and though icicles may be hanging from beard and moustache to the furs beneath one's chin, there is no sensation of extreme cold.

MAP ACCOMPANYING "OUR LIFE IN THE SWISS HIGHLANDS," BY J. A. SYMONDS AND HIS DAUGHTER MARGARET. (A. AND C. BLACK.)

Our Life in the Swiss Highlands

During the earlier frosts of the season, after the first snows have fallen, but when there is still plenty of moisture in the ground, the loveliest fern-fronds of pure rime may be found in myriads on the meadows. They are fashioned like perfect vegetable structures, opening fan-shaped upon crystal stems, and catching the sunbeams with the brilliancy of diamonds. Taken at certain angles, they decompose light into iridescent colours, appearing now like emeralds, rubies, or topazes, and now like Labrador spar, blending all hues in a wondrous sheen. When the lake freezes for the first time, its surface is, of course, quite black, and so transparent that it is easy to see the fishes swimming in the deep beneath ; but here and there, where rime has fallen, there sparkle these fantastic flowers and ferns and mosses made of purest frost. Nothing, indeed, can be more fascinating than the new world revealed by winter. In shaded places of the valley you may walk through larches and leafless alder thickets by silent farms, all silvered over with hoar spangles—fairy forests, where the flowers and foliage are rime. The streams are flowing half-frozen over rocks sheeted with opaque green ice. Here it is strange to watch the swirl of water freeing itself from these translucent shackles, and to see it eddying beneath the overhanging eaves of frailest crystal-frosted snow. All is so silent, still, and weird in this white world, that one marvels when the spirit of winter will appear, or what shrill voices in the air will make his unimaginable magic audible. Nothing happens, however, to disturb the charm, save when a sunbeam cuts the chain of diamonds on an alder bough, and down they drift in a thin cloud of dust. It may be also that the air is full of floating crystals, like tiniest most restless fire-flies, rising and falling and passing crosswise in the sun-illumined shade of tree or mountain-side.

Davos in Winter

It is not easy to describe these beauties of the winter-world ; and yet one word must be said about the sunsets. Let us walk out, therefore, towards the lake at four o'clock in mid-December. The thermometer is standing at 3°, and there is neither breath of wind nor cloud. Venus is just visible in rose and sapphire, and the thin young moon is beside her. To east and south the snowy ranges burn with yellow fire, deepening to orange and crimson hues, which die away and leave a greenish pallor. At last, the higher snows alone are livid with a last faint tinge of light, and all beneath is quite white. But the tide of glory turns. While the west grows momentarily more pale, the eastern heavens flush with afterglow, suffuse their spaces with pink and violet. Daffodil and tenderest emerald intermingle ; and these colours spread until the west again has rose and primrose and sapphire wonderfully blent, and from the burning skies a light is cast upon the valley—a phantom light, less real, more like the hues of molten gems, than were the stationary flames of sunset. Venus and the moon meanwhile are silvery clear. Then the whole illumination fades like magic.

All the charms of which I have been writing are combined in a sledge drive. With an arrowy gliding motion one passes through the snow-world as through a dream. In the sunlight the snow surface sparkles with its myriad stars of crystals. In the shadow it ceases to glitter, and assumes a blueness scarcely less blue than the sky. The journey is like sailing through alternate tracts of light-irradiate heavens, and interstellar spaces of the clearest and most flawless ether. The air is like the keen air of the highest glaciers. As we go, the bells keep up a drowsy tinkling at the horse's head. The whole landscape is transfigured—lifted high up out of commonplaceness. The little hills are Monte Rosa sand Mont Blancs. Scale is

17

annihilated, and nothing tells but form. There is hardly any colour except the blue of sky and shadow. Everything is traced in vanishing tints, passing from the almost amber of the distant sunlight through glittering white into pale grey and brighter blues and deep ethereal azure. The pines stand in black platoons upon the hillsides, with a tinge of red or orange on their sable. Some carry masses of snow. Others have shaken their plumes free. The châlets are like fairy houses or toys ; waist-deep in stores of winter fuel, with their mellow tones of madder and umber relieved against the white, with the fantastic icicles and folds of snow depending from their eaves, or curled like coverlids from roof and window-sill, they are far more picturesque than in the summer. Colour, wherever it is found, whether in these cottages or in a block of serpentine by the roadside, or in the golden bulrush-blades by the lake shore, takes more than double value. It is shed upon the pallid landscape like a spiritual and transparent veil. Most beautiful of all are the sweeping lines of pure untroubled snow, fold over fold of undulating softness, billowing along the skirts of the peaked hills. There is no conveying the charm of immaterial, aerial, lucid beauty, the feeling of purity and aloofness from sordid things, conveyed by the fine touch on all our senses of light, colour, form, and air, and motion, and rare tinkling sound. The enchantment is like a spirit mood of Shelley's lyric verse. And, what is perhaps most wonderful, this delicate delight may be enjoyed without fear in the coldest weather. It does not matter how low the temperature may be, if the sun is shining, the air dry, and the wind asleep.

In conclusion, I ought perhaps to modify the tone of enthusiasm taken in this article. I can well conceive that many invalids would not profit to the same extent

Davos in Winter

as I have done. Those especially who feel even dry cold very acutely ; those who by previous experience have found a residence in the high Alps trying to their health or spirits ; those who cannot do without distractions and society ; and those who have not strength enough for moderate exercise, ought, in my opinion, to be very careful before they enter on a winter season at Davos. In any case it is prudent to visit it as early as August, in order that the effect of the climate may be tried while there is still time to form other plans for the winter. It is, however, worth observing here that five hours' driving will in all seasons bring people who wish for change to the railway at Landquart. The verdict of the Davos physicians as to the probability of a cure may, I am confident, be trusted. They are extremely averse from encouraging patients to stay who would not be likely to thrive and do credit to the place. Lastly, it is well to be provided with some mental occupation ; for, though my own experience is that one suffers less ennui in the bracing monotony of the high Alps than in the more ennervating but attractive climates of the South, yet there is no doubt that the cheerful spirits so important to recovery from illness are severely tried in a winter of the Grisons. (April, 1878.)

I have allowed this essay to stand almost exactly as I wrote it nearly fourteen years ago, because it possesses some small historical interest, as having powerfully stimulated the formation of an English colony in Davos.

When I found, after several experiments, that I could not hope to settle down again in my own home, I built a house here. The experience I have gained during this considerable space of time has not shaken my faith in the principle of what is called the Alpine cure. But it

Our Life in the Swiss Highlands

has to a large extent modified my opinion about Davos as a health resort. The rapid development of the place, which has brought a railway up the Prättigau, and bestowed upon us the blessings of electrical illumination and the telephone, besides multiplying the resident and floating population, I dare not say how many times, has naturally increased the dwelling-houses to a very serious —I might say dangerous—extent. They stand too closely packed together, and in winter the heating apparatuses of all these houses render it absurd to speak of "flawless purity of air."

Still, the climate, irrespective of these drawbacks, due to the swift expansion of the village, has not altered in any essential respect. It must be added, also, that the authorities of Davos show great spirit as well as an enlightened intelligence in doing all they can for its conveniences and sanitary requirements.

Under my eyes the village has become a town. Modest hotels have grown into huge European caravanserais. Prices have risen, and the wine current in houses of entertainment has deteriorated. Social life imitates upon a small scale the manners of a city. Not a few points in my article of 1878 are almost ludicrously out of date now. The modest information I was then able to communicate regarding the method of treatment for invalids, the atmospheric condition of the valley, and so forth, have long ago become the common property, not only of experts, but also of the general public.

Nevertheless, I let this essay take the first place in our book, partly because in the main my old impressions are not altered, and partly because it indicates the real beginning of "Our Life in the Swiss Highlands." (January, 1892.)   J. A. S.

DAVOS IN THE OLDEN DAYS

WHAT was life at Davos like in the past, in those olden days, before foreigners began to frequent these valleys, and when Davos Platz formed the headquarters of a free and powerful government ?

Anyone attempting to answer the question must glance briefly at the early history of the Landschaft of Davos, in order that the political and social condition of its people may be intelligible.

Landschaft is the name given to a district, which combines several scattered hamlets and villages, under one jurisdiction. Now Davos, from very ancient times, consisted of the same component parts as now. That is to say, it extended from Laret, on the road to Klosters, to Schmelzboden, at the opening of the gorge which leads to Wiesen and the valley of the Albula. What we now call Davos-Dörfli is in the old books known as *zu St. Joder* or *Theodor*, from the patron Saint of its church. Round this centre were grouped Laret, the outlying farms of the Lake basin, and the dwellings of the Fluela Thal.

Davos-Platz was known as *zu St. Johann*, also from its church. It included the Dischma Thal and the main valley down to Frauenkirch. This has always been the head place of the Landschaft, where the two yearly markets or Kilbis were held, and where all public business was carried on in the Rathhaus.

Our Life in the Swiss Highlands

Frauenkirch, or the Church of our Lady, embraced the side valley of Sertig.

Next came Davos-Glarus, or, as the old books phrase it, *zu St. Niklaus*. The little outlying hamlet of Monstein was in former days dependent parochially on Glarus, but after the year 1631 it had a church of its own.

Such were the primitive divisions of the Landschaft; for political purposes these were again subdivided into fourteen neighbourhoods, with which we need not concern ourselves.

According to a calculation made in 1830, the whole Landschaft numbered 1,646 inhabitants, which is considerably less than half of the resident aliens and winter visitors in a good season now. I ought also to mention that the remote and secluded valley of Arosa, hidden away beyond the mountains above Frauenkirch, was dependent on Davos. Its population of fifty-one souls (in 1830) were, politically, members of the Davos community, with *bürgerrecht*, or rights of citizenship.

Concerning the name of Davos much has been written and many theories have been advanced. In the Romanisch language Davos means "behind." If, for instance, you want to say in Romanisch "my hat is behind the stove," you still use the word *davos*. There is, accordingly, a legend that certain hunters in the thirteenth century discovered our valley, and told their master that it lay up there behind. This etymology, however, must be doubted, for the old way of writing the name was not Davos, but Dafaas or Tavas, and thus it is still locally pronounced. In the despatches of the Venetian ambassadors the name is Italianised Tava. The Romanisch people of Graubünden to this day call it Taváu.

Whatever the derivation of Davos may be, many local names in the valley prove that the Romans introduced

PIZ KESCH FROM THE SERTIG PASS.

Davos in the Olden Days

their language here before it was superseded by the German of Teutonic feudalism. I will only point to Scaletta, from Scala or ladder ; Clavadel, from Clavis or key ; Pedra and Pedara, from Petra or rock.

Davos enters into the light of history at the end of the thirteenth century. After the fall of the Imperial family of Hohenstauffen, when Conradin the chivalrous and beautiful perished on a Neapolitan scaffold in 1268, the German Empire suffered a period of eclipse. The feudatories of the Empire now began to create independent principalities in various parts of the distracted realm. This tendency made itself felt even among our mountains.

They originally formed a substantial province of the Roman Empire under the name of Rhætia. Later on they recognised that shadow of ancient Rome which historians call the Holy Roman Empire. Under the Swabian Emperors, the passes and fertile valleys of the Alps had been held by crown vassals, counts, and barons. These crown vassals, upon the extinction of the Hohenstauffen dynasty, began to look out for themselves, and there was one baronial family, in particular, which at this period extended its suzerainty over Davos. This house acknowledged for its chief the Freiherr of Vatz, whose castles occupied the high land between the Lenzer Heide and the valley of the Albula, above Tiefenkasten. The Freiherr Walther von Vatz resolved to establish a colony of Germans in Davos. According to tradition, he sent up twelve families, of whom four were nobles and eight peasants. Among the nobles of this emigration we may reckon the family of Guler, which is still extant in the Prättigau. A few years later, they were joined by two other noble families, the Buols and the Sprechers.

This colony of German soldiers might be compared to one of the old military colonies of the Romans. The

Our Life in the Swiss Highlands

land of Davos and the people were given over to its members to have and to hold as chattels.

The colonists, on their side, were bound to repay their overlords, the Barons of Vatz, with feudal service of armed men in war, and with a yearly tribute. In deeds and contracts of the period the colonists are termed Walser. This designation has led some historians to suppose that the Germans in question were natives of the Rhone Valley or Wallis. But I do not feel sure that this derivation of the word Walser is tenable. We find in other districts besides Davos that similar military colonists acting in the German interest were called Walser, and that the special laws under which they lived were termed Walser-recht. It is possible that Walser, by the analogy of Wale and Welch, meant foreign sojourners, alien to the districts they occupied, and speaking a language different from that of the aborigines.

There is a charter extant, dated 1289, signed and sealed by Walther von Vatz, which consigns the whole Landschaft of Davos to a certain Landammann Wilhelm and his fellows, to enjoy freely, to rule as they think best without external interference, to choose and order their own form of government, and to exercise judicial functions in all cases, murder and theft excepted. In return for these privileges, the Landammann and his fellows bind themselves to help their feudal overlords with military aid, and to pay a yearly tribute from the produce of their lands—473 cheeses, 168 yards of cloth, and 56 young lambs.

This charter may be styled the Magna Charta of the German military colony which was now established in full possession of Davos. What happened to the aborigines, the Romanisch-speaking natives of the valley, we do not know. It is probable that they were absorbed by

24

Davos in the Olden Days

the German immigrants. It is certain that their language soon succumbed to German. That elder Latin dialect, as I have already said, can only now be traced in certain local names. The Davos speech itself is a comparatively pure form of old German, highly interesting to students of the period when the *Nibelungen Lied* was finally reduced to form, and when Minnesingers flourished at Thuringian and Swabian Courts. Peasants on the fields in Davos still use vowel sounds and grammatical inflections which carry a scholar back to the heroic age of German literature.

But to return to the Charter of 1289. This placed the German colonists, under their Landammann, in a position of practical autonomy. So long as they supported their overlords of Vatz in war, and paid their yearly tribute of produce, they were free to manage their own affairs and to govern the Landschaft as they thought best. The feudal tenure was accordingly of the slightest, and the isolation of Davos among its mountains, separated from the valley of the Albula by the deep gorge of the Züge, left the colony to organise itself more thoroughly each year into an independent state. These circumstances account for the comparative ease with which Davos asserted its freedom in the fifteenth century.

The feudal claims upon it, which resided in the Lords of Vatz, finally devolved by marriage upon the Counts of Montfort, who sold them in 1477 to Sigismund, Duke of Austria. Before that year, 1477, the whole of the mountain district, which we now call Graubünden, had been shaken by a series of revolutions. The people rose up against their feudal masters, destroyed their castles, and constituted themselves into three leagues. The earliest to form itself was that of God's House, which had its centre in Chur under the protection of the Bishop there.

Our Life in the Swiss Highlands

The Gottes-haus-bund, as it is called, dates from the beginning of the fifteenth century. The second took definite shape in 1424 at Trons, in the Vorderrheinthal, and is known as the Grey League, or in Romanisch as the Ligia Grigia. The third was organised at Davos in 1436, upon the death of the last male representative of the Vatz family, Count Friedrich von Toggenburg. This third league, called the League of the Zehngerichte or Ten Jurisdictions, included several parcels of the wide territory which had accrued to the Toggenburgs by their inheritance from the house of Vatz. Its principal component parts were Belfort, Davos, the Prättigau, Schanfig, Churwalden, Malans, and Mayenfeld. Finally, in 1471, the representatives of these three leagues—the Gottes-haus-bund, the Ligia Grigia, and the Zehngerichte—met together at Vazerol, above the Schyn Pass, and struck a common bond and covenant to stand together against the world.

The title given to this triple alliance was derived from the Ligia Grigia of the Vorderrheinthal. Probably because the Ligia Grigia was the first to assert its entire and democratic independence of authority.

From 1471 the three Grey Leagues started upon their political and historical career as Graubünden, i Signori Grigioni, les Grisons. It will be perceived from this rapid sketch that the rights which Archduke Sigismund of Austria acquired in 1477 by purchase over Davos were somewhat shadowy. At that period the whole of Graubünden had risen against the nobles, and had constructed self-government upon the strictest democratic principles.

Davos, in particular, I may add, was now regarded as the capital and seat of administration for the group known as Zehngerichte.

Although the Grey Leagues made alliance with the

Davos in the Olden Days

Swiss Confederation they did not enter that body ; and this is a fact to be particularly noticed in the past history of the Canton. The leagues occupied a singular and anomalous position ; they had asserted their rights of local independence and self-government, yet they regarded themselves as an integral portion of the Holy Roman Empire, while the Zehngerichte, with which we are specially concerned, acknowledged the feudal overlordship of Austria. This supremacy led them into frequent quarrels, which might have resulted in their annexation to Tyrol, if the Austrians had been at leisure to prosecute their conquest. That, however, was not the case, and in 1499 Austria recognised the confederation of the three Grey Leagues, reserving its own rights of feudal overlordship in the Zehngerichte. In 1525, after the battle of Pavia, our mountaineers took possession of the Valtelline, which, together with the Val Bregaglia and its capital Chiavenna, was afterwards ruled by them as despots.

We must now conceive of Davos, this modern wateringplace in the mountains to which people come for health, with its big hotels and meritorious imitation of cosmopolitan civility, as a centre of important political transactions in the sixteenth and seventeenth centuries. While Henry VIII. in England was divorcing his wives and disestablishing the old Church, Davos saw the envoys of France and Venice, Milan, Spain, and the German Courts, seated in her Rathhaus.

Ambassadors went forth in their turn from Davos to the crowned heads of Europe. The ruling families of the Landschaft sent their proconsuls and prætors, podestás and provveditori, as they were styled, to administer wealthy Italian provinces. Of these ruling families three of the most eminent are still represented here—the Buols, the Sprechers, and the Gulers. We find their coat-armour, as well as their names, on many monuments and private houses of the Landschaft.

I do not mean to continue the history of Davos in detail further than the year 1525. This was a year in which the Grey Leagues acquired the Valtelline. A little later the old statute-book of Davos was reduced to form, and it is from its pages that I wish to reconstruct some features of the mediæval mode of life here. I must, however, conclude this historical introduction by remarking that in 1644 Davos lost its rights of presidency over the Zehngerichte ; that in 1797 Napoleon Buonaparte took the Valtelline from Graubünden and joined it to the Cisalpine Republic ; and that in 1799 the three Grey Leagues were incorporated in the Helvetian Republic under the title of Canton Graubünden.

We must bear in mind that during the sixteenth century Davos was one of the three chief centres of a sovereign federated state, dealing on equal terms with princes, and swaying distant provinces in Italy with the autocratic might of tyrants. Into the social conditions of the Landschaft, at this highest point of its independence and political activity, I now desire to penetrate. For this purpose I shall avail myself of the book of statutes, reduced to order in the year 1596.

It clearly indicates a state of things which had then prevailed from remote antiquity, and nothing exists to prove that the manners and customs of the people altered until the irruption of foreign invalids and tourists about twenty years ago.

The most curious point about Davos at this period of its political importance was the social simplicity of its inhabitants. We know that members of its noble families —the Buols, the Gulers, the Sprechers—received knighthood and titles of nobility from kings. We know that

Davos in the Olden Days

they had their portraits painted in armour or the dress of ambassadors by good Italian artists. Such pictures may be seen in the dining-room of Hôtel Buol—they are the portraits of Herr Buol's ancestors. We know that many of them were men of high accomplishments, writing Latin with elegance and ease, like Fortunat von Sprecher, whose Rhætian History was published by the Elzevirs at Amsterdam. We know that the Courts of Spain, France, Austria, and Venice quarrelled for their support because of the vast strategical importance of the Valtelline. Yet, there is no sign in the whole Landschaft— if we except the church and the Rathhaus, and a single panelled room in what is called the Schlössli—that this place was once the seat of a wealthy and powerful oligarchy. It is possible that irreparable damage was inflicted on the ancient dwellings of Davos when Austrian troops took possession of the valley in 1622. Seventy buildings are said to have been burned on that occasion, including the houses of the Buols, the Gulers, and the Sprechers. But I am inclined to believe that while the Davos nobles exercised the reality of power, they were careful to mask it under a republican simplicity. The constitution of the Grey Leagues was strictly democratic, being based on the absolute equality, political and social, of every citizen who belonged by birth or ascription to any one of the component communes. For a Buol, a Sprecher, or a Guler to display in Davos, at the centre of government, the luxury or elegance to which he was accustomed elsewhere, would have awakened the suspicions of the jealous mountaineers. Accordingly we must travel to Parpan in order to visit a country palace of the Buols, to Luzein or Mayenfeld to see in what agreeable houses the Sprechers dwelt, to Zizèrs if we wish to examine a sumptuous villa of Von Salis, constructed on the Italian model,

Our Life in the Swiss Highlands

with marble staircases and balconies, and finished down to its smallest details in exquisite Renaissance style.

The upland valley of Davos, in the sixteenth century, was a kind of Sparta, with no eminent public or private edifices—with nothing, in fact, which should attest by ruins to the former greatness of its martial people.

It was isolated from the world around it. One poor road, on which country carts could be driven, led from the lake, across Laret, to Klosters.

We still trace it along the Schwarz See, through the wood, where a massive pillar of carved larch indicates the frontier of Davos and Prättigau.

All the other roads were bridle-paths until within the last few years. You rode on horseback over Fluela and Scaletta, on horseback along the dizzy heights 1,000 feet above the Landwasser, where the old way connecting Davos with Wiesen and Belfort can still be followed in summer. The wine of the Valtelline came in winter across the Bernina and Scaletta Passes on horseback, or on little sledges like toboggans. At the end of their long journey in the snows the pack-horses were stabled upon the meadows between my house and the Schiabach, which is still called the Ross-weid, or horse pasture.

I shall now proceed to examine the Landbuch of Davos, or Digest of its common law, which was first compiled in the year 1596. This collection of statutes presents us with a faithful picture of the Landschaft between the fifteenth and nineteenth centuries—from the time of its formation as an independent state to the date of its absorption in the Canton as one member of the Swiss Confederation.

The smallness of the community is proved by special stipulations with regard to kith and kinship, which in certain degrees of proximity relieved relatives by blood or marriage from denouncing wrong-doers to the courts of justice. These ties of relationship were termed Bluots-fründschafft and Kemegschafft or Schwägerschafft. It is clear, from the minute attention paid to kith and kinship, that the principal families must have been closely connected by intermarriage ; a fact which is amply borne out by the study of any Davos pedigree. It also results from these regulations that the community was expected to police itself. We are, in fact, introduced to an extremely simple society, which resembled one large household, whereof the several members were bound to report irregularities to its patriarchal chief, the Landammann.

The roughness of manners is proved by a series of rigorous laws against raising quarrels on the roads and in other public places. Stone-throwing in anger, beard-plucking in scorn, are specially prohibited. Wearing of arms, except when men are going on a journey, is forbidden. Any contravention of these regulations upon a Sunday is punished with greater severity, probably because hot-blooded young men met together on this day in idleness.

Before the Kilbi, or biennial market of Davos, a special proclamation used to be made by the Landweibel, or Beadle of the Landschaft, dressed in the parti-coloured blue and orange livery of the commune.

The proclamation ran as follows : " My gracious Lords, the Landammann and Council of this Landschaft Davos, command me to announce that whosoever shall inflame strife, battery, or assault, by word or deed, thereby incurs the fine of twenty crowns, without grace or favour. Under the like penalty are also forbidden gaming and dancing, ungodly cursing and swearing, inordinate eating and drinking, and other vicious acts. Whoso cannot pay the fine out of his goods shall be punished in his body, and this proclamation holds good three days and nights for natives and strangers. Therefore let every man take heed hereto, and look that he protect himself beforehand against shame and loss of substance."

The Kilbis were seasons of merry-making; they were also occasions for paying debts and settling affairs of business. It was therefore necessary to secure the peace at these times by extraordinary penalties. But sumptuary and moral laws in detail regulated the conduct of the Davosers at all seasons. Playing at dice or cards for money was forbidden. So was dancing in public or private, without special permission from the Kleine Rath or Privy Council. I find one order against masquing and mumming—*maschgerada oder Buzen gahn;* another, against any person over the age of twelve going about on New Year's Eve to sing at house doors.

In like manner the custom of walking round to congratulate young people on their wedding was prohibited on the ground that it encouraged excessive drinking, and put the bridal couple to too much expense for *Hofwein*. Wakes and feasts at funerals were forbidden for similar reasons. Sundays were treated with special respect. Everybody capable of going to church was obliged to do so under pain of fine. No work of any sort was allowed; and nothing except the necessaries of life, bread and wine, might be sold.

While the personal conduct of the Davosers received this careful attention, their safety was considered in some curious particulars.

There is, for instance, a law forbidding people to venture upon the lake until the ice shall have been proclaimed fit to bear—*Authentisch,* in the old German phrase.

The two chief buildings of Davos-Platz, the church and the Rathhaus, were protected by a series of carefully considered ordinances. With regard to the church it is

Davos in the Olden Days

not necessary to say much. Only one pathetic little law may be pointed out. The *Messmer* or sexton was bound to bury people in summer on the north side of the church-yard, so that in winter the less frozen south side might be used. No pigs were suffered to feed in the churchyard. The rules for the Rathhaus deserve fuller notice. These are still in force at the present day. The Rathhaus was not only the town hall and seat of government, but also the chief or only public-house where wine could be bought and lodgings be procured. It was therefore let from time to time to an innkeeper, called the *Rathwirth*, who undertook to keep it clean and in good order. He was obliged to furnish guarantees for his solvency and conduct. The rate at which he might sell wine, bread, cheese, and meat was fixed. He had to see that no one scratched the furniture, scribbled on the walls, or impaired the fabric. Smoking, or, as the statute phrased it, "*Tubakch trinken*," in the Rathhaus, was forbidden. So was dancing. I may say that dancing is even now probibited in the Rathhaus ; but you have only to go there at the meeting of the Gemeinde, in order to obtain demonstration that the rule about "drinking tobacco" has been relaxed.

The Rathhaus served also as the prison of Davos. Malefactors were confined in one or other of two places, which may still be visited. These were respectively called the *Kichen-falle*, or strong chamber, for mild cases, and the *Kiche*, a sort of oubliette beneath it, for worse criminals. Nearly all offences could be compounded by payment of fines ; but when the offenders would not or could not pay, they were flogged and put on bread-and-water diet in these dungeons. There was also a pillory standing before the Rathhaus, with a strong iron cage, into which the offender's head was tightly screwed. The remnants of this ponderous machine were recently in the

33   C

possession of my friend Herr Richter Florian Prader of Herti, below the Hôtel d'Angleterre.

If we wish to bring before our imagination an act of high justice as it was carried out at Davos-Platz, we have ample materials furnished by the Landbuch. I think that the following record, carrying us back to the period when the Landammann exercised jurisdiction in capital cases, may interest my readers.

On the day appointed for sentencing a criminal, a table was prepared in the middle of the open place before the Rathhaus; upon this table were laid a fair and naked sword and a judge's staff; round it in a circle were arranged armchairs—the chair intended for the Landammann being raised above the rest. Then the Landammann, accompanied by his assessors, descended from the Rathhaus and took seats at the table. The Landschreiber, or public notary, who acted as Secretary of State, produced the documents of impeachment and trial, and laid them beside him on a stool. After this the prisoner, who is always called "the poor person," *die arme Person*, in this curious document, was brought before the Court with hands tightly bound. The beadle of the Landschaft, arrayed in a gorgeous tabard of orange and azure, preceded him, while six trusty members of the Great Council, in full armour, carrying halberds, marched behind. After the prisoner had been seated in a chair, the halberdiers took their station behind the judge; the Landammann rose to his feet, and proceeded to open the Court. He described the offences for which the prisoner stood arraigned, gave a brief summary of his examination and trial, and wound up with a formal declaration, that the Court would act according to Imperial law and the well-established customs of our enfranchised lands. Then he turned to his assessors on the right hand, and put his

34

question to each in turn : "Wherefore I ask you, Herr
So-and-so, is it your opinion that, at this time and hour, I,
as Landammann of this Landschaft, in the name of all here
seated, should take sword and staff into my hand, and
pronounce sentence upon bloodshed and other crimes,
which shall be brought before me, according to Imperial
law and the well-established customs of our free lands ?"
Similar questions were put to the assessors on the left
hand ; and after receiving their assent the Landammann
sat down, raised the sword in air, and replaced it on the
table, doing likewise with the staff. He then exhorted
his assessors to help him with their counsel, in case his
own judgment should fail through want of wisdom or
knowledge. Finally, he bade the Landschreiber read the
Imperial law or proclamation, announcing that the Session
of the Court was open. After this the Treasurers of the
Landschaft were summoned, it being their duty to act as
public prosecutors. Their spokesman prayed that the
accused person might be judged according to the Word of
God, Imperial law, and the tenor of his previous trial.
The beadle then summoned two advocates for the
prisoner, and the public notary forthwith proceeded to
read aloud his indictment and the evidence against him.
Thereupon the prisoner's advocates sued for mercy,
appealing to the clemency of God, and the natural weak-
ness of human nature ; the prosecutors replied ; and
both parties submitted to the verdict of the Court.
Nothing now remained but to pronounce sentence. Accordingly the Court withdrew into the Rathhaus, settled
their verdict, and returned to take their places at the
table. Then the Landammann ordered the public executioner to appear, and gave the " poor person " over to
his custody, commanding him to proceed at once to the
place of execution, and to carry out the sentence of the

Our Life in the Swiss Highlands

Court. This sentence might either be that the prisoner should be burned and his ashes scattered to the winds or buried in the earth ; or else that his neck should be severed with the sword, so that a waggon wheel might pass between his head and his body. After the sentence had been pronounced the Court rose. The Landammann took his staff in hand ; the assessors followed, attended by the armed halberdiers ; lastly came the executioner, leading the "poor person" by a rope. A circle was formed round the executioner, who carried out the sentence, and then asked whether he had performed his duty according to Imperial law and the verdict of the Court. The Landammann said : "You have executed judgment according to Imperial law and the verdict ; may God have mercy on the dead man's soul !" In his turn the Landammann asked whether he had judged that day according to Imperial law and the well-established customs of our lands. The assessors answered, "Yes !" Next he asked if the beadles, apparitors, halberdiers, and artisans who had been concerned in this act of high justice should be held blameless. On receiving the answer, "Yes !" he finally asked if the hour for ringing the sunset bell, *Feierabend*, had arrived. When the people answered "Yes !" the Landammann broke his staff and dismissed the bystanders with a few words of solemn exhortation.

Before quitting the Rathhaus there is yet another feature in this building which carries us back to primitive Davos. A row of wolves' heads are ranged along its wall under the projecting roof. These relics remind us of the time when Davos was thickly forested, and when wolves and bears formed a serious danger to the inhabitants. Hunters who produced the skin of a wolf, *Huot oder Balg*, at the Rathhaus, were substantially rewarded ; and any

Davos in the Olden Days

fine specimens of these ferocious beasts received the honour of having their heads nailed up as trophies. Packed away in the garrets of the Rathhaus, another remnant from that elder state of society may still be seen. It is part of the old *Garn*, or wolf-net, which plays a distinguished part in the statutes of the Landbuch. Landammann Müller once told me that, when he was a boy, this wolf-net used to be suspended from iron hooks in front of the Rathhaus. He and other lads were in the habit of swinging in it on the sly—turning it, in fact, into a hammock. The net was heavy with iron traps, and each of its strands was made of stout hemp, as thick as one's little finger. I will now describe how the Davosers went a-hunting in the olden days.

When news arrived in Platz that some wild beast, bear or wolf (*Gwilt* is the general name for it), had appeared in the forest, orders were given to ring a tocsin from the church tower. "*Man Sturm lütet*," says the Landbuch. The attention of the Landschaft was thus aroused, and the word went round that the Landammann meant to collect the folk for hunting. Each neighbourhood, of which there were fourteen in the Landschaft, then selected a headman or *Caporal*—one who was sure to be willingly obeyed, "*der guten Volg hat.*" He enrolled the men and boys of his district, appointing some to be setters of the net, others to be watchers, and others to be drivers of the wolf. The watchers were placed under *Huotmeister*, the drivers under *Hetzmeister;* and it was carefully provided that two boys should never be told off alone to any station. Boys and men were equally distributed for these functions. Meanwhile the great wolf-net, or *Garn*, had to be removed from the Rathhaus, and carried to that quarter of the forest where the beast was advertised. Small sums of money were paid to the men who undertook this duty and returned the net to the Rathwirth's custody after the hunt was over. It will readily be imagined that when the church bells rang their tocsin, all the young men and lads of the Landschaft were eager for the sport. But elaborate rules provided that this should be conducted in no tumultuary fashion. It was the duty of the headman (or *Caporal*) of the neighbourhood in which the wild beast had been advertised, to lay the net. His fellows from the surrounding neighbourhoods were bound to assist him with watchers and drivers placed at convenient points of vantage in the woods. Great attention was finally paid to securing the orderly service of the beaters and the guards.

It is clear from these elaborate regulations for hunting matters that the Landschaft was capable of swift and practical organisation in an emergency. Each of the fourteen neighbourhoods had its own administrative machinery, and all together were responsible to the Landammann. He signified his intention to put the whole machine in motion by causing the church bells to be violently rung. This happened, and still happens, in case of fire. I remember one occasion in March, when a forest in the Sertig Thal took fire. The church bells clashed continuously for upwards of an hour, and in a short space of time all the roads to Clavadel were occupied by carts and men hurrying to the scene of action.

These facts account for the seemingly exaggerated height and size of the church steeple in Davos. That tower, with its belfry and spire, symbolises the voice of the supreme authority. There is a special and important statute upon *Sturm lüthen*, or ringing of the tocsin. When that brazen clang was heard in the valley, all the members of the *Landsgemeindschaft*—that is, every Davos citizen from the age of fourteen to seventy—was bound

Davos in the Olden Days

to obey the Landammann's call. He must leave his work or business, his merry-makings or his sorrowings at death-beds. The Landammann needed him for public matters of importance—perhaps to take some weighty decision in affairs of war ; perhaps to hunt the wolf or extinguish a fire ; perhaps to free a couple of houses from an avalanche ; perhaps to mend roads impaired by swollen rivulets in summer ; perhaps to dig roads out of the huge drifts of snow which mound them up in winter. No one between the age of fourteen and seventy was exempt from public service upon occasions of these kinds, and the Landammann made his orders heard through the voice of the bells rung jangling.

One can see that old Davos resembled a beehive or an ant's nest, in which the machinery of government is carried on by the simplest organisation of its members. The community, in fact, governed itself under the direction of its chosen chief magistrate. All citizens, from the age of fourteen upwards, had a vote in the election of the Landammann, and a vote in the passing of new laws or the revision of old laws. Down to the smallest particulars of daily life the Landschaft was self-regulative. The rate of interest was fixed ; hay was valued each year publicly ; the prices of bread, wine, and other commodities were established according to the seasons ; the amount of hay which any single man might purchase was limited ; in times of bad crops no one was permitted to sell hay outside the Landschaft. Thus we have to add the analogy of a co-operative company to our previous analogy of a beehive or an ant's nest. For many centuries Davos realised the ideal of an isolated, independent, self-sufficing, and self-regulating community, in which all things were ordered upon equitable principles for the welfare of the whole and the well-being of the parts.

Our Life in the Swiss Highlands

There was no competition, no trade, no complicated system of feudal tenure.

The foreign concerns of the little state and the ambition of its great families brought it indeed into manifold troubles ; but when those disturbing elements had been eliminated, the old elastic organisation of the Landschaft remained intact. I take it that Davos at the end of the last century resembled Davos at the beginning of the sixteenth century more closely than it did during the stormy political period of the seventeenth century, which has added historical lustre to its annals.

There are a few points of general interest in the Land-buch to which attention may be drawn.

One of these regards the laws against strangers. Strangers did not mean merely foreigners, but members of another community—the burghers, for instance, of Klosters or of Schmitten. On the principle of an ant's nest or a co-operative company, the Davosers favoured their own people. Severe ordinances were passed against strangers who attempted to undersell the natives. It was also laid down as a principle that real property and houses might not be sold to strangers if any injury to a Davoser could be proved. The tenor of contracts in such cases should always be interpreted in favour of a native.

A second point regards the maintenance of roads and public cleanliness. Trustees were appointed to keep the lake and the big well by the Rathhaus in good order. Foreigners were not permitted to fish in Davos waters. No rubbish might be thrown into the Landwasser. The public road through the Landschaft had to be of a certain width, and kept in sound condition by the several neigh-bourhoods. Nobody might mow grass upon its borders, litter it with rubbish, turn out cattle to feed there, or obstruct it with wood and stones. Very special directions provided for maintaining communications open with Wiesen. I have already remarked that the old road to Wiesen was carried from the hamlet of Glarus at the height of about 1,000 feet above the Landwasser. The post-road which we use at present was only made in 1865. An intermediate road, starting from Schmelzboden, was constructed about 1820 by a mining company ; but this has long since fallen into ruins. Meanwhile, the old road by which the Davosers of the Middle Ages travelled is still fit for foot-passengers, and well repays a visit. To keep this road open in winter was an affair of serious difficulty. It runs along a narrow ledge high above the forests, with trenched ravines descending sheer upon the torrent. Down these ravines sweep avalanches, and all the winds play freely on the bare exposed slopes of the naked mountains. The statutes of Davos provided, therefore, that both Wiesen at one end of this road and Glarus at the other should be bound to keep it in constant repair. Should an avalanche fall, or if a reasonable fear of avalanches should arise, notice had at once to be sent to the Landammann. He was then at liberty to proclaim the road unsafe, or to send men to dig it out. Some of the few romantic stories I have heard in this place are connected with the old road to Wiesen. It was believed to be haunted with evil spirits ; in particular by *Wild-männli*, or wild men of the woods. A fairly good representation of savage men, forming part of the heraldic bearing of Davos, may be seen upon the front of the Rathhaus. My friend Christian Palmy, of Wiesen, told me that during his father's lifetime the following circumstance happened : His father kept a village hostelry at Wiesen, and was sitting up one night to welcome a friend from Davos, of the respected family of Balzer. At last, long after the hour when he had been expected, Herr

Our Life in the Swiss Highlands

Balzer knocked at the house door, and descended in sorry plight from his horse. He was at once put to bed and cared for. But he never got up again. After a short while he died ; and this is what he told about his journey on his death-bed. He had left Glarus alone, and after traversing a piece of forest, emerged upon the bleak precipitous slopes above the Züge. When he came to one *mauvais pas*, which crossed a ravine, his horse shuddered, and a horrible uncertain creature leaped on to its crupper from the shadow of the wall. Herr Balzer succeeded in knocking the creature off ; but when he came to a second place of the same sort, he saw the same dreadful form awaiting him upon the bridge. He spurred his horse forward, hoping to ride quickly past. The Wildmännli— for such the creature was—this time sprang upon him, and clasped him round the waist and chest. He felt the thing's arms, long as the arms of a skeleton, chill him through blood and marrow, so that he fainted from cold, and fear, and pain. It was only after he had ridden another hour unconscious, and had come in sight of Wiesen, that he recovered his senses. The story is as worthy of credence as any such stories are. We may perhaps suppose that Herr Balzer caught his death by a chill that night above the Züge, and that his fevered imagination translated the fact of his seizure into terms supplied by current superstition.

I have told one ghost story about the old road to Wiesen. Another comes into my mind with which I will conclude this paper. People of Davos believe that certain men are born from time to time among them who have a supernatural gift for seeing the dead walk at night. Persons with this gift are called seers of the *Todten-volk*. A friend of mine here told me, not many days ago, that one of his cousins in the Prättigau possesses it. A peculiar call, or

THE TÖDI FROM GLARIS.

Davos in the Olden Days

intimation, warns the seer when this vision will be granted. He is then bound to rise from bed, or to leave the society of friends. He must go forth alone to a certain place where the dead walk. There he beholds the inhabitants of the churchyard pass before him. Each long since buried face gazes at him full in the eyes. The face of the last walker in this dread procession is that of a *living* man or woman ; and when the seer recognises it, he knows that So-and-so will shortly die and join the fellowship of the dead folk. But—and this is a terribly pathetic fate imposed upon the seer—the last and living member of the train may avert his face and pass unrecognised. If that happens, the seer knows that it is now his turn to die and join the fellowship of the dead folk. At Davos it is supposed that the dead take their departure from the churchyard, cross the Landwasser, and pace the solitary road which leads to the Waldhaus and the Dischma Thal. I sometimes indulge in thoughts of the curious unfamiliar impression our modern watering-place must make upon those ghostly survivors from the antique past. Now and again they awake from slumber under earth to revisit the pale glimpses of the moon. Mixed with familiar moonlight they behold gas-lamps and electric illumination. Their old houses of wood and low-roofed stone are still discernible. But huge hotels overtop these humble dwellings. Their descendants are still alive and at work here. But a crowd of people from far distant countries mingle with the scions of that antique stock ; and the ashes of many of these strangers are yearly committed to the same earth as that which covers Buol and Beeli, Guler and Sprecher. Do the foreigners who die here walk also at night ? and does the seer of the Todten-volk discern them ? This is the eerie question which I ask myself. J. A. S.

SNOW, FROST, STORM, AND AVALANCHE

(WRITTEN IN THE SUMMER OF 1888)

I

IT is wellnigh impossible, while treating of Alpine scenery in winter, to avoid monotony. The snow-world is colourless and almost formless ; and to describe things which have no shape or hue strains the resources of language. Besides, the life of human beings in these mountains—the life, that is to say, of the children of the fells and workers in the forests—has a singular intensity, a serious abiding sense of man's relation to the material universe. which is unknown to the inhabitants of flat countries and temperate climates. Language fails in the attempt to reproduce impressions and moods of the mind, which are thrilling enough in the midst of this austerely simple nature, but which have nothing to do with common experience upon the highways of the world. It is as difficult to write adequately about the winter Alps and mountaineers as about the stormy ocean and sailors.

The winter of 1887-88 was unusually severe over Northern and Central Europe. In the Canton of Grau-bünden it was exceptional, for three main reasons—the large amount of snow which fell, the long continuance of intense cold, and the frequency of avalanches, by

Snow, Frost, Storm, and Avalanche

which many lives were lost and vast damage was inflicted upon property. Dr. Ludwig, of Pontresina, in his "Meteorological Report" for February, says: "It is an ascertained fact that the oldest people do not remember such a long, severe winter, with so much snow, so many snow-storms, and so little sun. The same is the case with this winter's avalanches, which have exceeded in number and size all previously recorded in this district, and in several instances have fallen in unusual tracks."

The reason why avalanches were exceptional in size and numbers, and why they came down in unexpected quarters, can be explained. Only a moderate amount of snow fell in the autumn and early winter ; about New Year there was considerably less than the average quantity. On the heights of the mountains this coating of scanty snow hardened, under the action of sun, wind, and intense frost, into a smooth, solid, icy crust. Therefore, when a heavy snow-fall began in February, which lasted without intermission for six days and nights, accumulating an average depth of five or six feet on the crust of earlier snow I have described, this new deposit was everywhere insecure. It slipped in immense masses from the polished surface of the old snow, having no support, no roughness to which it could adhere, and rushed by its own weight into the valleys at points where ordinary and more slowly acting causes are not wont to launch the thunderbolts of winter. For the same reason successive avalanches descended upon the same tracks. As soon as one deposit had glided from its slippery ice-foundation and another snow-fall happened, the phenomenon was repeated, the crust of old snow still remaining treacherously firm and smooth upon the steep declivities. A postillion. who drove the post all this winter over the Fluela Pass (the highest in Grau-

Our Life in the Swiss Highlands

bünden, and the highest which is open for regular winter traffic in Europe), told me that he had counted between fifty and sixty avalanches, which traversed the actual post-road, and some of these were repeated half a dozen times. As the same conditions affected all the other passes of Graubünden—Bernina, Albula, Julier, Splügen, and Bernhardin—it will readily be conceived that traffic was occasionally suspended for several days together, that the arrivals and departures of the post were irregular, and that many lives were sacrificed. Singularly enough, no fatal accidents happened to the Swiss post-service. Those who suffered were men employed to mend the roads, carters, and peasants engaged in felling wood. Few valleys in the Canton escaped without the loss of some lives, and the tale is still incomplete ; for the more remote regions were entirely shut off for months together from the outer world by enormous avalanches, which interrupted all communications. We do not yet know, and, unless an official report be published on the subject, we shall probably never know how many human beings fell victims to the fury of the elements this winter.[1]

If we may speak of avalanche-showers in the same way as we speak of meteor-showers, it is possible to distinguish two great occurrences of this kind in the spring of 1888. They grouped themselves around two dates, February 16-17 and March 27-28. Intermittingly and sporadically, avalanches fell throughout the Canton almost daily in the months of February, March, and April. Some of the more destructive cannot be reckoned to the main showers I have mentioned. Yet the dates given above mark distinct crises in the avalanche-plague ; and for two well-defined meteorological reasons. Between

[1] This was written in June, 1888. But see the notes appended to the article.

Snow, Frost, Storm, and Avalanche

February 4 and February 9, snow fell continuously and universally, heaping up, as I have already described, immense stores of soft unsettled drifts upon the smooth surface of the autumn deposit. Given calm frost weather for a period of several weeks, this large snow-fall might have hardened in its turn, until the warm breezes of April loosened it in Schlag-Lawinen. That, however, did not happen. Soon after the snow was down, storms set in ; the Föhn-wind raged upon the heights and swooped into the valleys. The mountains were stirred through all their length and breadth, and the Staub-Lawinen poured like torrents from the precipices. That caused the avalanche-shower of February 16-17. The second shower of March 27-28 was due to somewhat different causes. Much of the snow had been dislodged from places where the Föhn-wind played its wild capricious games in February. But incalculable masses still remained unshaken ; and upon these a violent and general rain-storm acted at the end of March. The result was that millions of tons of snow, sodden with rain, got slowly into motion, and discharged themselves in Schlag-Lawinen down the gullies of the hills. The exact meaning of these technical terms, Staub-Lawinen and Schlag-Lawinen, will be presently explained. For the moment, I must beg my readers to understand that the avalanche-shower of February differed in some essential respects from that of March. It is also worthy of notice that the valleys on the southern side of the watershed—Mesocco, Calanca, Bregaglia, Poschiavo—suffered far more in the second shower, while the greatest damages upon the northern side, on the chief post-roads, and so forth, were inflicted by the earlier.

Though I possess considerable data for describing in detail the main features of the avalanche-showers in

Our Life in the Swiss Highlands

1888, as they affected Graubünden, I feel that I should only perplex and weary English people by directing their attention to places the very names of which are unfamiliar. Besides, I should prolong this article, which promises already to become unwieldy, beyond the dimensions of an occasional essay. I propose, therefore, to confine myself to general observations about the several sorts of avalanches, and to illustrations from my personal experience which may help to bring their dangers vividly before my readers.

II

There are several sorts of avalanches, which have to be distinguished, and which are worthy of separate descriptions. One is called *Staub-Lawine*, or Dust-Avalanche. This descends when snow is loose and has recently fallen. It is attended with a whirlwind, which lifts the snow from a whole mountain-side and drives it onward through the air. It advances in a straight line, overwhelming every obstacle, mowing forests down like sedge, " leaping (as an old peasant once expressed it in my hearing) from hill to hill," burying men, beasts, and dwellings, and settling down at last into a formidable compact mass without colour and without outline. The snow which forms these Staub-Lawinen is dry and finely powdered. When it comes to rest upon the earth, it immediately hardens into something very like the consistency of ice, wrapping the objects which have been borne onward by its blast tightly round in a firm implacable clasp. A man or horse seized by a Staub-Lawine, if the breath has not been blown out of his body in the air, has it squeezed out by the even, clinging

Snow, Frost, Storm, and Avalanche

pressure of consolidating particles. A human victim of the dreadful thing, who was so lucky as to be saved from its clutch, once described to me the sensations he experienced. He was caught at the edge of the avalanche just when it was settling down to rest, carried off his feet, and rendered helpless by the swathing snow, which tied his legs, pinned his arms to his ribs, and crawled upward to his throat. There it stopped. His head emerged, and he could breathe; but as the mass set, he felt the impossibility of expanding his lungs, and knew that he must die of suffocation. At the point of losing consciousness, he became aware of comrades running to his rescue. They hacked the snow away around his thorax, and then rushed on to dig for another man who had been buried in the same disaster, leaving him able to breathe, but wholly powerless to stir hand or foot. This narrative reminded me of an anecdote told by Haydon the painter, who nearly sacrificed a negro's life by attempting to take an entire cast of the man's body at one moment from the feet to the chin. When the plaster-of-Paris began to set, the negro could not breathe, and he was only saved from asphyxiation by Haydon's tearing down the mould of brick in which he had been placed.

Another sort of avalanche is called the *Schlag-Lawine*, or Stroke-Avalanche. It falls generally in spring time, when the masses of winter snow have been loosened by warm winds or sodden by heavy rainfalls. The snow is not whirled into the air, but slips along the ground, following the direction given by ravines and gullies, or finding a way forward through the forest by its sheer weight. Lumbering and rolling, gathering volume as they go from all the barren fells within the reach of their tenacious undermining forces, these "slogging" ava-

D

lanches push blindly onward till they come to rest upon
a level. Then they spread themselves abroad, and heap
their vast accumulated masses by the might of pressure
from behind up into pyramids and spires. They bear
the aspect of a glacier with its seracs, or of a lava-stream
with its bristling ridges ; and their skirts are plumed with
stately pine-trees, nodding above the ruin they have
wrought. Woe to the fragile buildings, to the houses
and stables, which they meet upon their inert grovelling
career ! These are carried with them, incorporated, used
as battering-rams. Grooving like the snout of some
behemoth, the snow dislodges giants of the forest, and
forces them to act like ploughs upon its path. You may
see tongues and promontories of the avalanche protruding from the central body, and carried far across
frozen lakes or expanses of meadow by the help of some
huge pine or larch. The Schlag-Lawine is usually
greyish-white and softer in substance than its more
dreadful sister, the Staub-Lawine—that daughter of the
storm, with the breath of the tornado in her brief
delirious energy. It is often distinguished by a beautiful
bluish colour, as of opaque ice, in the fantastically-toppling
rounded towers which crown it ; whereas the Schlag-
Lawine looks like marble of Carrara, and presents a
uniform curved surface after it has fallen. Though the
Schlag-Lawine closely resembles a glacier at first sight,
practised eyes detect the difference at once by the dulled
hue which I have mentioned, and by the blunted outlines
of the pyramids. It might be compared to a glacier
which had been sucked or breathed upon by some colossal
fiery dragon. Less time has gone to make it ; it is composed of less elaborated substance, it has less of permanence in its structure than a glacier ; and close inspection
shows that it will not survive the impact of soft southern

Snow, Frost, Storm, and Avalanche

winds in May. In extent these Schlag-Lawinen are enormous. I have crossed some which measured a thousand feet in breadth and more than sixty feet in depth. All road-marks, telegraph-posts, parapets, etc., are, of course, abolished. The trees, if trees there were upon their track, have been obliterated. Broken stumps, snapped off like matches, show where woods once waved to heaven. Valleys are made even with the ridges which confined them. Streams are bridged over and converted into temporary lakes by the damming up of water.

A species of the Schlag-Lawine may be distinguished, to which the name of *Grund-Lawine*, or Ground-Avalanche, shall be given. There is no real distinction between *Schlag-* and *Grund-Lawine*. I only choose to differentiate them here because of marked outward differences to the eye. The peculiarity of a *Grund-Lavine* consists in the amount of earth and rubbish carried down by it. This kind is filthy and disreputable. It is coloured brown or slaty-grey by the rock and soil with which it is involved. Blocks of stone emerge in horrid bareness from the dreary waste of dirty snow and slush of water which compose it ; and the trees which have been so unlucky as to stand upon its path are splintered, bruised, rough-handled in a hideous fashion. The Staub-Lawine is fury-laden like a fiend in its first swirling onset, flat and stiff like a corpse in its ultimate repose of death, containing men and beasts and trees entombed beneath its stern unwrinkled taciturnity of marble. The Schlag-Lawine is picturesque, rising into romantic spires and turrets, with erratic pine-plumed firths protruding upon sleepy meadows. It may even lie pure and beautiful, heaving in pallid billows at the foot of majestic mountain slopes where it has injured nothing. But the Grund-Lawine is ugly, spiteful like an asp, tatterdemalion like a street Arab ; it is the worst, the most wicked of the sisterhood. To be killed by it would mean a ghastly death by scrunching and throttling, as in some grinding machine, with nothing of noble or impressive in the winding-sheet of foul snow and débris heaved above the mangled corpse.

I ought to mention a fourth sort of avalanche, which is called *Schnee-Rutsch*, or Snow-Slip. It does not differ materially from the Schlag-Lawine except in dimension, which is smaller, and in the fact that it may fall at any time and in nearly all kinds of weather by the mere detachment of some trifling mass of snow. The Schnee-Rutsch slides gently, expanding in a fan-like shape upon the slope it has to traverse, till it comes to rest upon a level. Small as the slip may be, it is very dangerous ; for it rises as it goes, catches the legs of a man, lifts him off his feet, and winds itself around him in a quiet but inexorable embrace. I once saw a coal-cart with two horses swept away by a very insignificant Schnee-Rutsch while standing at my window in the Hôtel Belvedère at Davos-Platz. The man and one horse kept their heads above the snow and were extricated. The other horse was dead before he could be dug out. There is a Davos proverb to the effect that "a pan of snow may kill a man " ; and certainly the incident which I have just mentioned, occurring on a public road in Davos-Platz, and close beneath the windows of one of its chief hotels, corroborates the proverb. While crossing the higher passes in sledges, where the road is often carried at a vast altitude along precipitous slopes, with a width of less than five feet for the vehicle to move upon, a snow-slip of this kind may cause very serious accidents. Yet I ought not to speak ill of Schnee-Rutschen, for I have started them myself upon the declivities of the hills above

Snow, Frost, Storm, and Avalanche

Davos, and have ridden down on them to my great delight, feeling the snow surge and swell beneath me like a horse or wave, until our breathless descent was over, and we stood nine feet above the level ground which brought us to quiescence. These, however, were tame, carefully-chosen, carefully-calculated snow-slips, far different from such as leap upon the traveller unaware, and flick him, as a towel flicks a fly, from precipice into river-bed.

A special form of the snow-slip is known as *Wind-Schild*. When the force of the wind has drifted a mass of snow together on an overhanging slope, or heaped it up along the ledges of a beetling precipice, the mass, too heavy to sustain itself in that position, slips downward like snow from a steep roof. This is called a Wind-Schild, and the sudden fall of such a snow-slip may overwhelm men, horses, and sledges if it strikes them at a point when they can be carried off their legs and borne beyond the barriers of the road.[1] The Wind-Schild gives no warning of its approach.

Having now described the principal kinds of avalanches, it may be well to give some further details about their structure and the damage they inflict. I enjoyed an excellent opportunity last March of inspecting the interior of a Staub-Lawine which fell in the valley of Davos below the village of Glarus. At its deepest point it lay about sixty feet above the post-road, and a gallery had been bored through it with great labour for the

---

[1] This actually happened in February, 1889, on the Fluela. The post was coming up from Süss with three sledges—the postillion's sledge, as usual, in front, the conductor's behind, and the luggage-sledge between them without a driver. A Wind-Schild fell just after the postillion's sledge had passed, and caught the luggage-sledge, hurling it into the abyss below and killing the horse. The conductor, who followed, escaped without damage to himself or his conveyance.

passage of sledges. The walls of this tunnel were a compact mass of compressed snow, which the workmen cut into with pickaxes. You could make no impression on it with your fingers, and the marks of the pick were as sharp as on a block of marble. I noticed the following objects embedded in the portion of the avalanche exposed to view : large and small fragments of gneiss and limestone ; occasionally a huge boulder ; trunks of trees, mostly larch and pine, sawn flush with the snow walls ; branches ; innumerable twigs of cembra, larch, spruce, fir, and alder, so evenly distributed over the whole surface that the trees from which they had been torn must have been stripped by the whirl of wind and snow dust ;—these fragments were so firmly clutched that you could not scoop them out ; lastly, and most impressive, massive blocks of pure transparent ice, one of them six feet in length, three feet in depth, and how broad I do not know. This ice must have been torn by the blast from frozen waterfalls in the gullies of the Rutschtobel. The avalanche probably started at some 3000 feet above the Landwasser, descending from a district known as the Ausserberg, which is dominated by the two peaks of the Leidbachhorn and Aelplihorn.

It was clear on seeing how stones, stems, branches, twigs, blocks of ice, etc., were firmly wrought into the snow mass, that a man's body would be inextricably clasped by the same frozen substance. Standing in the gallery and reflecting on these things, I remembered with a thrill of awe that somewhere or another, at no great distance, the corpse of a man lay actually embedded there. He was called Caspar Valär, and he had been buried in the avalanche upon February 7. Gangs of peasants to the number of fifty had dug incessantly for seven days in the hopes of alighting on his body. Passing

Snow, Frost, Storm, and Avalanche

along the road, we had seen them at the stream side sounding the snow with poles, breaking it up with pickaxes, and delving into it with spades, and their sad resigned faces told how they sorrowed for their comrade. His fate might so easily be theirs too ! The savage Alpine winter claims its victims yearly. Therefore, *hodie tibi cras mihi, quod eras sum quod es ero* (to-day for thee, to-morrow for me ; what thou wast I am, what thou art I shall be) seemed written on their earnest features. At last this labour of the search, willingly and without wage given by the men of Glarus, had to be abandoned as impracticable. Caspar Valär was left to slumber in his icy sepulchre until the melting avalanche relaxed its hold in the springtime. His widow, meanwhile, with two young children, went on living in their wooden châlet on the hill which overlooks the dreadful thing which robbed her of her husband. On the 3rd of May she gave birth to a stillborn child, and on the same day her husband's corpse was brought to light. He had been carried across the stream by the rush of the Staub-Lawine, and his body was in excellent preservation.

Strange things are related of corpses which lie, like Caspar Valär's, for three months or more in avalanches. A man, on whose veracity I can count, told me that he knew a pair of brothers, one of whom was swept away by a Staub-Lawine. The other dug him out in the springtime, and found the corpse with a thick curling beard. Yet he remembered perfectly well that, on the day before his brother met his death, they had both of them shaved together. Of this he was confident ; and he told my informant the particulars with every mark of circumstantiality.

To be well embedded in an avalanche is better than to be immured, as sometimes happens, in a cranny or cliff or cavern which the avalanche has sealed by passing over it. Horrible stories are whispered regarding the bodies of men who have slowly died of hunger in such circumstances. Yet, so long as life lasts, there is always hope ; no pains are spared in ransacking the snow where human beings may be breathing out their last ; and cases of almost miraculous deliverance occasionally occur. Last February a young man called Domiziano Roberti, in the neighbourhood of Giornico, saw an avalanche descending on him. He crept under a great stone, above which there fell a large tree in such a position that it and the stone together roofed him from the snow, which soon swept over him and shut him up. There he remained 103 hours in a kind of semi-somnolence, and was eventually dug out, speechless and frightfully frost-bitten, but alive.

I find another still more curious story of salvation from the snow death on my notes. There is an elderly man at Küblis, in the Prättigau, unless perchance he died last winter, who haunted the village public-house and was only too ready to relate the following experience of his earlier days. The Fluela Pass, which is now a post-road, was in those years a mere bridle-path in summer, while in winter the people brought wine from the Valtelline across it on horseback or on little sledges not much larger than what we wrongly call toboggans now. The man in question, whom I will christen Hans Truog, though that is not his actual name, had been enveloped in a Schnee-Rutsch while making his way upward from the Engadine one stormy day in February. His body, disentangled from the snow stark and livid, was carried to the Hospiz and there left for dead. Hans was a native of the Prättigau, and soon after this had happened, another man from Prättigau came in behind

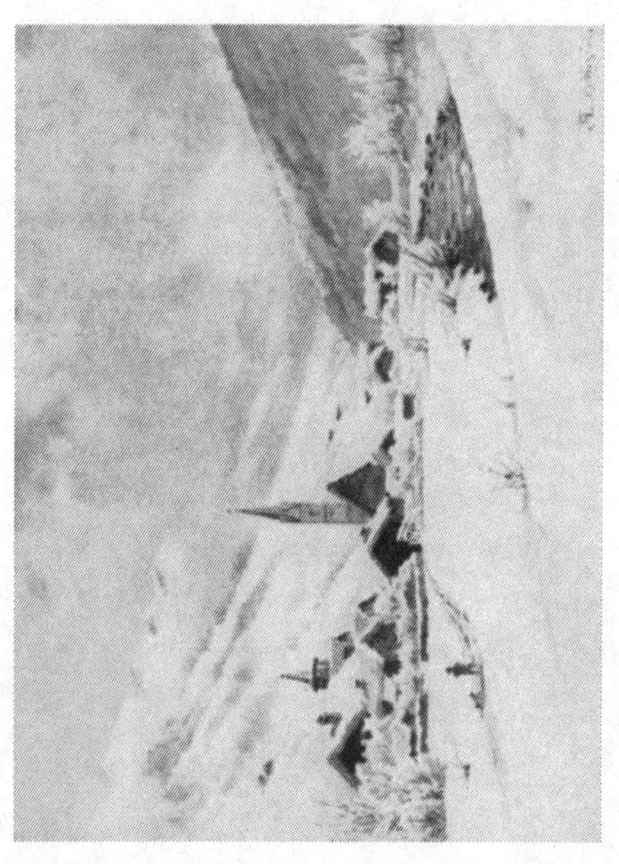

"KÜBLIS IN THE PRÄTTIGAU."

Snow, Frost, Storm, and Avalanche

him, bound for Davos and their home in the same valley. We will call him, for the sake of clearness, Christian Caduff. The folk of the refuge asked this Christian whether he would carry the dead man back to their common village in the Prättigau. Christian looked at the corpse, recognised the features of Hans Truog, and replied that he was willing to do so, but that, Hans having been a surly, ill-conditioned fellow in his lifetime, it would serve him well to drag his dead body down at the tail of the wine sledge. Accordingly, he lashed the frozen body firmly with a rope to the end of his own sledge, and after refreshing himself with wine in the Hospiz, set off at a quick trot across the snow to Tschuggen, a lonely inn about half-way between the Fluela and Davos-Dörfli. The snow upon these mountain tracks is very smooth and easy to glide over, therefore poor Hans Truog risked no injury to head or limb as he swiftly followed his churlish conductor's chariot. Nor was Christian Caduff so savage as Achilles when he dragged dead Hector round the walls of windy Troy through sand and stones. What could the tightly-knotted cords about the ankles matter to a corpse ? When Christian Caduff reached Tschuggen, he unyoked his horse and looked to his wine barrels, intending to pass the night there, for evening had already fallen. He also proceeded to untie the body of Hans Truog and stow it in the stable ; humanity touched his stolid heart so far at least as not to leave a dead man under the moon and stars. But what was his amazement when he perceived that the corpse was stirring, drowsily shifting as in some uneasy dream ! Having disentangled it from the sledge and drawn it into the warm living room, Hans gradually revived. The most he suffered from was the injury to his swollen and frost-bitten feet. This kept him several weeks at Tschuggen. But eventually he was able to

Our Life in the Swiss Highlands

walk home to Prättigau, where he lives, as I have said, to tell the tale. Christian Caduff, on the other hand, has long since joined his forefathers in the village graveyard. Had it not been for this man's churlishness, had Christian placed the corpse beside him on the wine-sledge, in all probability Hans Truog would never have revived from his frost sleep. Each minute in the cold air would have congealed the blood in his torpid veins more thoroughly, whereas the rapid passage of his body across the snow, the strong continuous friction of his skin, brought the blood again to the surface and stimulated vital circulation. Therefore to the barbarity of his neighbour he owed that life which the brute force of the avalanche had casually spared.

I have frequently mentioned the blast which avalanches bring with them, and which runs before the snow mass like a messenger of death. This phenomenon of the *Lawinen-Dunst*, as it is called, deserves some illustration. The fact is well authenticated, but its results seem almost incredible. Therefore I will confine myself to details on which I can positively rely. A carter, whom I know well for an honest fellow, told me that he was driving his sledge with two horses on the Albula Pass when an avalanche fell upon the opposite side of the gorge. It did not catch him. But the blast carried him and his horses and the sledge at one swoop over into deep snow, whence they emerged with difficulty. Another man, whom I count among my friends here, showed me a spot in the Schanfigg valley (between Chur and the Strela Pass) where one of his female relatives had been caught by the Lawinen-Dunst. She was walking to church when this happened, the people of her hamlet having taken the same path about a quarter of an hour before. The blast lifted her into the air, swept her

Snow, Frost, Storm, and Avalanche

from the road, and landed her at the top of a lofty pine, to which she clung with all the energy of desperation. The snow rushed under her and left the pine standing. It must have been an inconsiderable avalanche. Her neighbours, on their way back from church, saw her clutching for bare life to the slender apex of the tree, and rescued her. Many such cases could be mentioned ; a road-maker, named Schorta, this winter (February 17, 1888) was blown in like manner into the air below Brail, in the Engadine, and saved himself by grappling to a fir tree, else he would have been dashed to pieces against the face of a precipice ; as it was, he only lost his hat. A good friend of mine, the guide, Leonhard Guler, of Klosters, told me that, when he was a boy, he went with his father and a tall fellow from their village, in the winter, to bring down wild grass they had previously cut and stored upon the cliffs above Novai. They packed the hay in huge pieces of sacking carried for that purpose. On their return journey the blast of an avalanche caught their tall companion up and dashed him against a cliff, where he was literally smashed to pieces. Young Guler and his father collected the fragments, unbound a truss of hay, and carried the man's remains in it down to the village. There is no doubt that the story is true. I have been shown a place near Ems, in the Rhine Valley, above Chur, where a miller's house was carried bodily some distance through the air by the Lawinen-Dunst. Its inhabitants were all killed, except an old man about sixty and an infant of two years. Again, I may mention that the tower of the monastery at Dissentis was on one occasion blown down by the same cause. Cases are frequently met with where walls of houses, windows, and doors, have been smashed in by the wind of avalanches falling on the opposite flank of

Our Life in the Swiss Highlands

a narrow ravine.[1] I have myself seen a house wrecked by a Staub-Lawine, its roof removed in one piece by the blast, and its back wall and one side stove in by the weight of snow and stones and tiles which followed.

In order to understand the force of the Lawinen-Dunst, we must bear in mind that hundreds of thousands of tons of snow are suddenly set in motion in contracted chasms. The air displaced before these solid masses acts upon objects in their way like breath blown into a pea-shooter. From certain appearances in the torn and mangled trees which droop disconsolately above ravines down which an avalanche has thundered, it would also appear that the draught created by its passage acts like a vortex, and sucks in the stationary vegetation on either hand.

I will follow up these general details with a circumstantial account of what occurred here on February 6 last. The Fluela Pass, which connects Davos with the Lower Engadine, was closed to traffic on that day. But a man with whom I was acquainted, called Anton Broher (nicknamed the "Schaufel-Bauer" or "Knave of Spades," because of his black bushy beard), had started for the pass before this fact was generally known. Just before noon an avalanche caught him at a spot where avalanches rarely, if ever, fall, within a short distance of the inn at Tschuggen. An eye-witness saw him carried by the blast, together with his horse and sledge, 200 yards in the air across the mountain stream. The snow which followed buried him. He was subsequently dug out

[1] I quote this sentence from the *Davoser Wochenblatt* of March 7, 1888: "In Misox hat der Luftdruck einer Lawine, die unmittelbar neben dem Dorfe niederging, an einer ganzen Anzahl von Häusern die Wände eingedruckt." Misox, or Mesocco, is the chief place in the valley of that name on the Italian side of the San Bernardino Pass.

dead, with his horse dead, and the sledge beside him. The harness had been blown to ribbons in the air, for nothing could be found of it except the head-piece on the horse's neck.

I was curious to survey the spot where this had happened. Accordingly, when the state of the road permitted, I proceeded to the scene of action. Avalanches had fallen all along the opposite side of the valley in a continuous line, blocking up the river. The snow-banks over which I crawled were strewn with branches of cembra whirled across the ravine by the Lawinen-Dunst, and with boughs, twigs, débris of all sorts, torn from the larches under which I passed. In some places there was quite a heap of firewood brought together, and not a tree appeared uninjured. I extricated the leader of a fine young spruce, about eight feet long, from a snow-drift, and could see the broken stem from which it had been wrenched, across the water, in a direct line, at the distance of at least a thousand feet. The blast of the avalanches seemed to have exerted a sweeping upward force upon our side of the valley, as though, descending from the other side, it had been thwarted and compelled to ascend for want of space. The boughs from the torn trees were lifted into the snow at some height above us, and their cleavage showed that the wrench had come from below. When I reached the avalanche which carried Anton Broher across the water and killed him, I was astonished by its smallness and by the space he had traversed in the air. Yet there was the hole upon the other side, close to the stream, out of which his corpse, with horse and sledge, had been excavated.

Thanks to the prudence of our forefathers, villages are rarely placed in peril from avalanches. If we could read into the prehistoric annals of the Canton, it would be found, I think, that long before the Romans came here with their conquering legions, the safest sites for human habitation had been already selected and occupied through several centuries. Yet the elements are not to be depended on, and a few cases have occurred this winter in which whole communities have been exposed to the direst danger. I will select one instance as a specimen. Selma is a village of the Calancathal, which diverges, not far above Bellinzona, from the main valley of Mesocco to the north-west. On February 26 three avalanches descended on this spot. The largest fell at seven in the morning. The inhabitants of the opposite village, Landarenca, who had better opportunities for observing changes in the snow upon the heights above Selma, saw that a catastrophe was about to happen. They rang a tocsin on their church bells which alarmed the folk of Selma. Rushing out of their houses, these poor people were deafened with the roar of the descending snow mass. It swept onward, ploughing up their woods, gathering in volume and in speed, until it broke upon the solid building of their church. This bore the brunt of the attack and was demolished. But it acted like a breakwater. The avalanche, arrested in its course, yet not brought to quiescence, surged round the church and poured into the village. Houses were buried and partly shattered. On reckoning their numbers the escaped villagers perceived that four persons were missing—three women and an old man of eighty. One woman was subsequently discovered alive behind the stove of her shattered kitchen. A second was buried in a stable and extricated alive. A third had also taken refuge in a stable, whence she was dug out. The old man remained in bed with the snow piled high above him. He wondered that the night lasted so long, and was astonished when the rescue party came and hauled him through a window out upon a tunnel they had excavated to his dwelling.[1]

The Calancathal, in which this happened, suffered severely later in the spring. On March 31 eight great avalanches swept at once into it from both sides, burying houses and stables. The telegraph announcing this catastrophe ran as follows :—" Calancathal is one huge avalanche."[2]

It is worthy of observation that Schlag-Lawinen are comparatively slow in movement, and give intimations of their coming. This accounts for the fact that, while great damage is done to buildings, human lives are rarely sacrificed in considerable numbers. Fetan, in the Lower Engadine (between Schuls and Süss), is an upland village, which has suffered cruelly from both fire and snow ; and its history may be worth recording.[3] In the year 1682 a great avalanche swept over it. Six persons were killed, but the rest of the villagers, expecting some such catastrophe, had abandoned their houses. In one dwelling nothing was left standing but the living-room and one bedroom. These, however, contained the mother of the family and all her children, who escaped unhurt. In 1720 an avalanche demolished fifteen houses at one swoop. In one of them a party of twenty-six young men and women were assembled. They were all buried in the snow, and only three survived. Altogether thirty-six persons perished at that time, of whom thirty-two were consigned to a common grave upon the 11th of February. In 1812 a similar catastrophe occurred, destroying houses and stables. But on this occasion the inhabitants had been forewarned and left the village. A curious story is told about the avalanche of 1812. One of the

---

[1] See *Freier Rhätier*, March 10, 1888.

[2] *Ibid.*, April 1.　　　　　　　[3] *Ibid.*, March 6.

folk of Fetan, after abandoning his homestead to its fate, remembered that he had forgotten to bring away his Bible. The man was named Nuot Cla, or vulgarly Nuot Sar Chasper. In the teeth of the impending danger, through the dark night, he waded back across the snow-drifts, and saved the precious volume. Nearly the whole of Fetan was consumed by a conflagration on September 23, 1885, and this year it has again been devastated by avalanches. Yet the people stick to their old site, rebuilding their dwellings which the elements destroy.

It would be easy to multiply details of this kind. The annals of Davos, where I am writing, abound in striking records of the avalanches of past years. I will confine myself to a single extract from one of the local chronicles, which, though it has the air of legend, may well be founded on a real historical event. There was a family living at Ob-Laret, beyond Wolfgang, on the road to Klosters, in a wooden châlet, which was entirely sub-merged by snow and avalanche. They could not extri-cate themselves with all their toil, and soon consumed the provisions which the house contained. Famine stared them in the face. The mother of the family, in this dire contingency, decided that one member should be sacri-ficed for the benefit of all. But first she brought her children together in prayer, and then drew lots. The lot fell upon a little girl, who knelt down and declared her willingness to yield her life up, when suddenly a loud noise in the chimney was heard, and a chamois came tumbling down into their midst. This animal removed the necessity of human sacrifice, provided an immediate supply of food, and indicated a way out into the open air.

Snow, Frost, Storm, and Avalanche

III

I cannot do better than continue these observations with some account of my personal experiences upon the mountain roads. With this object in view, it will be well to describe the mode of travelling in use here. The snow-tracks which cross the higher passes are very narrow; and for this reason little low open sledges drawn by one horse are commonly employed. The sledge is a box, shaped somewhat like a car in a merry-go-round, into which a pair of travellers are shut by means of a wooden frame or lid moving up and down on hinges. This lid rises to the breast of a seated person, and protects his legs from falling snow. The upper part of his body is exposed. When the sledge upsets, which is not unfrequently the case, the whole falls quietly upon one side, and discharges its contents. The wooden frame or lid, being movable upon its hinges, enables a man to disengage himself without difficulty. The driver stands upon a ledge behind, passing the reins between the shoulders of the passengers. There are no springs to the vehicle, which bumps and thumps solidly in the troughs of the road, dispelling all illusions as to the facile motion of a sledge. If it is needful to pass another vehicle, the horse plunges up to his belly in soft snow upon one side, then struggles furiously, gains his feet, and lifts the sledge with quick spasmodic effort to the beaten track again. These sledges carry no luggage. A second horse is used, who follows close behind, and draws a truck on runners laden with all kinds of baggage. He has no driver; and the result is that these luggage-sledges frequently upset. It is always safest to travel with the post in winter, because the horses know each yard of the road from one stage to another. But a nervous traveller may even thus be exposed to trials of his courage ; for economy makes the postmaster provide the smallest possible number of postillions, and passengers are sometimes sent across a mountain in a sledge without a driver, following the sledge in front. I once crossed the Julier in a dark night of January, without a postillion and without any reins to guide the horse by. My reason told me that the beast knew his business better than I did. But, none the less, I felt forlornly helpless when he was floundering about in depths of snow I could not realise. It is always best to take things as they come, however ; and I comforted myself by reflecting that even an Englishman is a parcel which post-masters are bound to deliver safely at its destination.

Some of the pleasantest days of my life have been spent in these post-sledges on the passes of Graubünden. The glory of unclouded sunlight, the grimness of storm, and the mystery of midnight among the peaks of Albula, Fluela, Julier, Bernina, Maloja, Splügen, Bernhardin, are known to me through them. They are not luxurious ; but I can recommend them with authority in preference to the stuffy top-heavy closed carriages on runners which the inexperience of foreigners is now bringing into fashion. Though I have been out in very bad weather in these open sledges I never took any harm. The following notes of a day's journey on March 13, 1888, show that the risk of catching cold may be considerable ; yet I would back myself to catch cold in a German or Swiss railway-carriage more easily at the same season of the year. " I drove in an open sledge from Landquart to Davos, about nine hours, while it snowed incessantly, thick wet snow, very soft and sweet to breathe in, lovely on the woods

Snow, Frost, Storm, and Avalanche

of beech and pine, fantastic on the blue-green frozen cataracts. A dreamy day of long grey pearly distances, snow-laden orchards, hamlets slumbering in snow, and tall fir forests drooping their snow-laden branches over me. My outer garments were soaking wet ; fur cap and hair too. When we reached Laret these wet things began to freeze. When we reached Wolfgang a mighty blast tore snow from the meadows and whirled it round us, chilling me to the marrow. When we arrived at Davos-Dörfli I was harnessed in solid mail of ice, and my forehead bristled with icicles."

In the winter of 1887-88 I undertook many short journeys with the view of inspecting the unusual phenomena of avalanches. The most interesting of these was the last, when I left Davos with one of my daughters for Italy by the routes of Landwasser, Julier, and Maloja. We set off at 6 a.m., under a clear frosty sky, upon April 5. Owing to Föhn-wind and constant traffic the snow-road was broken into deep ruts and holes, which made our sledges leap, jump, bump, buck, lurch, and thud in ways quite indescribable to those who have not experienced the process. The luggage-sledge behind upset three times in the course of the first five miles. The great avalanche at Glarus we passed by means of the gallery which I have described above,[1] and were soon engaged in the dreary gorges of the Züge. This name has been given to the narrow and precipitous ravine through which the Landwasser goes thundering to join the Albula and Rhine, because on either hand, for the distance of about two miles, its steep sides are swept by avalanches. Zug is the local expression for the track followed by an avalanche, and the ravine in question is a continuous series of Züge. I have seen nothing in the

Our Life in the Swiss Highlands

Alps which impressed me so strongly with the force—the cruel blind force of nature—as the aspect of the Züge on that April morning. Avalanche upon avalanche had been pouring down into the valley from 3000 feet above. The stream was buried beneath Staub-Lawinen, Schlag-Lawinen, Grund-Lawinen, to the depth of scores of feet. Here and there the torrent burst with clamorous roar from the jaws of one dark icy cavern only to plunge again into the silence and the blackness of another yawning mass of desolation. Millions of tons of snow, of uprooted rocks, and of mangled forests were lying huddled together, left to rot beneath the fretting influence of rain or south winds, slowly losing dignity of outline and substance in a blur of mottled, besmirched, pitted hideousness. Here there was a tunnel in the cliff, festooned with frozen stalactites, and clogged with the débris of ice dislodged by its own weight from the dripping roof. There the walls of marble snow, where excavation had been made in avalanches, rose to a height of twenty feet above our heads. Next came a horrid Grund-Lawine, filthy, cynical, with its wreck of stones and rubble, gnawed stems, shattered parapets, and snapped telegraph-posts. Over these we had to crawl as well as we could ; the horses could only just contrive to get across the ridged deluge, climbing and descending, climbing and descending, on narrow tracks delved by the road-makers. These tracks are encumbered with enormous blocks of limestone and round boulders, which fall independently of avalanches from the scars left by avalanches on the heights above. And always rocks rolling in the ravines with a sullen roar ; always, the snow-slips shifting on the cliffs around us ; always, from time to time, the sullen clamour of the maddened torrent as it leapt from one black cavern to another. There are several tunnels

PIZ JULIER FROM THE HOSPICE.

Snow, Frost, Storm, and Avalanche

pierced in the living rock, and just before the mouth of the last of these, a Grund-Lawine had fallen two hours earlier. It had carried away the road and parapets, depositing a sharply-inclined slope of snow and dirty débris in their place. This we clambered over as well as we could, on foot. The horses, helped by their brawny drivers, had great difficulty in dragging the sledges across its uneven treacherous slope, which extended in a straight line to the stream-bed twenty yards below. The whole ravine left a sad and horrifying impression of mere ruin on the mind—nature-forces spending themselves in waste, acting now as they have acted for past millions of years, blindly clashing together, apparently with no result except destruction, certainly with no regard for man's convenience, and still more certainly with serious imperilment to human life. Yet we must not forget that these deluges of snow have their beneficent aspect. By relieving the upper regions of the Alps of their accumulated burdens, they prevent the snow of exceptional winters from forming into névées, which would sooner or later settle down as glaciers, covering the central chains, and altering the climate of the whole country.

I was glad to emerge from the Züge and to gain those larch woods on the way to Wiesen, from which a distant and glorious prospect may be enjoyed of the pure mountain summits glittering in morning light. To think that those calm tracts of silver snow, so exquisitely moulded into peaks and "finely-pencilled valleys" above their sombre pine-woods, should be responsible for all the havoc and the horror of the Züge !

I shall not dwell upon the next stages of this day's journey, which were performed in carriages ; for the snow had melted on the post-road from Wiesen to Tiefenkasten and half-way up the Julier. The evidences of damage caused by avalanches were interesting, but need not be recorded. It began to snow when we approached the village of Schweiningen. Enormous flakes swirled lazily and heavily through still grey air. As I caught them against the blackness of the pine woods, they looked like a countless multitude of Apollo butterflies. The flakes were hardly less in size, and had the same clumsy, helpless flight. From this time forward snow fell more or less continuously till the end of our long journey. Just below Mühlen we crossed an avalanche, which had cut its track out of a forest of young pines and larches. The section through which we passed revealed on both sides a compact mass of stems, sawn through to make the road. There was more of solid wood than snow, and the damage must have been mainly caused by the Lawinen-Dunst.

At Mühlen we had to take an open sledge again. Here, as the day was drawing to its close, I doubted whether it was prudent to fare forward in the whirling snow. But there is fascination in completing journeys once begun ; besides, we wished to cross the Julier before the snow could mound us up and stop our going. So we called fresh horses, and went forth into the twilight. The evening slowly dwindled, while we jolted, lunging and lurching along the troughed and deeply-cloven road to Stalla. Imagination quails before those bumps and jumps. They threw the horse upon his knees, ourselves upon our faces in the sledge, and the driver from his stand behind it. At Stalla there was the opportunity again of resting for the night. But the same impulse swayed us now as before at Mühlen. Our spirits rose, while the sleet fell thickly and the wind wailed grimly, at the thought of threading those mysterious snow-ways of the pass in darkness. Onward, then, we drove,

Snow, Frost, Storm, and Avalanche

silencing the postillion, who more than recommended the wisdom of a halt. Night closed round, and up we travelled for two hours, at a foot's pace, turning corners which we could not see or feel, exploring trackless wastes of drift, with stinging snow-shafts on our faces. The Hospiz was reached at last; and here we had a third chance of suspending our journey and resting for the night. Imagine a hut of rough-hewn stone, crowded with burly carters, swarming out to greet us by the light of one dim lantern. Over the roof of the hovel surged the mounded snow, and curved itself in billowy lines of beauty—like the breasts, I thought, of Amphitrite's nymphs, as Pheidias might have moulded them—above those granite eaves. The carters emerged from a cellar, as it seemed, climbing up six feet of snow by steps cut out to reach the level of the road. As they stood in the doorway, stalwart fellows clad in shaggy serge, like bears, the snow-wreaths curling from the rafters touched their hairy heads. I had no adverse mind to staying there and fraternizing with these comrades through a winter's night. Nor did I fear for my daughter's comfort. I knew that she would be well; our beds, though cold, would certainly be dry. Winter on the tops of mountains has this merit, that damp can find no place there. And the hearts of mountaineers, beneath their husk of roughness, are the hearts of gentlemen. But the impulse to fare forward, the dream-like sense of something to be blindly done, the more practical fear that we might be snowed up for days in this frostbound "cave of care," bade me order out fresh horses. They were ready at my call, for we were travelling extrapost, and the telegraph-wires, though drowned in snow, discharge their messages. I liked the new postillion. I did not fancy the horse which was harnessed to our

71

sledge. He was a tall, lean chestnut ; and chestnuts, as I know by experience, are apt to feel impatient if they get embarrassed in deep snow. As the sequel proved, I made a false shot ; for this chestnut showed himself up to every trick and turning in the road we had to follow. Another horse was yoked to the luggage-sledge behind us, then left to do as best he could, without a driver—such is the custom on these mountains. He did his best by following the beast in front. I cared little about luggage at that moment ; what I wanted was to arrive at Silvaplana safely with my daughter.

The descent from the Hospiz was grimly solemn and impressive. Passing from the friendly light of that one stable-lantern, we now entered the dim obscurity of dreamland—a mist of whirling snowflakes, driven onward by the wind which grew in violence. It is never wholly dark upon the snow ; but the lustreless pallor of the untracked wilderness, fading off on every side into formless haze, and the complete effacement of all objects to which the sight is accustomed in these regions, are peculiarly trying to eyes and nerves. Here and there we could perceive the tops of black stakes and telegraph-posts emerging from the undulating drift. Here and there for considerable intervals they were completely hidden. As these posts average thirty feet in height, some conception of the snow-depth may be formed. There was also, at times, a faint suggestion of impending crags and masses of black rock on this hand or on that. Like the hulls of vessels seen through fog at sea, they swam into sight and shrank out of it again phantasmally. Nothing more was visible ; nothing on which the sense of sight could seize for comfort and support. The track was obliterated, buried in fresh-fallen snow and storm-drift. Everything seemed changing, shifting, yielding to

Snow, Frost, Storm, and Avalanche

the uniformity of elemental treacherousness. The winter road upon the Julier plunges straight downward, cutting across the windings of the summer post-road, which lies with all its bridges, barricades, and parapets five fathoms deep below. At one spot, where absolutely nothing appeared to indicate the existence of a track, the postillion muttered in our ears, " Now we must trust to the horse ; if he misses, it is over with us—*es ist mit uns um*." The reins were laid upon the chestnut's shoulders, and he succeeded in feeling, scenting out the way. Pausing, sounding at each step with his fore feet, putting his nose down to smell, sometimes hardly stirring, sometimes breaking into a trot for a few seconds, then coming to a sudden halt again, then moving cautiously as though in doubt, he went with interruptions forward. The sledge-bells had been left behind at the Hospiz for fear of avalanches ; their tinkling or the crack of a whip suffices in such weather to dislodge a snow-slip. The other horse with the baggage-sledge followed behind, attending eagerly to every movement of his comrade. And so we passed silently, glidingly, mysteriously downward into the gulf of utter gloom, without making the least sound. The only noise we heard was the eldritch shrieking of the wind, and a horrible æolian music from the telegraph-wires close at our ears. We could touch these wires with our fingers when they were not buried in snow, and they thrilled with a sharp metallic shudder like the voices of banshees or lost wailing women, uttering shrill threats and curses, murmuring their drowsy runes of doom. Sometimes we ascended avalanches, and there there was blank vacancy and utter silence—every object huddled in ruin, and the path smoothed out by softly-curving wreaths. The horse was up to his belly in unwrinkled drifts. Only through changes of movement in the sledge did we know that we were climbing steeply up or plunging perilously down. On the dizzy top of one of these avalanches it happened that the clouds above us broke, and far aloft, in a solitary space of sky, the Great Bear swam into sight for a few moments. This little starlight was enough to reveal the desolation of the place, and the yawning chasms on our right and left. I knew by experience how narrow, how high-uplifted, is the thread of traversable pathway in such passages. A false step to this side or to that would plunge us into oceans of soft smothering snow from which in darkness we could not hope to extricate ourselves. Yet the two brave horses kept the track. Ursa Major was swallowed up in mist again. The wind rallied with fierce clutching grasps, while we cautiously descended from the avalanche and resumed what must have been the winter road. although we could not see or feel it. Just then cembras began to show their dark masses on the cliffs, and something more sombre even than the night loomed far ahead before us. The cembras told me that we were nearing Silvaplana, and the obscurity in front must surely be the bulk of the Bernina group beyond the Engadine. Courage ! We shall soon be under shelter ! But, even as I said these words, the whirlwind scooped the snow again in blinding drifts around us, and the telegraph-banshees shrieked with redoubled spitefulness : " Come away, come away to us ! Come and be buried as we have been ! Come and be damned in the prisons of frost with us ! The wind that makes us croon our weird song shall wind the snow-wreaths over you !" That was not to be our destiny, however ; for, after jolting through another avalanche, the excavated walls of which touched our sledges on each hand, we made a few sharp turns, saw lights ahead, and came lurching into the little street

Snow, Frost, Storm, and Avalanche

of Silvaplana opposite the hospitable "Wilde Mann." We had been driving for fourteen hours over every conceivable kind of road—rough, broken, precipitous, trackless—and we were glad enough to get a late supper and a warm bed. In this account of a night passage of the Julier I have not spoken about cold or exposure to weather. Indeed, we did not think about these things, nor did we suffer from them. Of course we were snowed over, and almost throttled sometimes by the wind. But cold is little felt on mountain passes when the air is dry and the traveller wears proper clothing.

The storm howled on all night, but died away before the morning. Long ere the sun had risen on the Engadine, his glorious rays were scattering clouds and silvering mists above the glaciers of Bernina. They fled like smoke, or formed themselves in squadrons, which went slowly rolling down the ridges of the hills before a wakening breeze which blew from Italy. That day's journey was accomplished in brilliant light; and the huge avalanches we had to traverse—eleven of them between Silvaplana and Maloja, not counting minor snow-slips—were as white and glittering as alabaster. These were either Staub-Lawinen which had fallen in February, or Schlag-Lawinen brought down by the warm weather of the last week. At Maloja the extent of the winter snowfall made itself very obvious. Large houses and stables were literally buried; the mass of snow upon their roofs was connected in a long even line with the snow upon the meadows, while deep galleries had been cut out for access to the doors or windows. The sudden drop from Maloja's mountain parapet into an Italian valley is always impressive. To-day it was remarkably so; for the hanging woods and precipices, along which the road winds by a series of cleverly engineered zigzags, were encumbered with soft curving, beautifully moulded snow—fold over fold ; lip stretching down to lip ; so heavy, so voluminous, so airily suspended, that they seemed to keep their balance by a miracle. Indeed, in several places the forest had been cut by avalanches. But the grandest sight was just above Casaccia. On the night of March 27 two huge Schlag-Lawinen fell from different quarters in the neighbourhood of this village ; and on the night of the 28th a third descended from the Canaletta gorge, and stormed around the ruined church of San Gaudenzio. All these were visible as we approached Casaccia ; and the last of them had to be traversed at its greatest breadth. It was here that I studied a newly-fallen Schlag-Lawine in its most picturesque form and in a highly-romantic position.[1] Travellers by the Maloja will certainly remember the deserted church of San Gaudenzio, and the delicate tracery of its windows, on their right hand coming from the Engadine. It has escaped from total destruction by a miracle. Through a fortunate deflection of the avalanche the main stream, with its burden of trees and stones, swept past the building. Yet the snow is piled so high around it that a man can step from the level of the avalanche on to its highest wall, while its single door is mounded up.[2] Rarely have I contemplated anything of beauty more fairy-like and fantastic than this Schlag-Lawine, white and luminous beneath the cheerful sunbeams, curling round the grey ruin, and stretching long firths and pine-plumed pinnacles into the valley !

The winter is over and gone. Among the cities of Italy, upon the lagoons of Venice, the memory of those grey months of snow and storm has melted like a dream of midnight. Meanwhile the same forces which un-

[1] See above, page 49.
[2] See letter from Bergell to *Freier Rhätier*, April 11, 1888.

THE PIZ BERNINA AND THE MORTERATCH
GLACIER.

Snow, Frost, Storm, and Avalanche

leashed the avalanches, and sent them thundering down their paths of ruin, have been slowly but surely consuming their frail substance. Warm wind, the *Schnee-fresser*, and April rains, have made them vanish into dew. Where the Adige sweeps toward the sea at Brondolo, where swollen Brenta licks Bassano's wooden bridge, perhaps we pause to think one moment of our friends, the Staub-Lawine, Schlag-Lawine, Grund-Lawine, Schnee-Rutsch. This, then, this flood of water, racing to the ocean, is what they have become !

Returning to the Alps in summer, we look for them wellnigh in vain. Here and there, like the carcase of a whale rotting upon the sea-shore, some mighty but diminished monster may still be seen, with the havoc it has wrought, the splintered pines, rocks, displumed larches, battered alders, strewn around it. Perhaps we cross a desolate high pass where winter dwells rebellious in unwillingness to quit his hold on earth. The torrent is bridged over there with snow, and heavy masses clog the gullies. On June 8, in this same year, I traversed the Fluela, and had an hour in open sledges at the top. Thus, after nine weeks' wandering in paradise, I re-entered my mountain home by the same way as out I went in April.

A dead avalanche upon an upland hillside is an almost pathetic spectacle. It has furrowed its way through the pine wood, and grooved a track of desolation in the valley. The stream is choked with its compact incumbency of snow. Birch-trees and forlorn fir branches nod upon its broad, dusky-white back, bending leafless boughs, or tossing draggled plumes in drear disarray. All round and far below, the meadows smile with flowers and waving grasses. Yet here at least, in the midst of spring, lies winter ! Then, as the June sun rises day by

Our Life in the Swiss Highlands

day with stronger beams, the avalanche decays and trickles into rivulets. You see little flowers thrusting their jewelled heads from the brown fringe of withered sward around its frozen borders. First come the lilac bells of soldanella, and crocuses like white shells on some sea-shore of romance. Each successive day brings a new fringe of blossoms round the retreating snow, and each evening sees them pass away into green grasses. So brief is the bloom-time of the earliest flowers ; so active is the life of earth in summer ! Then globed ranunculus and pale anemone, geranium and pearl-white lily, gentians with their enamelled cups of peacock blue, pink primroses and creamy butterworts, start in rainbow circles from the fresh young sward. Soon, all too soon, the tall grass gains upon these vernal flowers. The mowers with their scythes ascend the Alp, and before July is over we have to wait for winter, when the avalanche will surely fall again. J. A. S.

NOTES

I

The preceding article was written in June, 1888. Since then an official report has been published of the damage inflicted on the Canton by avalanches during the winter of 1887-88.

Six hundred avalanches are included in this estimate ; but many thousands are not reckoned, because they fell in places where no injury to life or property had to be considered.

Twenty men, it seems, were involved. Of these, seven were extricated alive, and thirteen perished.

The injury to live stock was small : one horse, two cows, eight sheep, nine goats, and a swarm of bees.

The number of buildings wrecked was as follows :—Four chapels, fifteen dwelling-houses, one hundred and seventeen large stables, eighteen hay-barns, thirteen huts upon the Alpine pastures, two flour-mills, two saw-mills, one distillery, and ten wooden bridges.

The total loss to the Canton, including public and private property, amounted to £14,300 in round figures. It is impossible, however, to state with accuracy the value of the forests destroyed.

II

Avalanches are unlike glaciers in this respect, that they offer none of the problems which streams of ice in motion have presented to the scientific observer.

Given certain conditions of weather, certain accumulations of snow on the higher levels of the mountain ranges, and certain disturbing causes, the simple force of gravity is sufficient to account for the descent of these formidable torrents.

The disturbing cause may be either violent wind acting upon unwieldy masses of suspended snow ; or rain soddening similar masses, and adding to their weight and solidity ; or the passage of animals across ledges and wreaths whence snow is easily detached ; or even the vibrations of a man's voice, a horse-bell, or a carter's whip. It may, again, be the spontaneous subsidence of a sheet of snow too cumbrous to support itself upon a steep declivity.

The small amount of snow dislodged in the first instance by any one of these causes sets an avalanche in motion. In ninety-nine cases out of a hundred, the snow slides a little distance, and then is arrested by some inequality in the ground. But if circumstances are favourable to its advance, it accumulates more and more material from the surrounding slopes, acquires momentum, and eventually rushes forward with irresistible force. In order to generate an overwhelming avalanche, dangerous to whole villages and forests, the original snow-slip must have occurred at a considerable distance, measured by thousands of feet, and must have been so situated as to draw a large area of snow-field into motion.

Roughly speaking, then, all avalanches, however distinguished by specific names, originate in snow-slips, which, unless they are arrested near the source, convulse a large portion of their neighbourhood, and discharge themselves with fatal fury on the valley.

III

Several artificial means have been tried for securing life, traffic, and property against avalanches.

We have seen that the mischief begins high up on the bare cliffs and slopes above the forests. The passing of a chamois, the halloo of a hunter, the crack of a postillion's whip, is sufficient to set snow enough going there to overwhelm a village.

Measures are not usually taken at the altitude where avalanches originate.

The first and most important line of defence is the forest itself; and for this reason the forest laws of Switzerland are very severe. A man is not allowed to fell a tree in his own wood without the forester's consent. Everything is done to preserve the natural rampart afforded by a mass of pines.

In the second place, where avalanches descend regularly every year, stone galleries are built, or tunnels are mined out of the solid rock to protect roads. We have examples of these galleries and tunnels in the Züge, near Davos.

Scientific engineers are eager to change these plans of defence. They believe that the root of the mischief ought to be attacked. In places where avalanches are expected, at the tops of the Züge, they recommend the building of terraces and dwarf-walls, so as to arrest the earliest snow-slip. Lower down, in the forest zone, piles should be driven into the ground, and fenced with wattling. If these pre-

Snow, Frost, Storm, and Avalanche

cautions were taken, it is believed that the avalanche would be arrested at its commencement and impeded in its descent.

Fifty or sixty well-known avalanche tracks have been successfully treated by these means in Switzerland.

J. A. S.

IV

The following letter describes our passage of the Julier in storm at night. It was written upon the day after the event :—

CHIAVENNA, *April* 6, 1888.

DEAREST L.—Yesterday was indeed " a trying day." As I sit in this Italian inn, with my windows wide open, and a warm spring rain pattering down on the boys at play in the piazza, I can scarcely believe that the bumpy and exciting events of our journey over the mountains into this land are true. To begin with, then, the road from Davos to Wiesen excelled all my powers of word-painting for atrociousness. We were much delayed, as our luggage was upset three times, entailing much skurrying, hoisting, and rearrangement on each successive occasion. " Immer dieselbe Geschichte," remarked the postillion, grimly sarcastic, each time. And how could it be otherwise, considering that the road was a ploughed field and the luggage-horse had no driver ? We changed to wheels before Wiesen, and continued on them to Crapaneira, thence to Alveneu. At Alveneu the hepaticas were bursting into bloom. Here we got into our extra-post, and on to Tiefenkasten. At that place we lunched. The weather, which had been fine before, was now rapidly turning bad. The only horses which we could procure were three which had just brought a party down from Mühlen. They were consequently not of the freshest. Before we had got far it had begun to rain. As we advanced up the pass the rain turned to snow, and increased into a tremendous snow-

81

storm. I allow that I often exaggerate, but indeed the flakes
were enormous this time. Father compared them to Apollo
butterflies. They were not smaller than that. The fresh
snow increased the badness of the road. Our great unwieldy
Sechsplätziger (or carriage made to hold six people) trailed
wearifully onward. The postillion either could not, or else
would not, make his horses move at more than a foot's pace.
We crossed the remains of three great avalanches. They
had done tremendous damage to the young forest, tearing
up and snapping off masses of trees, which lay about the
tracks of the avalanches and across the valley, as though
to bear a living record of the wicked strength of that fallen
snow. At Mühlen we changed to sledges, and decided to
push on again, as it was only four o'clock, and there seemed
to be no reason for staying there, especially as no one even
warned us against proceeding.

From Mühlen to Stalla the road was so ghastly in its ditches
and bumps that one forgot the world could be smooth. We
found that standing upright in our sledge somewhat broke
the horror of the forward lurch. Added to this, the storm
grew thicker, and twilight crept imperceptibly over us. We
had an old weather-worn man for driver. He suddenly began
to upbraid us. "How dared you start over the pass," he
cried, "on such a night and at such an hour ? I cannot
promise that we shall get over." It was impossible to argue.
His was one of those domineering spirits. Whatever I suggested he saw reason to contradict, even if I said the very
same things as he had said himself. He finally declared that
our last chance was to sleep at the Hospiz. "Very well,
then," I roared ; for the wind roared too, and the driving
snow froze in ice across my lips ; also, he was deaf. "It is
not very well ; it is quite impossible," he retorted, fiercely.
"With this weather you will be snowed up. There you will
remain ! You will never get down !"—"Then go on while
it is yet possible."—"I cannot go on ; I do not know the
pass well. I have no boots." This was a final stroke.
Father was mute, partly because of the storm, and partly

PIZ JULIER AND PIZ ALBANA IN WINTER.

Snow, Frost, Storm, and Avalanche

because conversation of this sort carried on in sheer despair leads to nothing. So, finally, we all relapsed into deadly silence. The almost invisible track wound grandly up over such masses of snow that one became utterly confused. Mighty avalanches of pure white stood out like towers into the twilight at times, and then were lost. Still we wound on.

But what have been perhaps the most dangerous minutes of my life were yet to come. It is a fine thing to know that one has gone through a thing so grand in one's life that one cannot forget it ; and such a thing, I really think, was this. Our horses were good, and finally the Hospiz loomed grey and dull far above us. This Hospiz, more than most Swiss Hospizes, can be fitly described as a " cave of care." With frozen snow wheeling round its walls in eddies, its low roof draped in icicles, which fell to meet the drifts upon the ground, it could scarcely have struck an outsider as being attractive. To us at that minute it meant human life and comfort. From its snow-buried door issued a crowd of interested and burly men, all talking, laughing, and all hopeful ; amongst them a cheerful postillion. Our tormentor now threw the reins gladly over to this one, who guaranteed to take us down the pass. Hope had at last returned to us, and in our folly we again started into the night and the storm. It is this drive that I never can forget. There was so much fresh snow that the road (if indeed there was any) had quite disappeared. The horse found his way without any help, the luggage-horse following all by himself. The postillion whispered into my ear : " One false step—*und es ist um mit uns !*" The winter road goes *quite* perpendicular and straight down over the wilderness of eternal snows. As we crouched forward, I could stretch my arm forth *over* the telegraph-wires, and the poles, you know, are about thirty feet high, and this was sheer depth of snow, not avalanche. There was utter solitude and silence. Sometimes the wind rose behind us, and came hurrying through the telegraph-wires, uttering wild screams as though phantom women were racing at our backs. Not a bell on the horses for fear of avalanches, and a driving snow falling over all. Once, when something was wrong with the harness, and we had to stop a second or two, I looked up into the sky. The wind had torn the clouds apart, and there, in a bit of black sky, all the stars of the Great Bear were shining quite placidly and still. They were soon lost in the storm, however, and we continued our descent. One tremendous avalanche choked the whole valley at one point, and this we had to cross. When at last we saw the broad stretch of the Engadine and its scattered lights, it seemed an unreal and a strange thing. I have never hardly felt as tired as I did when I got out of the sledge at Silvaplana. "What a good thing great-auntie isn't with us," as our small cousin said on that dreary walk across the sun-baked moor. Perhaps those were my thoughts about my family, if indeed I thought at all; but I was so stupid that I found the old landlady pulling me along by one arm, whilst telling her daughter to take the other.

Well, it was all a splendid experience. We both enjoyed it, and I never felt frightened once, though I may have felt disheartened sometimes. We were in bed by ten, and up to-day at five again, and off in the post across the Maloja. It was a beautiful morning at starting, and such a grand drive! bumpy, but peaceful, after our previous experience. We crossed eleven real big avalanches after Silvaplana, and had two upsets of the luggage-cart—otherwise quiet. The snow round Maloja lies a great depth, the houses are buried up to their roofs, and it is also very deep on the Stütze to Casaccia. The most magnificent avalanche I ever saw was here. It lay like a large blue glacier full of sad old trees which had lived their quiet lives up there on the mountain-side for ages, and were now caught and carried off to wither in this terrific fiend's embrace.

Well—you will now be saying, like Mr. Gosse and the mesembryanthemums, "We cannot bear avalanches." So I will write no more upon them.

I have been out and seen the spring. Here in Chiavenna the snow-flakes grow in millions, all up and down the hill-

Snow, Frost, Storm, and Avalanche

sides, below the chestnut-trees, and along the mossy banks of little running streams in meadows. There are crocuses, hepaticas, cowslips, and a wealth of primulas. The earth is warm and brown and moist. It is a joy to kneel upon it and to snuff up the delicious scent of growing things. The grass is already green down here in Italy. Snows and frosts and sledges seem hundreds of miles away. M. S.

CHIAVENNA IN APRIL

THE majority of people who winter in the High Alps do so at present on account of health—their own health or that of relatives in whom they are interested.

One of their chief difficulties at the termination of the winter season is to know where and how to pass the early spring. Human nature cannot endure more than six or seven months of snow ; and there are few men or women, except, perhaps, incipient lovers, who do not want a change of hotel society after so long a period.

When the days lengthen, when the sun rises higher in the heavens, and our white-sheeted valleys grow monotonous, and the softer south winds whisper in the afternoon, folk begin to reflect that flowers are blossoming, and birds singing, and peach-trees clothing their bare boughs with crimson, in happier regions not so far away. How easy it would be to get to Italy, we cry ! One day will carry us outside this dream-world of dead snows into lands thrilling and budding with newly-awakened life.

The usual thing is for the winter visitors to consult their doctor in these circumstances, and to ask him where they ought to go. They act rightly ; for the doctor judges better than they can what is safe and unexceptionable for their health-conditions. Yet the doctor himself is under difficulties. He has not always enjoyed the opportunity of living in the climates which his clients wish

Chiavenna in April

to visit. Not unfrequently he knows far less about them, except on hearsay—that is, upon the statements and statistics furnished by medical papers and self-styled authorities—than many of his patients do, who have travelled through those countries, or have dwelt there for their pastime or instruction.

It follows, therefore, that the doctors in these Alpine health resorts recommend only what they can conscientiously advise—some place they are acquainted with, some place upon the way to England, some place where the food is tolerably good, some place where the miscellaneous inquirers may be safely housed under the supervision of their medical adviser.

I have written these words by way of preface to a description of Chiavenna in the spring. It is a resort which seems to me unreasonably neglected ; for the advantages it offers are manifold. The climate is not so damp and languid as that of the Italian Lakes, nor so bleak as that of the Rhine valley. Proximity to the Gothard railway renders it a first stage on the road to most lands. Chiavenna is almost at our doors. But one may go farther and fare worse in April.

Chiavenna is a little Italian town enclosed by romantic mountains, which soar into towers and spires and pyramids above it. Yet the place is so situated at the meeting-point of two main valleys (the Splügen Pass and Val Bregaglia) that southwards the prospect expands alluringly toward the Lake of Como and the plain of Lombardy. In Chiavenna we have always an open vista enticing us to Italy ; always the majestic precipices overhead, wreathed with leaden or silver or golden mists, shooting their sharp needles into the blue of heaven, beckoning to us from the Alpine regions we have left behind. A torrent of the purest water flows through the town :

Our Life in the Swiss Highlands

so pure, if the truth must be told, that it serves one or more breweries, and makes the beer of Chiavenna widely celebrated. This may or may not be an attraction to visitors. But I can assure them that the beer is sound. There is a spacious hotel to pass the time and sleep in ; an old posting-house, formerly a palace, now transformed to suit modern requirements, with an attentive host, who takes pride in his kitchen and his cellar and the comfort of his guests. I need not add that this is the Hôtel Conradi, and that Herr Weber keeps it.

I have lived much in Italy, and have traversed that enchanted land of nature and the arts down from its Alpine barriers to the sea which beats about the promontory of Sicilian Lilybaeum. But I have found in all my wanderings no better frontispiece to the long series of Italian pictures than this of Chiavenna—no place in which one leaps so suddenly from north to south, from the mystery of the mountains into the Italian charm. Crossing Maloja, we leave the stony hills which gather fountain-heads for Rhine and Danube and Adige and Po. We glide insensibly into the Italian garden. When we reach it, there are vine trellises and almond orchards, peach-trees laden with bloom or fruit, big-bellied gourds asleep on sunny stones, taciturn cypresses near dwellings built for secrecy and love, tall bell-towers reaching to the skies among the voiceless habitations of the dead, bridges entwined with creeping weeds through which the deep-tongued torrents clamour, castles on toppling rocks recalling deeds of antique story. The whole of Italy, to one who knows Italy well, is suggested in epitome here. And Chiavenna has the additional attraction of combining with this Italian magic something of Alpine purity and freshness. Everywhere come streamlets pouring down from snows in spring. The black rocks are fringed

88

Chiavenna in April

with rhododendron, tufted with crimson primulas and heaths, embossed with budding saxifrages. Under the grey boles of Spanish chestnut-trees the sward spreads soft and green. This velvet lawn is starred with crocuses, lilac and white ; and where transparent waters irrigate the fields, one may wander for hours among dancing beds of snow-flakes, raising their shell-like blossoms from frail stalks above the grassy cushions whence they spring. There is a ruin of old granitic rocks around you, the spilth and waste of mountains shaken in past ages by earth-splitting throes. But these have been mossed over, smoothed by "the unimaginable touch of time," mellowed to sombre greys and glowing tones of purple. Feathery birch-trees sprout from the chasms which divide those monumental blocks. Fir-trees plume them. Rare ferns nestle in their crevices. Blue hepaticas and delicate wood-sorrel shelter round them. Dark violets, where the turf is moist and deep by overhanging walls, fill the spring air with fragrance. And man may pass from spot to spot, exploring and inquiring, finding no end to his delightful rambles.

Nearly three centuries ago—that is to say, in the year 1618—this fair land was visited by one of those terrible catastrophes which make us mortals wonder whether we are not the sport of some malignant destiny. At the time of which I speak the little town of Plurs, distant less than three miles from Chiavenna, was a flourishing commune, tenanted by perhaps about 1,200 persons. During the evening of the 4th of September in that year, a huge mass of mountain above Plurs detached itself from the main body, and rolled down in rocks and dust upon the town. Plurs was stoned to death, and 930 of its inhabitants were buried in the ruins of the hill to which they formerly looked up for safeguard and protection. A contemporary chronicler, Fortunat Sprecher, who was stationed in Chiavenna on this fatal day, relates that the thunder of the falling mountain reached his ears like the explosion of a park of artillery.

One of the pleasantest excursions from Chiavenna is to a country-house which stands upon the outskirts of the desolated town of Plurs. It is a villa, belonging to the descendants of a gentle family who had their principal possessions in the ruined commune. You reach this lonely dwelling by a path which leads through secular chestnut-trees—grey-bearded giants of the forest, who have survived a score of revolutions, and borne the brunt of changeful seasons through at least four centuries of human life. Turfy are the ways beneath them, and mossy the unmortared walls which close those labyrinths of winding paths. In the autumn, when the gnarled boughs shed their russet foliage, this journey is poetical and solemn. The fallen leaves rustle beneath one's pushing feet, green and gold and amber ; pale lilac crocuses touched with rime peep through, as though to bid farewell to summer. Then we reach the homestead. The mass of masonry seems too large for its surroundings. It was evidently built as the adjunct to some strenuous phase of life in the submerged town of Plurs—a place to which its masters came for solace and expansion. Now it stands alone here, among the chestnut boles, close by the dusty waste of stones which swallowed Plurs up, itself abandoned to Heaven knows what kind of occupancy. We knock, and enter : find ourselves in a wide echoing hall : are introduced into an apartment panelled with carved woodwork in the broad style of the late Renaissance. An English or American *parvenu*, if he could clothe his reception-rooms with that panelling, would feel himself possessed with ancestors, provided with

Chiavenna in April

some immemorial tradition from the past. But the place is too solemn to linger long in, and the frescoes upon the walls are too grotesque to invite an art student's attention. Let us abandon the weird old house. Nevertheless, when we turn our backs upon it, we shall perforce admit that few things have been seen by us in fact more like what we had dreamed of in romance and story.

Not there, not on the outskirts of buried Plurs, lies the true spell of Chiavenna. I do not invite the prisoners of winter in the High Alps down to these decayed habitations. Such ruins supply at best an episode for poets, a subject for the painter's palette. It is the noble land, the plenteous nature, the luxuriant vegetation, the good water and the wholesome air, the excellent quarters and the ease in your inn, and lastly, and above all, the escapement into beautiful Italy, which form the permanent attractions of Chiavenna—Chiavenna, the key of Italy and Alpine secrets, as its name implies. *Clavis, Chiave, Clav, Clef.* I leave my readers to find what further mysteries this key unlocks.   J. A. S.

CATCHING A MARMOT

It was already growing hot when we left Davos at 7.15 a.m. to ascend the Seehorn, and we were very hot indeed when we reached the summit at 10. There we were flattered into a feeling of coolness by a pleasant wind, and we sat long on the mossy ground, lazily looking down on the lake at our feet, whilst we devoured some very acid plums and discoursed, as I now remember, upon the cruelty of sport.

We decided to descend the mountain on the western side—there where the rocks break so suddenly the shining strips of turf. We had not gone far down before we came upon a fine marmot, who had strolled out to enjoy the pleasures of the day like ourselves. He beat a hasty retreat, and we followed, regretting that marmots are always so unapproachable.

After that we lingered long upon the slopes, picking flowers. We noticed that our dog had disappeared, and became aware of loud sharp barkings, mixed with a curious whistling sound, ascending from the wood far below us. The noise was so strange that we hastened down to discover the cause. The sounds grew ever more excited as we approached ; sometimes ceasing, then beginning again with redoubled force. Great was our interest, for we knew the dog to be a Venetian by birth, and therefore no sportsman. Yet somehow the sounds savoured of sport.

Catching a Marmot

We were now in the wood, and suddenly breaking through some thick trees we came upon a very extra-ordinary scene. The broad stem of a fir-tree jutted out over a small precipice. Against this fir-tree, on his hind legs, with fore paws waving in anger, stood a large marmot at bay. He whistled furiously. Our black spitz-dog stood trembling at a safe distance, his shrill bark clashing with the squeal of the marmot. To the general noise there was now added our screams. We had left our morality on the top of the peak, and were both seized with the same intense desire to possess that nice fat marmot.

The chase began. At first stealthily, then furiously. One of us got above the precipice, and one below. Just as we felt ourselves sure of him, off went the marmot, while only his tail received a parting salute from the end of an alpenstock. The sun blazed down over the hot rocks. Our footing was most insecure. Hats, alpen-stocks, baskets, flowers—all were abandoned and went bowling down, unnoticed, into the forest. Tally ho ! All things but the marmot were forgotten. And pre-sently we came upon him. He had got into a narrow crevice between the rocks. In vain did we pull his tail enticingly. Other means than these must be tried.

And, moreover, with us it was a matter of, " First make a bag for your marmot, *then* catch him." Necessity being the mother of invention, a grand plan was hit upon. Hair-pins have always acted as friends in need—hairpins run hastily through a petticoat—and the effect was supreme. Superfluous garments become an incubus when hunting a marmot in a sun heat of 140° Fahr.

For half an hour we worked to oust that marmot. We used gentle means, and he used his teeth and his whistle. The dog barked. We screamed. For thirty minutes

93

Our Life in the Swiss Highlands

Bedlam was let loose on the rocks of the Seehorn. Then silence. The last stone which covered his retreat had to be removed, and with it the last chance, perhaps, of our ever catching a marmot. The ledge of narrow rock whereon one of us crouched in a trembling agony of excitement offered small room for action. The creek, where the other was engaged in driving up the marmot from behind, perhaps even less.

The bag, prepared with so much genius, was now laid cautiously along the ground ; the last stone was hurled in pursuit of our lost properties. From the crack into which the marmot had retreated his fat body at last emerged and scuttled into the snare prepared for him. A bit of string, a tight knot, and the bag was closed.

Well, at mid-day on July 8, 1889, two heated damsels were to be seen toiling along the Davos-Dörfli road, one bearing, slung over her shoulder, a mysterious striped bag, the contents of which wriggled furiously, and weighed twelve Swiss pounds.   M. S.

VIGNETTES IN PROSE AND VERSE

DAVOS REVISITED

THOSE who are obliged, as I have been, to live for their health's sake in an Alpine valley, escape from it with alacrity from time to time. There is a sense of being imprisoned, a feeling of physical and mental stifling, owing to the narrow limits of the landscape and the monotony of everlasting pine woods. The view is bounded upon all sides by the craggy hills, shutting out the distance and preventing one from gazing on the miracles of sunrise and sunset. You only infer that the sun has risen by a flush of rose along the eastern crests, and that he has sunk by the same change of colour in the western sky. This in itself is irksome to eyes familiar with the broad landscapes of England or the horizons of a southern sea. Then the scenery, though grand, is simple in its majesty, severe in colouring, varied with few picturesque details, ill adapted to the purposes of art. Of course, too, the many interests of city life are wanting. There are no statues or pictures, no historic buildings ; the libraries are scantily furnished, the theatre is inadequate, the music third-rate, even in a place so far advanced as Davos-Platz. Most people, especially those of an æsthetic temperament, find it very difficult to maintain their intellectual energy under these conditions. They

Our Life in the Swiss Highlands

pine and droop. Even those who, like myself, have literary work to do, and find that they can do it here with less expenditure of force than at a lower level, fret now and then, and long to get away. It is, therefore, an immense pleasure to descend into the spacious plains of Lombardy, to float upon the mirrors of Venetian lagoons, with that illimitable vault of burning sky above, or to wander through the ancient towns of Central Italy. Nevertheless, the mountains take a lasting hold upon their foster-children, and foreigners who have lived among them long acquire something of the Nostalgia, or *Heimweh*, which the natives feel for Switzerland. It is pleasant to return to the tranquil never-changing scene, the perpetuity of nature.

> Yet once more, world of whiteness, world of snow,
> World of calm winter sunlight, clear and low,
> Where winds are hushed and waters fret no more
> These yellowing reeds beside the frozen shore ;
> Thee I salute, as one who late hath found
> Rest for nerves over-wrought by sight and sound ;
> Who fain would sleep, yet not all sleep, but be
> Cradled in wise insensibility ;
> For whom the days monotonously dear
> Shall fill the cycle of a vacant year,
> In blank well-being, thoughtless, deedless, still,
> Untouched by ache of good, by pang of ill.

THE ALPINE WREATH

There are two brief intervals of colour beauty in the High Alps. One is during late autumn, toward the close of September, when the upland pastures above the forest line and the grey precipices of barren rocks assume hues of orange, russet, purple. This is due to the decay of innumerable little shrubs and herbs. All kinds of um-

Vignettes in Prose and Verse

belliferous plants turn a brilliant yellow. The bilberry
takes a tint of bluish red ; the arctostaphylos burns in
cataracts and patches of pure scarlet ; the mountain ash
puts on a coat of crimson. This is the appearance they
present when you walk through them. But seen in mass
together from any considerable distance, they lend a
peculiarly rich and varied tone to the stern landscape.
It is like a glow of warmth and atmospheric violet diffused upon the scene. Unluckily, as the frost strengthens,
the leaves wither and fall. The glory hardly lasts a fort-
night. The other interval of which I speak is in early
June. The long seven months' winter, with its grim
monotony of snow—interminable whiteness, varied only
by bright blue shadows—has yielded at length. Then
suddenly the meadows bourgeon into flower-beds. It is
impossible to describe the variety and brilliance of these
summer flowers, and the delightful impression which they
leave on eyes and brain starved in the craving colour-sense.
One wanders singing through field and forest. Every
day seems to bring some new and lovely blossom to light.

A garland I will weave of mountain flowers :
    Pure golden-hearted dryas, silverly
    Touched o' the nether leaf ; androsacë,
    That deepens from cream-white through summer hours
To crimson ; with the dark soul-nourishing powers
    Of azure gentian, bright-eyed euphrasy,
    Pink Alpine clover, pale anemone,
    And saxifrages fed by flying showers.
These I love best ; for these when snows withdraw,
    When down the vexed paths of the avalanche
    Shy deities of spring renew their dance,
Cheer those gaunt crumbling cliffs that tempests blanch,
    Where black streams thunder through the glacier's jaw
    And sun-gleams o'er the world-old cembra glance.

Our Life in the Swiss Highlands

We started late one February afternoon for a toboggan run to Klosters. The sun had set when we left Wolfgang; but all the sky was rosy with its after-glow, the peaks and snow-fields which surrounded us shining in every hue of saffron and crimson. Then, as we rushed down the steep descent, there swam rapidly upon our sight from behind the vast bulk of a black mountain pass, the full moon, a huge transpicuous dew-pearl of intensest green, bathed in fiery colours of the glowing heavens. People who summer in the Arctic Circle describe these luminous effects. Our swift motion beneath the celestial wonders, over the myriad-tinted snow-path, added intoxicating glory to the vision. It was like flying through a sphere of iridescent beryl. But we soon passed downward from those airy heights, and plunged into the forest, where all the splendours of the sky and the path we sped upon were swallowed in chasms of black shadow. From these we emerged into the silver of the moon, striving victoriously at that lower level to surpass the sunset incandescence we had left above. . . .

I rose at four o'clock one summer morning. Dawn was going up behind the Tyrolese frontier, and in the south-west a buoyant vast balloon of moon, greenish, like a lustrous globe of aqua-marine, hung swathed in rosy air upon the flat slope of Altein. The Davos valley, blurred and vaporous with cold white mists of night and thunderstorm; the church spire piercing them, telling that men and women lived there shrouded. But up above, on all the heights, Nature played her own divine symphony; the full moon sinking glorified, the dawn ascending red and tired already. Has it often been noticed how very tired the earth looks at sunrise ? Like Michael Angelo's wild female figure on the tomb at San Lorenzo, dragging herself with anguish out of slumber. I felt this most three years ago, after spending a summer night upon the Feldberg, those enormous German plains outspread around me. When the morning came at last, its infinite sadness was almost heartbreaking.

A February Morning

The Via Mala at 6 a.m. was ghostly glorious. The undefined light of approaching dawn dilated all its heights and depths, and a waning moon hung far away to westward in a melancholy space of sky between the beetling crags and nodding precipices. Everywhere the frozen cataracts and huge ice-columns gleamed with spectral, garish lustre out of the grey twilight. We were the only things alive, except the stationary pines, in that long, tortuous descent. Primeval forces seemed to clip us round ; the grey-green architecture of the ice, in which all life of leaping streams hung spell-bound and suspended, added intensity of grimness to the deathly cold and stillness of the scene.

> With a sense of things that are over
>   A touch of the years long dead,
> A perfume of withered clover,
>   An echo of kindness fled,
>
> We wake on this morn when snow-wreaths
>   Silently thaw to rain,
> And the love that the old years know breathes
>   Dying, not born again.
>
> Cold and grey is the morning,
>   Grey with evanishing rose ;
> We wake, and I feel her warning,
>   I know what the doomed man knows.

Our Life in the Swiss Highlands

Strayed are the streams of madness,
Dried is the fount of tears ;
But oh, at the heart what sadness !
And oh, in the soul what fears !

IN THE AVERSER THAL

There is nothing in the way of river scenery among the mountains to equal this. The Averser Rhein, at one point of its course, transcends in fairy-like charm the Sesia and the Mastalone, and all those lovely torrents of the Dolomites. It has a tremendous volume of the clearest azure water, which sometimes hides in obscure caverns and cembra-tufted gorges ; sometimes swims through grassy meadows with wide swishing curves that hollow out the turfy margin to their liking ; sometimes carves a monumental way through cliffs of pure white marble, white and pure as Pentelican or Parian, foaming on paved work of smooth, flawless lustre ; sometimes falls thundering in cataracts arched with changeful rainbows ; sometimes glides, deep and solemn, in dark pools that make the spirit dream of death, and long to dive in them and pluck the heart out of their mystery.

We slept, my guide and I, at Canicul, in a room which held the archives of the valley in a chest, and had the Eucharistic vessels of the commune (ancient pewter wine-jugs of a peculiar shape) on the window-sill. Our host was the Landammann.

IN A GRAUBÜNDEN STABLE

l often smoke my pipe in the stable of an evening. The company of hinds and grooms offers an agreeable contrast to the popes and despots, sculptors and poets,

Vignettes in Prose and Verse

historians and diplomatists of the sixteenth century with
whom I pass my working hours. These men have a
great deal to tell that is interesting about the habits of
their animals, the incidents of their rough life, the perils
of the mountain passes in winter, and the dangerous
labour of bringing blocks of larch or pine down from
the craggy forests. Then the beasts in a Swiss stable
are usually well cared for ; the mild-eyed cows lie comfortably ruminating, with their tails tied up to the stalls.
The horses are almost overfed, and love their masters.
To express the mood of these evenings I composed this
sonnet late one night, seated alone upon the corn-
chest :—

A flat, rug-cushioned corn-bin ; one dim lamp
    Darting malign light ; harness-hung low walls,
    Panelled with pine, where gleam of satin falls
    Subdued from rays scarce struggling through the damp.
Six stalwart horses : how they feed and stamp,
    Nuzzling their noses to the brimful stalls ;
    Skin smooth as silk, sleek tails : hark ! Sepperl calls,
    Whinnying to Popp, his mate ; then turns to champ.
This is the gloom to dream in, sending up
    Fragrant smoke-incense to far rafters dun.
    The cat purrs in her sleep ; the tired grooms sup
Their bed-ward ale ; then, lounging, one by one,
    Slouch to yon hay-loft in the roof above.
    I, only I, am left—with Night and Love.

Autumn Mists

An impressive feature of early autumn in these high
regions, dividing that soft, slow season from the summer,
is the frequent invasion of the valleys by white, dry,
fleecy clouds of vapour. They are formed in lower
Switzerland, upon the lakes of Constance, Zürich, and

Our Life in the Swiss Highlands

Wallenstadt ; whence they come stealing, like a flooding tide, up every creek and crevice of the mountains. They do not reach the summits. Standing upon the crest of some tall hill, you may gaze upon the congregated peaks around, emergent from a sea of woolly whiteness. The clasp and curl of these vapour billows, their lazy, crawling movement along the hillsides, the way in which they overflood some barrier such as a mound or pine-clad buttress, render them peculiarly attractive to watch. The sight has a subtle power of evoking sad but restful thoughts, inviting the soul to reverie.

> Oh sweet, oh soft, this interbreathing space
> > Between deep draughts of labour ; soft and sweet
> > This pause the year makes with slow sauntering steps
> > 'Twixt summer, autumn, and pure snow's embrace.
> Now the grey mists blown from some far-off place
> > Of Bodensee or Rhienthal, merging, meet
> > At dew-fall round the mountains, flow and fleet,
> > Stream into air when morn ascends apace.
> Now thoughts that summer through like hounds did chase
> > Their quarry, dream, or silent sessions keep.
> > Love now clings cloud-like round the soul ; one face,
> That troubled, trembled, questioned, floats with deep
> > Tender persuasion o'er the fields of sleep.
> > Oh soft, oh sweet, this transient autumn grace.

A NIGHT UPON THE SCHWARTZHORN

I reached the Hospiz of the Fluela at seven, supped, and went to bed at eight. Slept at once profoundly, till Josias Hold's voice woke me, bidding me to coffee, on the stroke of midnight. The gymnasts had arrived, some twenty-eight young fellows. We started for the peak in fair full moonlight. It was very still and solemn, wind-

THE SCHWARTZHORN FROM FLUELA
HOSPICE.

ing slowly upwards to the snow-slopes and the glacier. All sounds have a peculiar value in the twilight of an August night. There was something particularly thrilling in the murmur of a streamlet rushing beneath huge wrecks of boulders which we crossed. Behind us, above the mountains of the Lower Engadine, hung a marvellous star of dawn. It " flamed in the forehead of the morning sky," ascending ever over peak and precipice, as flying from the slow reluctant dayspring. The moon was nearly full, and made a lantern useless. Nothing equals the solemnity of these midnight marches on the high uplifted horns. Nor did the gymnasts break the spell. They moved like soldiers, keeping step, and spoke with the low sweet voices of country folk. On the glacier we found a heavy coating of snow, which forced us to walk warily. Then came the saddle and the steep arête : slippery rocks and frosted ledges, hanging sheer above the Dischma Thal. I was not sorry to leave them for a tract of steep hard snow which led to the summit. We all gathered round the cairn, and waited in silence for the sunrise. Eastward there first appeared a band of white, which looked like moonshine on a belt of mist, but was really a token of the dawn : for while the pyramids of Pitz Linard and Buin cut into it with their silvered cones, it toned to green, and passed from citron to mellow orange, widening, broadening, creeping round about the circuit of the sky, but leaving the moon still mistress of the upper heavens. Then Bernina, Ortler, and Tödi began to glow with a faint half-conscious rose. So the dawn stole gradually onward, fading the flying star and westering moon, disclosing all the peaks of Switzerland and Tyrol, lingering through that inexplicably prolonged space of time which sunrise always occupies. When the east was already full of coming light, there shot with

Our Life in the Swiss Highlands

broad impulsive sweep from the zenith full into the core
of hidden fire a luminous, majestic meteor—a thrilling
episode in this dawn-drama—as though some star had
left her station, yearning to engulf her radiance in our
planetary sphere. At last a crest in Tyrol dazzled with
true sunlight; and in a few moments the whole Alp-
world lay bathed in rosy-golden day. I then discerned,
far, far away, a tiny blue comb of crags upon the south-
eastern verge of the Italian plain—a Dolomite beyond
the Etzsch Thal—perhaps the Rosengarten. It was
freezing hard all this while. But the sun brought
warmth, and showed the Schwartzhorn hoary with
night's frost, which melted literally, like a dream,
away.

'Neath an uncertain moon, in light malign,
    We trod those rifted granite crags, whereunder,
    Startling the midnight air with muffled thunder,
Flowed infant founts of Danube and of Rhine.
Our long-drawn file in slow deliberate line
    Scaled stair on stair, subdued to silent wonder;
    Wound among mouldering rocks that rolled asunder,
Rattling with hollow roar down death's decline.
Still as we rose, one white transcendent star
    Steered calmly heavenward through the empurpled gloom,
Escaping from the dim reluctant bar
Of morning, chill and ashen-pale as doom;
    Where the day's chargers, champing at his ear,
    Waited till Sol should quit night's banquet-room.

Pure on the frozen snows, the glacier-steep,
    Slept moonlight with the tense unearthly charm
    Of spells that have no power to bless or harm;
But, when we touched the ridge which tempests sweep,
Death o'er the murk vale, yawning wide and deep,
    Clung to frost-slippery shelves, and sharp alarm,
    Shuddering in eager air, drove life's blood warm
    Back to stout hearts and staunch will's fortress-keep.

Vignettes in Prose and Verse

Upward we clomb; till now the emergent morn,
    Belting the horror of dim jagged eastern heights,
    Broadened from green to saffron, primrose-pale,
Felt with faint finger-tips of rose each horn,
    Crept round the Alpine circuit, o'er each dale
    Dwelt with dumb broodings drearier even than night's.

Thus dawn had come; not yet the day: night's queen
    And morning's star their state in azure kept:
    Still on the mountain world weird silence slept;
    Earth, air, and heaven held back their song serene.
Then from the zenith, fiery-white between
    Moonshine and dayspring, with swift impulse swept
    A splendour of the skies that throbbing leapt
    Down to the core of passionate flame terrene—
A star that ruining from yon throne remote,
    Quenched her celestial yearnings in the pyre
    Of mortal pangs and pardons. At that sign
The orient sun with day's broad arrow smote
    Black Linard's arrogant brow, while influent fire
    Slaked the world's thirst for light with joy divine.

ON THE SILVRETTA GLACIER

My friend, Peter Minsch, drove us in a brake with a
pair of horses from Klosters up to Sardasca. It is a stiff
climb of two hours from the cow-huts to the glacier, over
rough grazing-ground, and along cliffs tufted with alpenrose and bilberry. The sun had sunk before we reached
the Club-Hütte, and all the Prättigau lay in deep shadow
under a shield of smouldering gold. We supped; and
while we were so engaged there came a German doctor
with his wife, two Tyrolese guides, and a half-drunken
fellow from Klosters. The scene was picturesque enough.
The hut is a low building with stone walls, roofed over
rather abruptly with rafters : a small stove in the corner
by the door; two lockers provided with wine and crockery;

two broad sleeping berths strewn with hay.[1] Candles were stuck about, lighting up the smoke-browned interior and the motley party there. Visiting-cards of former tourists adorned the panels. Outside roared the glacier torrent, and from the hut door we could see the distant lights of Klosters. At nine we all turned in to sleep. The hay was made into rough beds, and rugs were spread for our feet. Three groups were formed : one of my wife, myself, and Warren ; one of our guides ; the third of the Germans and their guides.

At three o'clock the guides brought us coffee. I looked out, and felt a raw wind blowing off the glacier. Smoky greyish clouds raced along the upper peaks, faintly tinged with feeble sunrise-light, blurring the stars and dimly-coloured sky. The morning star, close beside a thin moon in her last quarter, swam now clear of mist, now entangled. The prospect for a fine day was not bad. And yet one felt that the serene weather of the past week had suffered change.

We crossed the glacier stream, and after twenty minutes' walking over the moraine got upon dirty ice. Then followed two hours of continuous ascent over gradual snow-slopes, never very steep, until we reached the summit of the Silvretta Pass, about 10,200 feet above sea-level. The views, as we went climbing on, became singularly beautiful—looking back upon the green meadows of the Prättigau, with the Davoser Weissflüh and Casanna crowning its dark forests, and in the far distance Calanda and Tödi leading the eye onward to the Bernese Oberland—all this bathed in soft, almost Italian colouring, the hues of a dove's breast. On the other side, Scesaplana closed the prospect ; but here the finest episode

---

[1] This Club-hut is a thing of the past now. It has been replaced by a two-storied shelter, where excellent accommodation can be had.

Vignettes in Prose and Verse

was the group of the two Litzners, each double-peaked and bizarre with sharp splintered towers, swathed up in mists of violet and amber like huge stone imitations of the Mönch and Eiger. The long curves of the glacier formed a splendid foreground to this panorama, while the jagged precipices of the Silvrettahorn and Verstanklahorn enclosed it in a frame of snow-sprinkled sombre rock. Marching onward over the level snow-fields of the Pass, we enjoyed two different pictures slowly opening on our gaze. To the right hand, past the Gletscherhorn, the eye follows the steep ice-fall of Vadret Paitscha, and rises by a sudden spring up to the gigantic pyramid of Pitz Linard, a most noble and imposing mass of dark grey granite, mightily buttressed by sharp spines of jutting precipices. Facing him stands the comparatively insignificant block of Pitz Fliana, not powerful enough to impair his majesty, yet sufficient in bulk to supply the equipoise required for the suggestion of a superb portal, through which, beyond incalculable space of air, the whole Bernina range rose glittering and silver into clear cerulean heavens. This was splendid. Yet right in front through a second mighty portal formed by the same mass of Pitz Fliana fronting the red and orange-tinted peak of Klein Buin, appeared a picture softer and more beautiful. Above some serrated ranges of Engadine mountains, Ortler soared in his incomparably graceful sublimity ; and the low sun bathed each plane of the long landscape with suave light and crystal shadow. This, I thought, is capable of even being painted ; an almost perfect composition. We passed onward, and down the Plan Rai glacier, skirting Klein Buin, and gradually coming within sight of the nobler Pitz Buin. All the rocks here are red and tawny with iron ore, greenish in some places, as with serpentine or copper.

Our Life in the Swiss Highlands

The little cols and cheminées of ice, the undulating snow-tracts, and the hard blue sky above, formed with these variegated rocks a singular combination of colours. There is a tiresome steep moraine to descend after leaving the glacier ; then a long delightful walk over springy meadows and through larch woods, near a hurrying stream, to Guarda in the Lower Engadine.

CLOUD IRIDESCENCE

After many years spent in the High Alps I have come to regard this phenomenon as a very ordinary occurrence, especially in the winter. The clouds which display iridescence are usually motionless shoals, shuttle-shaped or fish-shaped, thinner at the edges than the interior. The iridescence, which is sometimes of quite extraordinary brilliancy, shows itself in most cases at the edge of the cloud, but sometimes is suffused like a sort of prismatic tinting over the whole surface. One may occasionally notice patches of the same variegated hues suspended in what is apparently cloudless blue sky, but which contains, I suppose, finely diffused vapour. I may also add that the same phenomena are observable with diminished minosity and brightness of hue by moonlight. The finest display of iridescent cloud I ever witnessed was on the 7th of December, 1879, from the summit of the Schwartzhorn, 10,300 feet above the sea. The sky, which, viewed from that altitude, spread like a canopy over the entire Alpine region—from the Gross Glockner eastward to Monte Rosa in the far west, from Tödi to the Ortler—was fretted with innumerable and isolated shuttle-shaped clouds, clearly defined against the hard deep purple of the firmament, and tinged with the most vivid nacreous

tints wherever the sun struck them at the proper angle.
Lying on my back and gazing upwards, I was reminded
of the appearance presented by some of the frailest
siliceous shell-structures when seen under a powerful
microscope. It may be added that this beautiful spectacle did not last very long, for the weather was on the
point of changing, and a blustering Föhn-wind blurred
and confused the cloud landscape. Cloud iridescence, I
need not add, is not to be confounded with either haloes
or fragmentary rainbows; nor need it be said that the
phenomenon is not confined to the High Alps. The first
time I ever noticed it was many years ago on the railway
descent to Dijon, about four o'clock on a fine October
afternoon, and I have sometimes observed it also in
England, but never so brilliantly or so commonly as
during winter in the Grisons.

THE PHENOMENAL SUNSETS OF 1884

Here at Davos the sun in mid-winter does not rise
above the mountain barrier till 10 a.m., and sinks again
below it at about 3.30 p.m. We therefore do not witness
either sunrise or sunset upon the horizon, but judge of
the effects of both by light and colour in the upper sky.
On the evenings of November 29 and 30, when the line
of hills to westward were quite black, and the stars were
shining in the heavens, a rosy flame, almost exactly like
the northern lights, but of a purer quality, overspread
the western sky, defined the hard black outline of the
mountain range, and glared upon the white expanse of
snow in the valley and along its eastern barriers. On
one occasion the young moon and some stars shone with
a pallor of extraordinary luminosity in the midst of this

rose-tinted veil. On another occasion the whole north-eastern region of the heavens was at the same time of the most vivid golden-green—the peculiar green of chrysoprase and some highly-tinted beryls. Each tone of light, rose and green, was reflected on the long broad basin of valley snow, the blending of both colours being of a strange bewildering brilliancy. At this height of more than 5,000 feet above the sea, the atmosphere has great purity and transparency. It therefore happens that on cloudless days the sun shines, a hard white ball of light in a darkly-tinted blue firmament. But I noticed during all the days when these phenomena were visible, that instead of presenting this ordinary appearance, the sun, from early morning till late evening, moved surrounded by a luminous, slightly opalescent haze—not at all resembling halo or iridescence of vapour. The quality of this haze was quite different, being far more evenly distributed, and such colour-tone as it possessed being far more finely graduated from centre to circumference. The morning phenomena, at the same period, were also noticeable for their beauty, but not so exceptional as those of the evening.

AN ODE TO THE FÖHN-WIND

The Föhn is a hot, dry wind which blows from the south. People used innocently to suppose that it was the Sirocco of the Mediterranean, coming heated from African deserts. This has been disproved, and the present theory is that the Föhn is generated in upper regions of the atmosphere under special meteorological conditions. Its violence and dryness make it exceedingly dangerous to villages. Hundreds have been burned down during its frequent and stormy visitations. I believe that in valleys where it

Vignettes in Prose and Verse

rages with more than usual force—those of Glarus, for
instance, and of Meiringen—people are forbidden to light
their fires in a strong Föhn. In the winter here they
call it the Schneefresser, or snow-devourer. It does more
to melt the snow upon the Alps and to launch avalanches
on the valleys than any other agency. Like the Sirocco,
it has a curious effect upon the nerves, at once irritating
and relaxing. Few people feel well while it is blowing.
In me it excites restless longings and vague desires for
the impossible. Something of this effect I have tried to
express in verse, using (with culpable temerity, perhaps)
the magnificent stanza created by Byron and appropriated by Swinburne :—

> Over this prison,
> Where suns new risen
> Can yield no vision
>   Beyond our vale,
> The south wind, winging
> His way, and bringing
> Echoes of singing,
>   Doth lightly sail :
> That rippling burden
> Full oft I've heard on
> The waves he stirred on
>   Italian sea.
> O light land-rover,
> O soft sea-lover,
> Soul of the South, I am fain for thee !
>
> Thou fickle stranger,
> Blithe ocean-ranger,
> From dread and danger
>   And man's doubt free !
> Thy wings enfold me,
> Thy whispers hold me ;
> What hast thou told me
>   Of Venice and thee ?

111

Our Life in the Swiss Highlands

A vault of thunder ;
Two lives thereunder,
That clasp and sunder
    In gloom and glare.
This hast thou sung to me,
This hast thou flung to me,
Swift as the lightning on earth and air !

For though years carry
Their load, and tarry
On hearts that marry
    With frore despair ;
Still 'neath thy pinion,
E'en misery's minion
Scorns her dominion,
    And smiles at care.
These lips with kisses,
Where love still misses
Hope's crown of blisses,
    Are faint and fain ;
For thou hast sought me,
Thy breath hath brought me
Lips of light loving above the main.

In life's Decembers
The heart remembers
That 'neath joy's embers
    Lurked fear and pain.
Yet, oh, my master,
Through all disaster
Thrills fast and faster
    The yearning strain.
I pine and sicken,
Keen memories thicken,
These dry roots quicken
    'Neath winter's bed.
For thou hast spoken,
Thy spells have broken
Frosts of the spirit that bound her dead.

Vignettes in Prose and Verse

Oh ! follow, follow !
From this white hollow
Fly like the swallow ;
    Lay Hope's tired head
In some south garden,
Where youth is warden,
And gates are barred on
    The north wind's tread !
Let music waft her
With light and laughter
Where, months hereafter,
    Some clinging scent
Of pines that languish
In summer's anguish
Shall tell of the years of the pains here spent.

Ah me, forsaken !
From dreams I waken :
Thy wings are shaken,
    Thy veil is rent :
Snows, snows surround me,
Winter hath bound me,
Old age hath found me,
    My brows are bent.
Haste, haste, sea-lover,
Lest snow-flakes cover
Thy wings that hover
    Above our vale !
For the north winds whistle,
The stout pines bristle,
Soul of the South, thou are frail and pale.

               J. A. S.

SUMMER IN THE PRÄTTIGAU

CONTERS is a small village in Prättigau. It is one of those tiny settlements of wooden houses, clustering round a doll's church, amid meadows and orchards such as one may always find in Swiss valleys, perched high above the river on the side of the hill, and quite separated from the rest of the world. Here one of my Swiss friends was born. Her father—Herr Brosi—is *Stadthalter* of the surrounding district. He is a well-read and well-educated man, with charming manners and conversation, and his greatest pleasure lies in the successful cultivation of fruit trees. When Fräulein Brosi married, she came to live up in Davos with her husband, who farms a small property on the lake. I had long promised to spend a day with her down in her old home when the cherries should be ripe. The time of cherries had come. It was the last day of July, and it was with a feeling of real pleasure that I made the plan over night with Frau Hold to drive on the following day into Prättigau, and spend some hours among its fruit trees and those more generous blossoms of July we cannot gather on these mountain heights.

At half-past four I awoke. Through my open window I saw the valley lie blue in shadow as though holding still to some dreams of the past night. The men were out already, mowing the frozen grass, and all the meadows

114

KLOSTERS FROM THE RAILROAD.

were white with summer hoar-frost. The sun just tipped
the mountain peaks, and they caught the light, and
tossed it back one from another, till every line beneath
the sky was rosy. Soon after five the carriage came
round, and I drove away in the early morning light.
There was that delicious sense of frost struggling with
the dawn of a warm summer day. The sun was sucking
thick milky mists out of the hollows where they clung
amongst the leaves and grasses. The lake was all in
shadow as I drove by, and very calm. Through the
steamy mists which rose upon its surface one could see
far down to where the water-weeds were growing.

Frau Hold, with her baby and various bundles (which
are always part of a Bündner lady when she visits her
relatives), met me at the other end of the lake, and we
drove on over the pass and down through the woods to
Klosters. Here the sun finally rose, or rather penetrated
into the heart of the valley, and I felt the summer day
had begun. It was interesting to me to trace the line
of the new railway which was that year still in a skeleton
state. Crowds of workmen were out on the line—hard-
working, large-eyed men from the south, carrying "Progress" with supreme indifference up into the old-souled
mountains, through green and sleepy meadows, past
wooden homesteads—"das schöne Gegend verderbend,"
as my companion fitly remarked. All the village gardens
by which we passed were full of bloom, and the carna-
tions hanging from the windows gave promise of innumerable flowers. We reached Küblis at nine, and waited to
water the horse, then started up the opposite side of the
valley for the village of Conters. The road is smooth
and good, but very steep, traversing steadily up and
along broad meadows and orchards with one dip through
a beech wood. Under the beech trees the sun came

shivering in flakes of golden green upon the faintly-trembling leaves. There were tufts of ferns in the walls, and cool trickling springs. Emerging from this shadow we came out again upon broad meadow-lands, in the midst of which Conters is built—that warm, wooden village, so daintily put down and smothered among fruit trees, over which its roofs emerge and peer down into the valley of Prättigau, or up towards the glaciers of Silvretta. The church lies a little below the houses. It is a squat white building with a sloping wooden roof, and a high wall round the ground where the people of Conters bury their dead.

As we had not warned the Brosi family of our arrival its members had gone out as usual to their work in the fields, leaving their house door locked. But whilst Frau Hold went off to fetch her people, I was most kindly welcomed by their neighbours the Sprechers, who live in a large wooden châlet across the street. I had walked all the way up from Küblis, under a burning sun, and it was very pleasant to sit down on the cool bench by the window of the panelled *Stube* and look out across the orchard. There was a lovely old lady there with grey hair and a rosy complexion. Her tall gaunt daughter placed Eierbrod and raspberry syrup before me on the wooden table, and also a pile of literature. These Sprecher ladies seemed to read a great deal during the long evenings of winter. When the Brosis returned from the fields I was summoned to their house next door. It is a pretty low homestead, built all of wood, which is burnt almost black by the sun. Hops grow abundantly over the stacked wood, clinging in green festoons from the eaves and tossing back long streamers from the beams. Lucia, Frau Hold's pretty young sister—a girl with lots of yellow hair plaited round her head like a crown—came out to meet me, and took

Summer in the Prättigau

me through a dark passage into the *Stube*, a sitting-room which is like most Graubünden sitting-rooms, panelled entirely with wood ; a green stove of solid serpentine in one corner, a cupboard with some inlaid work on its doors, and painted plates on the dresser, in another ; and a bench running round the wall behind the table. Quantities of flowers, grown in potted-meat tins, broke the sunlight in the windows, and here the bees buzzed dreamily. The Stadthalter then took me out into his garden to see the young trees, calling special attention to a wonderful Italian cherry-tree which bore cherries like liquid red light. I picked and ate them every one. This sounds greedy, but greediness is equivalent to etiquette when one visits in Bündnerland. Leaving the garden, I went with Lucia and the baby for a slow walk along a path which skirts straight across the hillside through the beech-woods till it reaches a point where there is a " view." Walks in search of views are not, as a rule, satisfactory affairs, but this one I thought was very beautiful. The rough bed of the Landquart river, so far below, seen through the tall trunks of the beech trees, was a novel and romantic sight. The day was warm ; we sat down on some fresh-mown hay, and ate the unripe hazel-nuts which grew around us. The child roared in a meaningless manner—babies have that way in all countries. Its phlegmatic young aunt paid it scant attention. The church bell rang for *Mittag*. Nothing otherwise disturbed the hot noonday stillness. Herr Brosi met us on our way back, and taking me into the Stube told me many interesting stories. He told me of the terrific avalanche which in the year 1722 rushed over Saas one day, doing infinite harm to the old village ; and when on the following day all hands were engaged in digging out the ruins, a second avalanche fell and killed

117

the men at work and ruined the entire village, choking up Prättigau. But the north side of the valley remained unharmed. Conters looked down in comfort over her neighbour's devastation, and found in one of her meadows next morning a hen's nest containing all its eggs intact, which had been swept out of some stables in Saas, and carried by the wind across the valley. Now Saas is all built up again—a new Saas, smothered in orchards, its houses burnt black by the sun, and where the old village stood is now a fertile cup of green meadow full of fruit trees, and only this much of the avalanche remains—a long white scar slanting along the mountain-side, where the great mass fell, and where the slow pine forest and scanty turf has never grown again. But below this again a new and narrower, and to me a still more terrible scar on the breast of the mountain, is seen—that of the railway. This, however, is Progress.

The mid-day meal was now announced. It consisted of fried *gediegenes Fleisch*, or died meat, soup, boiled ham, potatoes, and prunes, with a pile of red-currants for dessert. And after this the Stadthalter said, " Die Jagd wird jetzt losgehen." The ladies of the party were all provided with serviceable aprons ; Herr Brosi, and Julius our driver, each shouldered a ladder ; and off we went to the cherry-trees. The *Emt*, or second crop of hay, had already grown high, but our host being a gentleman of large property and vast hospitality, allowed us to plunge recklessly through the high grass of the orchards till the cherry-trees were reached. There, then, were the cherries ! They shone against the sky, they dipped and danced amongst the leaves. I was soon up in their midst, clambering to the topmost branches. I once had thought I could not have enough of cherries, but soon found I was likely to have too many, so stayed to contemplate the scene and do penance for former abuse of Lamartine's account of Swiss scenery. That gentleman, in one of his poems, described glaciers descending into oak forests. I almost found he spoke the truth, for here, as I stood up among the branches of my cherry-tree, I looked back and saw the broad white stretches of the Silvretta glacier gleaming through the leaves. It was like a thing one sees in dreams. Only one doesn't dream on such occasions, and I soon returned to my pickings, rapidly filling with fruit the long round basket which was strapped upon me. The others were up in the trees too, laughing and singing. The child lay rolling in the grass. Even the sober Julius had dropped his mask of habitual gloom. I picked and picked, and looked around and beyond, across the Prätti-gau, all swimming as it were in a green bath of heat, then up to the snowy mountains, and back to the church and my new friends. The other ladies of the party soon wearied of their labours, and only the Stadthalter and Julius, the ladders, baskets, and I, continued the " Jagd." All down soft meadow paths we went, picking and tasting, and cracking jokes, and whilst stretching up to the branches we shook down an occasional almond-bug— most loathsome of insects—in the place of a cherry. Sometimes we sat down in the cool grass to rest, then wandered off to new trees, till at last our baskets were full. Then we trailed lazily back up the road, dragging our spoils with us, till we reached the gate of the church-yard.

"There lie our dead so quietly," said Herr Brosi, looking in through the wooden doors. "And there are few stones, you will see ; there are mostly only flowers to show where they lie." So I looked, and saw within the cool tall grasses the thick pink rosebuds, too fat and lazy to bloom outright, but rolling on their stalks and scenting

the still air with sweetness, and there were white ever-
lastings, sword-grass, and periwinkles. I expressed a
great wish to enter, but the gate was locked, and there
was no other way for it than to climb in over the wall.
So the Stadthalter put his ladder against it, and Julius
placed his somehow on the other side, and we clambered
over into the shade—there where the people who have
lived their lives in the wooden village up above among
the cherry-trees come to lie when life is over, side by side,
with no stones and only the flowers above them. We
got into the tiny church, and went up to the window above
the altar to see a bit of old stained glass, which, by some
curious chance, is still preserved there—a *Muttergottes*
with streaming yellow hair and gorgeous crimson robe—
very old, very austere, and richly coloured. The little
church is cool and quiet. Many generations have come
and gone through its doors. It has been Catholic and now
is Protestant, but all have worshipped the God who
gave them life up there in sunny Conters. A feeling of
intensely living, yet calm happiness, had spread through
me—perhaps the black cherries had mixed the sweetness
of their juice in my brain. We scrambled back over the
high wall across the ladders, and when I remarked that we
had broken that wall together with the laws, the Stadthalter reassured me cheerfully by remarking that he was a
Schul-kamarad of the *Pfarrer*.

We were extremely hot, but that mattered little. By
the help of currant syrup I soon cooled down in the house.
It was four o'clock, and I was well aware that the time
for departure had come. Coffee was then produced,
together with very strong cheese, currant jelly, butter,
and bread. My tastes were remembered (to my despair),
and a large cup of thick clotted cream put before me.
The pretty Lucia had been to sleep and the baby was a

little cross, its mother flustered. In fact, there was the
general sense of a hot day of pleasure coming to an end.
But this is never to be despised. Herr Brosi was doing
up the cherries. Most of them we took with us, but some
went to Paris, to which city Conters exports much fruit.
I wonder who it was who brought them there, and whether
the cherries that I had gathered that day tasted sweet
on some French dinner-table.

The sun was still shining hotly over Conters when we
left it and started homewards down the hill. The family
walked down a bit of the road with us, as far as where the
cherry-trees grow in their orchards. Then they turned
back. Bits of shadow were creeping across the road ;
the beech wood was all in shade ; but beyond blazed
Prättigau, and a locomotive steamed along the line. We
joined the post at Küblis, and followed it and all its string
of carriages up in a cloud of dust. Some German men
and ladies in various shades of stiff and unbecoming
alpaca garments such as that nation delights to wear,
were admiring the *Bahn*. The valley was heavy with
heat-mist ; but above Conters, the peaks of Casanna stood
blue and calm, their great rocks stooping as it were across
the forest to kiss the quiet village. A thin young moon
was melting in the liquid sky above the tower of Saas.
As the vast lumbering diligence, followed by its train of
lesser carriages, bowled heavily round the bridge near
Mezzaselva, an insignificant and squeaking locomotive
bustled under it—and this was *Progress*. I saw them
together, the old and the new, for the last time, and the
sight depressed me. I should have liked at that minute
to be back in the cherry-trees, forgetful of trains, and
desirous of cherries only.

The sun cast a ruddy light of orange gold across the
valley, across the hills, across the men's faces on the line,

Our Life in the Swiss Highlands

and upon the trees and grasses. All seemed melting together in the great melting-pot of the sun-god. We stayed at Klosters to water the horse, then started off again, slowly, in the train of the post. Calm had come again—the chill of evening settling down after the July day, and darkness creeping steadily across the world. How still it was ! The very dust upon the road seemed fallen asleep. The clover leaves closed themselves ; the trees lost their shadows. The bells of the horses rang continuously, and so monotonously. A postillion hummed from time to time a disconnected *Jodel*. The German travellers had closed their carriages. At Laret all light was faded from the valley and the mountains. The ridges were cut out black and dreamy against the sallow sky, and the stars were beginning to stand forth in the blue.

"There are few stars to-night," remarked my friend. "It will probably be fine to-morrow. Many stars in the sky is a bad sign." She was quite pleased and willing to exile the stars from heaven for the sake of her hay.

A great shining planet rose over the Seehorn. It shone and rippled in the waters of the lake as we drove by. Frau Hold got out at Höhwald. The child howled dismally—it did not know much why ; but I suppose was tired and forgot. How strange that seemed. To be tired and to forget the day at Conters !　　　M. S.

AMONG THE ORCHARDS OF TYROL

THE little village of Schluderns stands at the meeting-point of many ways, upon the extreme western boundary of Tyrol. Ascending northward, one road crosses the windy Heath of St. Valentine, and bifurcates at Nauders for the Lower Engadine, whence it leads in due course up to Samaden and Maloja ; while its other branch descends the gorge of Finstermünz, whereby one reaches Landeck and the Arlberg railway. The same road, plunging southward across Vintschgau, threads the vine-clad slopes of Meran, and thence follows the Adige by Botzen to towered Verona. By the north-west, starting from Schluderns, the traveller gains Switzerland through Münster Thal, and the bleak bear-haunted forests of Buffalora. If he chooses the south-western route, he breaks at once into the narrow valley which conducts him by the Stelvio Pass, beneath impending glaciers of the Ortler range, to Italy's majestic Valtelline, where Adda races through leagues and leagues of vineyards to the Lake of Como.

It is clear that the position of Schluderns is one of geographical importance, now that the high central Alps from which the tributaries of the Po, the Adige, and the Danube descend, are being traversed in every direction by tourists. And yet its name is hardly known ; for the simple reason that until the summer of 1885 it boasted of no inn. An isolated hostelry, a single house called Spondinig, set down amid a waste of dwarf willows, sand, and boulders, at the distance of twenty minutes from this village, has usurped the traffic which should naturally have fallen to Schluderns. Often have I groaned, and probably have other travellers also, at the necessity which forced me to spend a night in so forlorn a " lodge in some lone wilderness " as is Spondinig. For, to tell the truth, one of the principal charms of Schluderns is that it smiles, a visible oasis in the desert. Above, the valley expands into bare, open grass-land. Below, the inundations of the Etzsch have spread perennial barrenness. Itself, nestled against the sides of sheltering slopes descending from the Weisskugel, can boast of broad and liberally watered meadows, where the Tyrolese mares and colts love to roam ; while its quaint old dwellings are embosomed in orchards of apple, pear, and walnut trees. In one of these orchards, at the end of the village, with a striking distant view of the Ortler, stands a white farm-house, which has recently been converted into a hotel under the name of Schweizerhof. It pretends to nothing beyond airy rooms, cleanliness, wholesome fare, and hospitality. Swiss folk keep it who have long plied their trade on the Hospiz of the Fluela in Canton Graubünden. To introduce this halting-place to travellers is one of my objects. They may be as glad as I was to light upon that old-fashioned *Stube*, with its projecting Gothic window in one corner, and a stove of green tiles in another, low cross-legged tables in the middle, and broad settles of walnut wood fixed against the panelled walls. Such a room presents a pleasant contrast to the dreary *salle-à-manger* which renders life burdensome in commonplace wayside caravanserais. It is difficult to say why, out of many Tyrolese villages, upon a summer journey, one un-

THE ORTLER FROM THE STELVIO ROAD.

Among the Orchards of Tyrol

pretending hamlet, with no claim to renown, should make so agreeable an impression as to leave a lasting memory. In the case of Schluderns I think the reason is that one can scarcely reach it except on routes which render its deep-embowered orchards grateful to the sense by contrast. Of all mountain passes Buffalora (or Ofenerberg) is the most severe and solitary. Nothing can be imagined more bleak than the Valentiner Heide. The Etzsch Thal from Meran ascends through a double row of barren hills in a river-plagued trough, where the cruel fight of man with nature seems to be symbolised in a never-ending series of ghastly, blood-bedabbled crucifixes. Even after the sublimities of the Stelvio, which is beyond comparison the grandest in scenery, as it is the highest of all carriage-passes in the Alps, this verdure of soft lawns and interlaced fruit-trees affords repose to nerves that have been overwrought by that ideal beauty.

The main object of interest at Schluderns is a feudal castle called the Churburg, which rises above the village, commanding a superb prospect over Upper Vintschgau and the Ortler range. To its antique walls and jutting outworks the leafy tops of pear trees and swaying boughs of walnuts, long untouched by pruning hands, sweep upward from the home-garth. The castle has always been inhabited, and is still occupied by counts who take their titles from Churburg and from many other Tyrolese strongholds. Their shield, "argent a fess dancettee gules," quarters innumerable coats, among which I noticed one of singular beauty—"argent, three wings expanded azure." These arms adorn the porcelain stoves, and are painted on the shutters of the building. They may also be seen, together with the eagle of the Empire, emblazoned on the battlements and gateways of the old walled town of Glurns. This proves the importance of the house of

Our Life in the Swiss Highlands

Trapp (for so the Counts of Churburg are named) in their immediate neighbourhood. Glurns, which lies at no great distance from Schluderns beyond the Etzsch, is an interesting specimen of the feudal burgh as distinguished from an open village. Its walls and the towers above its gates are still intact. The straggling street, dilapidated homesteads, and enclosed gardens of this medieval relic well deserve a visit. But we must return to the castle. The main structure is built about a square arcaded court, round which run open galleries, with pillars of rudely sculptured marble in Byzantine style. From these galleries the suites of apartments open in two upper stories. This central block is detached from the lodgings of the grooms and servants, the chapel, guard-room, entrance-tower, and stablings, by a grassy alley ; while a flight of broad stone steps, screened by strong walls, or curtains, slit with loop-holed windows, leads from its chambers into a slumbering pleasance on the southern side. Here orchard and flower-garden melt into each other, terrace after terrace, as the steep ground breaks away towards the village. It is a fascinating labyrinth to stroll in ; a solitude inviting us to dream of "ladies dead and lovely knights," who once were wont to pace these balustraded alleys. After a visit to the armoury above in the main building, we can fill our fancy with another set of visions, and behold the Counts of Churburg riding in full panoply to war beneath the arches of their portcullised barbican. Few private houses contain so rich a collection of complete suits of mail, all of them well preserved, belonging to known members of one family, and dating from the early Middle Ages. The changes in armour, both of man and horse, from the Crusades to the Renaissance, may here be studied. Weapons of all periods and kinds, damascened sword-blades, huge two-

126

Among the Orchards of Tyrol

handled glaives, daggers enriched with Italian niello, quaint German baskets for chiselled rapier-hilts, heraldic bearings side by side with crucifixes graven deep on gorget or cuirass, crossbows of wood inlaid with ivory, clumsy arquebuses, long-muzzled pistols and triangular stilettos, gauntlets and helmets of divers fashions, not to speak of lances, partisans, and halberds, crowd the walls in every space left vacant by well-burnished suits of knightly steel. In short, an amateur of armour will be repaid a visit to Schluderns if only he gain access to this chamber. Probably he will be introduced into the armoury by the daughter or the grand-daughter of that Josele Pichler who first ascended Ortler, and to whom a pillar in white marble has been erected on the Stelvio. Both of these women are denizens of the castle, from the ramparts of which they view the peak connected with their name.

I have written enough, perhaps, in recommendation of Schluderns to travellers who wish to break their journey in this portion of the Upper Etzsch Thal.

I will only add, with regard to mountain excursions in the neighbourhood, that it is an excellent station for the ascent of the Weisskugel. J. A. S.

MELCHIOR RAGETLI; OR, THE LIFE OF A SWISS PORTER

PART I

BEFORE I took up my residence in Switzerland I used often to wonder how that useful and important functionary, the concierge in a Swiss hotel, obtained his education. The familiarity with many languages displayed by Swiss porters, and their acquaintance with the ways and wants of different nations, struck me as singular. They could not have afforded to spend much money on their early training; and yet they seemed to have been everywhere, and to know a little about everything in Europe.

Lately I have been in a position to obtain much information from the men themselves regarding their past lives. And I think it may be interesting to condense this into a narrative, which shall explain every step in a porter's career from boyhood to the period when he stands in middle life with dignity at the entrance of some palatial hotel like the Schweizerhof at Lucerne.

It will be convenient to give the hero of my tale a name and birthplace, although I must premise that he is purely a fictitious personage. At the same time I shall be careful to record no incident which has not been related to me by some particular person as a detail of his own experience.

Melchior Ragetli

We will suppose, then, that he was born in 1860 at Emsenau, in the Rhine valley, above the ancient town of Chur. Emsenau is a large village surrounded by broad, open meadows and orchards—on the one side sweeping away to the turbulent river, on the other ascending gently to those solemn woods of pine and larch which climb the mountain-sides, until the summer pastures of the Alps are reached, with crags and tracts of snow to crown them. The commune or Gemeinde of Emsenau owns a wide extent of cultivated ground, large forests, and Alps sufficient to maintain a couple of thousand cows. Each of the burghers receives an allotment of nearly three acres, which he holds during his lifetime. He is also entitled to cut wood enough from the common forests to supply his homestead through the year; and he may send a certain number of cows to graze freely on the Alps in summer. Yet the inhabitants of Emsenau are poor; for it has often been observed that wealthy communes do not encourage industry. The men marry too early on the expectation of the allowances made them by the Gemeinde.

The father of my hero was a man who had collected a small competency in his youth by the somewhat singular industry of smuggling Swiss subjects over the frontier into Italy. He was, in fact, a secret recruiting-agent for King Bomba, and received handsome fees for each stalwart Graubündener whom he added to the Neapolitan army. Military service under foreign Governments being prohibited by the laws of the Confederation, Christopher Ragetli had to conduct his men by the most precipitous paths and inaccessible passes he could think of. Upon one occasion, as he told me, he marched two days and a night without halting. He is now a vigorous man of sixty, spare and sinewy, with grizzled hair and piercing black eyes.

Our Life in the Swiss Highlands

Before 1860 the Ragetlis had already been blessed with two sons, whom they christened respectively Caspar and Balthazar. Accordingly, when the subject of this history arrived upon the scene, he received the name of Melchior. These brothers are still called "The Three Kings," or "The Three Wise Men of the East," by their friends ; and I may mention that all three of them have been at some time porters. In the course of twelve years, two sisters and another brother were added to the family.

Christopher Ragetli built his own house upon his own land with some of King Bomba's Neapolitan ducats. It is a pleasant wooden dwelling, standing in an apple-orchard outside the village. A vine has been trained over the whole of the south front, and in June the garden blossoms with magnificent white lilies. There is a big barn for hay and firewood communicating with the house by a long open gallery. One of the ground-floor rooms is used as a carpenter's workshop ; and in the largest bedroom stands a loom at which the mother and daughters weave cloth for family wear. Such a homestead realises the ideal of peasant proprietorship. In it, although there is little money, frugal plenty abounds. Nothing has to be bought except coffee, sugar, spice, salt, and such things for the table, with a few indispensable articles of clothing and instruments of labour which cannot be fashioned at home. When shall we in England arrive at the like state of living, so earnestly and wisely desired by Mr. Ruskin ?

The people of Emsenau are Catholic, and use the Romanisch language. In its purest form, as spoken by the natives of the Vorder Rheinthal, Romanisch (or Ladinisch) is a well-preserved dialect of rustic Latin. In the Rhine valley, where Emsenau is situated, it has, however, been largely adulterated with German, while

Melchior Ragetli

in the Engadine it tends more and more to assimilation with Italian. There are several varieties of the dialect to be found in isolated valleys of the Grisons, all of them testifying to the long occupation of this Rhætic province by the Romans. The Romanisch population speak with pride of their tongue as the key to languages. There is truth in this boast; for Romanisch exhibits a remarkable richness of vowel sounds, which enables those who use it to catch with ease the accent of other races, while its vocabulary has much in common with French, Italian, and Spanish. In the schools German is taught, and sermons are frequently preached in that language.

Young Melchior was thus bilingual from his boyhood; and between the ages of seven and sixteen, when he entered and left school, he had also acquired a third tongue. The inhabitants of Graubünden speak, for the most part, German; about 30,000 speak Romanisch, and a smaller section, belonging to the valleys of Mesocco, Bregaglia, and Poschiavo, use Italian. Now the same education is given in all districts; and among the Italian Graubündeners there are both Protestant and Italian villages. It is therefore a frequent custom for German families to send one or two of their sons during the winter into an Italian family, receiving an equal number of Italian children in return. Business communications, which are continually going on across the passes of Bernina, Maloja, and Bernardino, facilitate this exchange; and thus, without any additional expense except that of the journey, two families may obtain for their lads the advantage of acquiring a foreign language. It seems that Christopher Ragetli, in his smuggling days, formed an intimate tie of comradeship with a hardy chamois-hunter of the Val Mesocco; and, since his friend had two sons of the same age as Balthazar and Melchior, the bargain

Our Life in the Swiss Highlands

was struck. He met Antonio Palmarin—such was the man's name—at Splügen, taking the two Italian boys back with him to Emsenau, and entrusting his own to Palmarin's care. One long winter spent at St. Bernardino in the snow-drifts sufficed to give Melchior and his brother a fair acquaintance with Italian. They had plenty of opportunities at home to use and improve this knowledge ; for a large percentage of summer workpeople in the Rhine valley are Italians.

It should be mentioned that the schools in mountain villages are only open during the long Alpine winter—that is, from the beginning of October till the following Easter. This, though it somewhat retards the scholar's advance in learning, is excellent for his health. All through the summer, lads and boys tend sheep or cows upon the fields, help their fathers to make hay, roam in the woods, and get their fill of air and sunshine. The schoolmasters have gone to their own villages, where they mow and gather in the crops like other peasants to whose households they belong. Such being the arrangements for Swiss schooling in the mountain districts, a handy lad of fourteen or fifteen may have the glorious opportunity of being taken to the breezy pastures where the cattle pass their summer. He will go as help to the Senn, or head herdsman, whose business it is to collect the milk and make the cheese for several families. Or he may be employed as goatherd, or be used to prevent the cows from straying beyond boundaries. No English child, setting out for a holiday at the sea-side, departs from home with a keener sense of exhilaration than little Melchior did one June morning in 1874, under the care of his father's friend, the Senn. They were bound for those high meadows above Panix, in the Vorder Rheinthal, which belong to Emsenau. It is a great event, this

Melchior Ragetli

translation of the cattle from their winter quarters to
the highlands, 6,000 feet above the sea, above the forest
line, within sight of glittering glaciers, and under overhanging crags of mighty precipices. The whole village
is astir long before daybreak ; and the animals, who know
well what a good time is in store for them, are as impatient as their masters. The procession sets forth in
a long train, cows lowing, bells tinkling, herdsmen shouting, old men and women giving the last directions about
their favourite beasts to the herdsmen. Rude pictures
of the *Zug auf die Alpen*, as it is called, may sometimes
be seen pasted, like a frieze or bas-relief, along the low
panelled walls of mountain cottages. These are the work,
in many cases, of the peasants themselves, who write the
names of the cattle over the head of each, attach pre-
posterously huge bells to the proud leaders of the herd,
and burden the hinds with vast loads of bread and
household gear, and implements for making cheese.
How many happy memories of summer holidays have
been worked into those clumsy but symbolic forms by
uncouth fingers in the silence of winter evenings, when
possibly Phyllis sat by and wondered at her Damon's
draughtsmanship ! It takes two whole days and nights
at least to get from Emsenau to the Panixer Alp. But
when this journey is accomplished, the human part of
the procession instals itself delightfully in little wooden
huts, which allow the pure air from the glaciers to whistle
through every cranny. The tired cows spread themselves over pastures which the snows have lately left,
feeding ravenously on the delicious young grass, starred
with gentians and primulas, and hosts of bright-eyed tiny
flowers. And then begins a rare time for men and cattle.

Auf den Alpen droben
Ist ein herrliches Leben !

Our Life in the Swiss Highlands

" On the Alps above there, is a glorious life ! " This is the opening distich of a favourite village song from Tyrol, which the Swiss have appropriated. Indeed, the phrase is true to fact. For through those lovely summer months, until the snow descends again in September, each day is passed there under the open skies, basking upon heathery slopes far, far above the valley-mists and dust and noise of tourists, bathing in sunlight, drinking the rich fresh milk, sleeping lightly, rising early, with a canopy of heaven above, and the majestic pageant of the mountains unrolled on every side. A Graubünden boy finds no formidable enemy even in bad weather. He is Nature's child enough, shaggily clad enough, and warm-blooded enough to bear the snow-storms of July and the drenching rains of August with indifference. Every aspect of his existence on the Alp is a new joy to him ; and I never heard that he caught cold there. Although the Swiss are not a sentimental, or in any high sense an imaginative race, it is no wonder that a couple of summers spent thus at the most impressible period of growth should instil into young minds that vague, deep-clinging passion for their hills which is so famous. If there are not more poets among the people it is not for the lack of poetic elements in their common life. Perhaps the reason is that such elements are too abundant ; just as Venice, the exact opposite of Graubünden, has notice-ably produced no poet. What is incontestable, however, is that this free life, in communion with open Nature, among the solitudes of the grandest mountains, has helped to form Swiss character. It has implanted self-reliance and the love of liberty in stalwart bosoms, while it has no less certainly contributed to the nerve and fibre of manly limbs. I also should derive the sedate, cautious, almost religious attitude of Swiss folk, face to face with

Melchior Ragetli

the great forces of the world, from solemn and inspiring influences in their boyhood. Some one told me of a young English scholar who professed that, if the globe were depopulated, he should like to repeople it by breeding from Swiss guides. The idea was not a bad one.

The summers of 1864 and 1865 passed thus upon the Panixer uplands, helped to transform Melchior from a child into a sinewy and vigorous youth. He was tall and spare, taking after his father, but more broad-shouldered ; and the hawk's glance of Christopher Ragetli had assumed in him a sort of stag-like wildness. Living bare-headed in rain and sunshine, his thick brown hair grew into a wavy tangle, rising from the centre of the forehead, and sweeping in heavy billows over low broad brows almost down to the deep-cut caverns of his eyes. He was indeed a striking lad, as he strode across the hillsides with that long slouching tread of the true mountaineer, which covers so much ground and never tires. Though alert enough and indefatigable, Melchior was not so supple or so agile in his movements as the men of our Scotch Highlands. The Swiss of Graubünden tend to massiveness ; and Melchior, in spite of his stag-like face and figure, and the proud toss of his head upon the firm elastic throat, was built too solidly and knit too tightly for flexibility or speed. But see him half-way up what looked like an inaccessible crag, or watch him getting a larch stem of twenty feet in length and six feet (average) in girth ready to launch down a torrent, and you would admire the address with which that ponderous strength is used. Then might you understand why the Austrian and Burgundian chivalry fell like swathes of grass before such mowers in the fifteenth century.

How was he fed at home ? should here perhaps be asked. I am prepared to answer that question with minute particulars. The Ragetlis, though not wealthy, were substantial peasants. They owned a farm of about £2,000 worth, which the father, mother, and eldest son worked in common, receiving occasional aid from the younger children. This made them better off than many of their neighbours. Education costing almost nothing to the Swiss, the Gemeinde supplying fuel, and the women of the family weaving sufficient homespun from the wool of their own sheep to clothe the men, it was easy to give the children a wholesome diet. The first meal, taken early in the morning, before school-time, included coffee, bread, a mash of maize and milk, and cheese. After school, the boys always found a hunch of bread, which they consumed while waiting for their dinner. This consisted of soup, potatoes, and perhaps some bacon. Pudding, or *Mehlspeisen*, of various sorts, completed the bill of fare. Among these, what the people call *Pitzokel*—that is, something like thin pancakes cut into long narrow ribbands—was conspicuous. In summer, vegetables were added from the garden ; but peasants do not greatly care for such relish to their food. I have often heard them say that fruit or salad *niutzt nichts* does not help to build a man up. Supper repeated breakfast. These three meals, it will be seen, were almost wholly without animal food. Wine and beer, too, were conspicuous by their absence. Christopher Ragetli kept neither in the cellar, but drank his glass from time to time at the *Wirthschaft*. They made an effervescing cider out of mixed apples and grapes at home, and distilled excellent medicinal spirits from the roots cf the gentian. But these liquors were bottled and reserved for great occasions. On Sundays, meat was added to the mid-day meal, in the form of dried hams of beef, mutton, and chamois, sausages of pork and beef mixed, all of which were prepared at home during the winter. It may here be remarked that the *gediegenes Fleisch* of Graubünden, which consists of joints of raw beef, carefully smoked in the chimney, cured with salt and spice, and finally dried in the cold clear winter air, is excellent, nourishing, and delicate.

It must not be thought that all the folk in Emsenau lived so well as the Ragetlis. Some families subsisted on almost nothing but potatoes and weak coffee. One poor fellow, who has now developed into a hearty man, told me that before he left home he hardly ever tasted bread or cheese or meat, and that he was a mere hungry skeleton with skin upon it. At school he had so little flesh and blood that when he cut his finger to the bone it did not bleed. This man also told me a strange tale, which I will relate. There was a family in the same village, as indigent as his own, but reckless and wild. The long, gaunt, lanky sons grew up like beasts of prey, stealing eggs, climbing into stables and sucking the cows' udders. One of them, more frantically famished than his brethren, confessed to having hacked with his knife a large slice out of the quarters of a richer neghbour's live pig. Whether the young brigand cooked this Abyssinian beefsteak or ate the delicious morsel raw, I forgot to ask. Another of the same brood used to supply himself with animal food by drinking the blood from slaughtered beasts, whenever he got permission to indulge his appetite that way. I was informed that this comparative vampire developed into the stoutest and comeliest fellow of the set ; and indeed blood, drunk warm from the veins of a sheep or bullock, ought to be highly nutritious. Has not a cure for consumption been established in America upon the principle ? A little of such diet will go a long way to support life.

Our Life in the Swiss Highlands

When Melchior completed his sixteenth year he left school. At this time he knew Italian fairly, and could speak and write German with correctness. He was well grounded in grammar, arithmetic, and Swiss history. He had been taught to compose business letters, and to draft the simpler forms of contracts. Singing also he had learned, and was beginning to develop a baritone voice of considerable strength and richness. Altogether, it must be allowed that he had received a very excellent education. The five summer months, or long vacation, enabled him to learn all that a Graubünden farmer needs to know regarding the treatment of cattle and horses, mowing and storing hay, sowing and reaping, felling and trimming trees ; and as this branch of his education was carried on under his father's eyes, he had been incidentally initiated into many interesting secrets of woodcraft, shooting, and so forth. The question now was, what line of life he would select. The farm of the Ragetli family did not need Melchior's labour. It was already sufficiently cared for by his father, mother, and eldest brother. He might become a carpenter, or go into service as *Stallknecht* on some distant property, or study to be a schoolmaster, or finally select the trade of porter. Such were the four principal alternatives which presented themselves to his mind. Melchior chose the last of these industries ; and this may be considered singular, when we remember what a fine creature the youth was, and how he had been exercised in open-air employment. But the fact is that to every lad in Emsenau porters represent the unknown world of cities and of alien lands. Porters are for Emsenauer boyhood, in the midst of landlocked Switzerland, what sailors are for boys in sea-girt England. They come home after six months' foreign service with plenty of cash in their pockets, clothes of

138

Melchior Ragetli

novel cut, hair curled and pommaded after the French
fashion, a new language, and tales of adventure in big
towns. They swagger, treat their village-comrades to a
glass of wine, and pose like world-experienced heroes.
Most of them have crossed the sea to London. All have
something to tell of Paris or of Nice, of Rome, or Vienna,
or Naples. I think it was an Oberländer's narrative of
his life in Venice, that miraculous city floating on the
sea, which made Melchior resolve to be a porter. And
for Venice, though he never went there, he still enter-
tains the vision of a dream. He had no other chance of
obtaining so much familiarity with men and manners as
the life of a hotel-porter offered to his fancy. None but
porters changed from place to place, and learned their
business the better the more they moved about. If he
became a carpenter, he would fashion wood into solid
houses and plane it into beautiful panelling, at wages
here in his own country. If he took to farm-service, he
would tend cattle and horses, and drive carts about the
Graubünden roads. To be a schoolmaster was an attractive prospect ; but this meant more money spent on
further education than his father could afford ; and
besides, the schoolboy knew what schools are, and had
no great desire to win a scanty pittance in some distant
village like his home. On one occasion of his youth he
thought of entering a seminary and qualifying himself
for the priesthood. His maternal uncle was Bishop of
Chur—that is possible in the Catholic Church : and occasional visits to the stately palace on the hill above the
old Roman city had inflamed his imagination. But
Melchior did not love the scent of incense, and already
felt that women ought to play a part in his life. His
father, too, reminded him that the ecclesiastical garb
was not sure to carry him, like Fortunatus's carpet, into

a palace and a throne in some cathedral. This momentary longing, therefore, was rejected by his wiser nature ; and, moreover, he thirsted to mix with men of all kinds ; the seminary smelt staler to his nostrils than a barrack or a prison. Only a porter's career offered opportunities of seeing the world, of enjoying his vigorous youth in various phases of experience, and of amassing money enough to make marriage with an Emsenauer girl at the age of thirty possible. This is what Swiss youths look forward to : fourteen or fifteen years spent in the stream of life, capital secured, and then domestic comfort on a portion of their own land in their own village with a wife of their own kindred. The further course of this narrative will show in what way they work the problem out. Melchior accordingly determined to select the porter's trade, and carried his magnificent adolescence into that humble industry. Sentimentally, we may think that he might better have remained in Arcady. But his choice had something of adventure and ambition in it.

There are several degrees of porters in hotels of the Swiss type. The highest of these is the concierge, or hall-porter, who is responsible for the main conduct of the house in its relations with the outer world. The second is the omnibus-porter, who goes backwards and forwards to trains and steamboats, and has considerable influence in bringing strangers to the house. Small hotels, managed upon economical principles, combine these two functionaries in a single person. Lowest in the grade come the Hausknechte, or floor-porters, answering to our " boots," who are principally concerned with luggage, cleaning shoes, carrying fuel, and sweeping up. Primitive inns may be found where one man does the work of all three kinds together. But the broad distinctions I have indicated exist in every first-class hotel organized upon a large scale of service.

Melchior had to begin at the bottom as Hausknecht, and to work his way gradually upwards. In order to secure a place as omnibus-porter or concierge, it was necessary that he should know some English and French ; for in either of these positions he would have to deal with strangers who might not be able to speak German. Every new language gained adds something to the stock-in-trade of a porter ; and lads who have no ready money for a foreign journey are bound to earn enough by manual labour to purchase the opportunity of acquiring these indispensables for more remunerative service. Many men who have not had the energy to seek these languages in foreign lands remain subordinates, and win small wages through their lifetime.

It was not difficult for a fellow of his build, six feet high and strong as a horse, to find situations. Melchior worked for three years as under-porter, during the winter at Davos-Platz, and during the summer at St. Moritz Bad, obeying the orders of upper-porters whom his father knew. He brushed clothes, blacked boots, cleaned lamps, shifted furniture, beat carpets, ran errands, and discharged the myriad indescribable duties of an odd-man in overworked establishments. It was a hard life, and to our sense of such things somewhat ignoble, when compared with the simple but dignified occupations of a peasant. Yet he had chosen this trade, and he now obtained an insight into its most complicated machinery. The whole organism of hotels, in which he was destined to spend many years, and from which he meant to draw a little fortune, lay open to his eyes. Nor had he any responsibility, so long as he did faithfully what he was bidden. Melchior, at this stage of his career, won the credit of being a stout, honest, active, willing, and intelligent servant, which afterwards stood him in good stead. He learned his business as thoroughly as only a penniless peasant bent on gain can do. Moreover, he enjoyed something of the novel experience which had attracted him to the career of porter. It was nothing for the lad of Emsenau to dance occasionally at the public balls of Davos and St. Moritz. These dreary little watering-places seemed to his untutored eyes the centres of wild thrilling dissipation. He even learned to waltz ; and after acquiring the habit, he began to circle with a finish and precision which might have roused the envy of town-bred mashers. No better dancing can be seen in London or Vienna than the muscular and music-loving peasants of the mountains display in their restrained and stately style of rhythm. Money, too, was more plentiful with Melchior now than of old times in his village. He could drink a glass of wine or beer on Sundays over a game of cards or skittles with companions. At this period of life I think he learned to play cards—Tresett and Yass— and for the first time ordered a suit of clothes at a tailor's. Earlier he had worn his mother's homespun, fabricated into the semblance of coat and trousers by a *Kleidermacherin*, or female clothes-maker.

After passing three years in this fashion, and forming valuable acquaintances, Melchior resolved to learn French. He had about two hundred francs of earnings in hand at the end of the time ; but his father could not help him with introductions into French families. The difficulty of taking the first step in a new country deters many young fellows of Melchior's stamp from risking what will afterwards secure them profit. The most fortunate are those who possess family connections in foreign lands. And the Swiss are so distributed over Europe in many

Melchior Ragetli

minor branches of trading industry that opportunities not unfrequently offer for a young man to obtain new languages at the price of personal service in some house of business. Melchior had not that chance. So, quite practically, he made his mind up to take a third-class ticket for Geneva, and to push his fortune there. Letters of recommendation were supplied by friends, and his own stalwart personality seemed to the young man a sufficient introduction. I ought previously to have mentioned that he was not liable for military service. At the age of nineteen he had duly presented himself for examination and enlistment among the candidates of his year. It happened, however, that just then the Confederation was not in need of more soldiers than the exact necessary. Accordingly, the army surgeons pronounced Melchior unfit for service on account of a very trifling defect in his eyesight. He had, indeed, at the termination of some childish fever, been unable to distinguish objects quite clearly at a certain distance. This never proved of the least practical annoyance to him ; nor would it in a season of more urgency have excused him from military duties. As it was, his freedom left him at liberty to pursue whatever course of life he chose, without hindrance.

He soon found a place in a second-class Genevan hotel, with a large restaurant attached to it. Men of all nationalities, refugees from Russia, Poland, Germany, and France, used to meet there ; and the one language in use was French. Melchior's rather hybrid French, which he does not speak with Parisian purity, may be ascribed to his training in the " Croix de Savoie." At first he filled the place of odd-man, and spent much of his time in scouring dishes and helping to serve in the restaurant. Afterwards, when the superintendent of the

143

cellar fell ill, he was chosen, for his probity, to take that duty. That happened in November, and he worked among casks and bottles during the winter. It cost him an attack of rheumatism in the legs, which became chronic ; but he learned much that was useful concerning the treatment of wine. His pocket at the same time profited ; for a cellar-master, however honest he may be, has ample opportunities of tasting the liquors under his charge, and wise masters do not scrutinize too narrowly. *De minimis non curat lex* is a maxim of wide application ; and we know in England that a butler who discreetly helps himself, while he prevents the world from cheating us, is a most valuable servant. On one occasion, when Melchior's rheumatism grew intolerable, he took a bottle of old cognac up to bed, and thought to cure himself by drinking it before the morning. Next day he was obliged to call a doctor in, who told him that a second dose of the same kind would probably have landed him in heart disease.

At the approach of spring Melchior felt the wandering impulse strong upon him. He was losing his health and making little progress with the French language in that Geneva cellar. Hearing then that a *marmiton* or kitchen-boy in the establishment wanted to go home to his native village in Provence, he proposed that they should take the trip together. Though each of them had saved some money, they resolved to live upon the way like *Wander-Burschen*, begging food and shelter. In order to abide by this determination, Melchior sent his earnings home to Emsenau. It speaks well for the kind-heartedness of folk in general that Melchior and his chum tramped on the hard hoof from Geneva to Lyons, and from Lyons down the Rhone to Marseilles, without spending a franc. They did odd jobs at farm-houses, slept in stables, and

Melchior Ragetli

enjoyed the pleasures of the open road, in that celestial weather of a southern April. Between Vienne and Avignon a good-natured bargeman gave them a lift in his boat. Then came the land of olives and weird stony wildernesses, and, at last, oh, heavens! the sea. That is what Melchior had long dreamed of. So he made up his mind to stay at Marseilles for a season; and being now well advanced in French, he got occupation in a Swiss pastry-cook shop.

As weeks rolled by, the burning summer of Provence, so different from those old summers on the Panixer Alps, made him yearn for home. The object of his year's wandering had been accomplished: he knew French, and his 200 francs had grown to over 400. In August, then, he wrote to his old master at Davos, asking for the same situation during the winter season. A favourable reply came; and he set forth on foot again, this time alone, for Geneva. The money he had saved at Marseilles was duly despatched by post to Emsenau, and he kept only five francs in his pocket. One night, near Tarascon, he slept under a hedge, and waking very hungry about daybreak, spied a pan of polenta at the door of a farmhouse. On this he breakfasted without asking leave, and put the pan back where he had found it. The way in which he recounted this act of petty larceny makes me feel sure that he has no worse sins of commission on his conscience. I entertain a real affection and respect for Melchior, knowing that he has the stuff of a strong, simple soldier, dutiful and loyal, with fine spiritual fibres rooted in the memories of his free mountain life in boyhood. He might have fought at Mürten or have perished with the Swiss Guard in the Tuileries. His porter's uniform, his polyglot accomplishments, and petty shifts for earning money, do not conceal from my sight what is heroic in the man.

Our Life in the Swiss Highlands

Therefore I have often reflected with sympathy upon the hardships of that autumn journey back to Geneva. He speaks little about it ; but the adventure must have been very different from the holiday tour he made in spring with his Provençal comrade. Folk were suspicious of his outlandish French and gaunt sinewy length of limb. His wild eyes troubled them. Not unfrequently he found himself run in, as a vagabond, by gendarmes, and had to spend the night in the casual ward of noisome houses of detention. He wore his shoes through, and suffered from sore feet. A touch of fever also, caught by drinking the marsh waters in the neighbourhood of Arles, reduced his strength. Without yielding to fatigue or hunger, he grew wistful, wondered whether he should fall ill by the roadside, drooped beneath the steady sultry glare of sunlight. The grapes were ripening, and the vintage had begun in many places. Still Melchior trudged onward, and when he reached the city he found it necessary to take train for Chur.

Then followed a couple of delightful weeks at Emsenau. His family made much of him, and his splendid constitution shook off the trifling ailments of the last three months like dew. In his turn he was able to pose as a travelled man, to treat his friends, and tell them stories about the sea and ships. The masses of his Faun's hair were cut and oiled, properly *frisirt*, and hideous to look on. Yet the lads of Emsenau admired him hugely, and the girls in church cast sidelong glances at the desirable young fellow. It was on this occasion, I believe, that he began to court a girl who had already struck his fancy in their school-days, and who afterwards became his wife. A good winter season at Davos brought the total capital at his disposal up to a round sum of 500 francs. With so much in his hand it was time to think of England.

THE SCHATZ ALP RUN DOWN TO DAVOS.

Melchior Ragetli

Four years had elapsed since he left school, and he was now twenty. This part of life had been spent in acquiring the rudiments of his profession, and in buying a knowledge of French. If he could but learn English also, he would be able to compete for the higher places which bring solid profit and consideration.

PART II

At this point I must interrupt the course of Melchior's narrative in order to communicate some general facts and more minute particulars concerning Swiss servants in London. The Swiss are highly appreciated in a small percentage of English families, because they take situations at low wages. They are known to be honest, sober, strong, simple, and industrious. The fact that they come to learn a language is in their favour. This supplies a kind of guarantee for steady conduct. But, on the other hand, they understand nothing of our habits, cannot answer the door properly at first, have no natural gifts for white-lying, and are certain to give warning when they think their knowledge of English is sufficient. Accordingly, it is only the less wealthy people, or those who see but little company, from whom they find employment. What the young Swiss dreams of, is to get a situation in some private house of good condition. The difficulty, however, of obtaining this prize is immense. Unless he starts with a definite engagement, procured by Englishmen who have taken interest in himself or his family during some Swiss tour, he must live at his own cost and answer all the advertisements he reads in the *Times*. Backwards and forwards, from the City to the West End, from Wimbledon to Hampstead, he is daily on the march. Weeks slip by ; the money in his slender purse grows small by degrees and beautifully less ; at last he borrows from friends who have found a place, and writes home for cash to pay these debts of honour. At this point he is generally forced to take some situation in public establishments, where the opportunities of learning our language are limited. The cook-shops of the Strand, the Charing Cross Hotel, and some of the Swiss restaurants in the neighbourhood of Leicester Square, afford him temporary refuge. This is the reason why a Swiss porter's English is so cockneyfied, so coarse, and so ludicrously defective in most cases. He has picked it up orally in the bustle of the lowest drudge's life.

If he is fortunate, one of the many advertisers takes him into service before the waters of the great city close over him. But even then his lot is far from being agreeable. Swiss man-servants, as I have said, are mostly engaged by the penurious or shabby-genteel. It would delight the soul of Thackeray if he could hear the stories about London households which have been told me by Swiss servants. I am in the position to corroborate the *Book of Snobs* with authentic *pièces justificatives*, appending names and residences. But this, of course, is not my object. It would be treasonable to betray confidences frankly and ingenuously given, in order to carry shame and confusion like bomb-shells into London drawing-rooms. Yet I think it may be amusing to relate one piece of experience I find upon my note-books, for this will show how very little English people understand the sort of men they may take into their service when they engage a cheap Swiss footman.

The man in question, whom I will call Peter, is descended from ancestors who have been German nobles

Melchior Ragetli

since the middle of the thirteenth century. Few English people are aware that Graubünden was an integral part of the Empire until the fifteenth century, when it declared its independence. Before that date it counted noble houses of the same importance as the earlier Hapsburgs. After that date it ranked among European States, sending its ambassadors to France, Venice, Milan, Vienna. Finally, at the end of Napoleon's career, Graubünden was included as a Canton in the Swiss Confederation. Well, Peter was a member of one of the oldest equestrian families of this Canton. The churches and manor-houses of the country-side were decorated with the coat-armour of his forefathers. They bore this shield : " Party per fesse or and sable, a knight in full armour swinging a two-handed sword across his left shoulder counterchanged." A pedigree, perfect from 1250, showed all the branches of the race of Wartenberg. Here and there the parchment was illustrated with coronets ; there had been a count of the Empire in one generation, a baron in the next, an Austrian field-marshal with a princess for bride in the last century. At the extreme end of the eldest line came Peter's own name. Among his father's papers lay a diploma of French nobility granted by Henri II. to "our well-beloved friend and servant, Salomon de Wartenberg, ambassador from our allies the Grisons to our Court in Paris." This Salomon was the immediate ancestor of the Wartenbergs of Luzein, to whom Peter belonged. These archives I have examined, and they are very interesting, since they show what a fighting race the family had been between 1300 and 1800. The coronets which individual members added to their ancient German Ritterthum had all been gained upon the battle-field. But after the incorporation of Graubünden into the Swiss Confederation, after

149

the introduction of the Code Napoléon, with its equal division of hereditary estates, the Luzein Wartenbergs sank into the condition of peasants. They lived with republican simplicity, retaining indeed the traditions of their past, and enjoying local consideration for their birth, but seeking no means to support a rank which is not officially recognised in Switzerland, by any acquisition of extraneous wealth. It was only when one of them happened to notice the Wartenberg arms emblazoned on the panels of a countess's carriage in Vienna or Berlin that he remembered the nobility of his extraction. Peter, accordingly, when he wanted to learn English, took the usual method, and got engaged as single-handed footman in South Kensington. It is not my intention to reveal the square or street, or the number thereof, in which Peter found a refuge. His masters were people of some pretension. Scotch by origin, they had acquired in the last generation a scrap of judicial ermine which gave them position in the upper middle-class. Little did they imagine that, so far as blood went, Peter, with a couple of thousand pounds in his pocket, could have claimed precedence before them in every Court of Europe. The Collops were not rich. They occupied a house too small for comfort, and their establishment was conducted on a scale of extreme parsimony. Accustomed as Peter was to Swiss frugality, he opened his eyes wide at some of the mean devices to which Lady Collop, widow of the judge, descended in order to save farthings. After a dinner-party, for example, in which there had been great show of liberality, she would slip down from the drawing-room and empty the heel-taps from claret and sherry glasses into the decanters, which she then locked up in the cellaret. Peter was a humorous fellow, and many whimsical tales had he to tell of the

Melchior Ragetli

shifts to which people are put who make hundreds pass for thousands in their income. He slept near an untrapped sink in a basement-room lighted from a mouldy back-yard. Poor Peter, whose old home in sunny Luzein had been so wholesome and so airy ! But he *would* come to London and learn English. He was man enough to know that these trifling annoyances had to be laughed at. What really hurt him was the stony indifference of his employers. "They never spoke a kind word to me. Indeed, I do not think it occurred to them that I was human." Even the solemn family prayers at which he was bound to attend seemed a matter of parade and drill. Having seen Molière acted at the Comédie Française, he now rocked himself to sleep among brushes, bottles, boots, blacking, heaps of his young master's clothes, beetles, and mephitic vapours, with a forlorn repetition of " Que diable allait-il faire dans cette galère ?" Early in the morning rose the barrister son, and rang his bell for shaving-water. Up jumped Peter. The coals for Lady Collop's morning fire had next to be extracted from the cellar and carried to the two-pair front. Then came interminable knives and boots to clean. Breakfast was laid in a scramble ; prayers were got through ; and Peter began to hand round coffee and toast. While this was going forward, several sordid skeletons used to step out from the Collop family's cupboards. It is incredible what delicate subjects English people will discuss before their servants. The Collops gave Peter a lesson in language every morning on themes chosen from the most secret and shabbiest recesses of their own lives. It would be wrong to repeat these in detail ; but take one insignificant item for an instance. When company had been dining with them the preceding evening, Miss Collop used to reckon how many glasses of champagne Captain M.

had consumed, and how much claret Sir Thomas N. had wasted. Much was pardoned to the latter, for he had rank, and was a most desirable *parti*. But the impecunious Captain, for whom one of the younger sisters had a sneaking partiality, received no mercy at Miss Collop's hands. The polite lies, the subterfuges, the hypocrisies, the little plans to throw dust in the eyes of their neighbours, by means of which the family maintained its outward show, were openly and cynically exposed. Life in Switzerland is so simple and so solid that Peter felt at first bewildered. He did not know whether to laugh or to be angry at so much baseness in great high and mighty London. But having more of Democritus than Heraclitus in his composition, he resolved to see the burlesque side only of these things. What he learned in South Kensington proved of service to him in after dealings with this sort of English people. Yet it was long before he discovered that we are not all formed upon the Collop type.

After this digression I will return to Melchior Ragetli, and describe how he fared subsequently to his arrival in London. He found himself at the end of his journey with rather less than 500 francs in his pocket. For the first three nights he put up at the Swiss Hotel in Old Compton Street, which forms a general meeting-place for his compatriots. His bedroom there cost him two shillings a day, and food seemed terribly expensive. Yet this first step was not a mistake ; for the *habitués* of the house, who dropped in to greet their friends and drink a glass of beer in the evening, soon made him acquainted with all the ways of the town. At the advice of an honest lad from his own Canton, Melchior resolved to move into a sort of *pension* kept by Mr. Goodchild. It is called the Christian Young Men's Association, and is situated in Sloane Terrace. By doing so he probably

Melchior Ragetli

avoided many of the risks to which strangers are exposed in London ; for Mr. Goodchild's establishment is conducted upon excellent principles, and though no undue discipline is imposed upon its inmates, they are properly looked after. Melchior's living now cost about 18s. a week, with something extra spent occasionally at the Swiss Hotel. He also began to take lessons in English. Accordingly, at the end of four months, his exchequer sank to a low ebb. All this while he was on the lookout for some situation, but, finding nothing to his liking, he deferred taking a place in one of the Soho Square restaurants which lay open to him. He thought it best, and wisely, to wait until affairs became desperate, rather than to lose his chance of better and more profitable occupation. Toward the end of July necessity drove him to clean knives and polish plates in the fiery furnace of the restaurant. Just, however, as the worst came to the worst, Melchior's prospects brightened. I happened to be passing through Soho Square late one afternoon upon the eve of my departure for the country, when I saw a face I thought I could remember staring out from behind a dubious and dingy window. The deep-set wild eyes reminded me of something I had seen in different circumstances. Then suddenly it flashed upon me that there was Melchior Ragetli, whom I had known two winters in my hotel at Davos. He recognised me also, and, leaving his work, rushed out into the square to speak to me. Three minutes sufficed to explain his position ; and I told him to meet me that evening at the Athenæum, if he could get leave from his employers.

Melchior turned up at the hour arranged. By this time I had formed a little plan for our mutual advantage. In Switzerland I liked the fellow's looks ; and I knew that my old man-servant in the country would want assistance. The house was going to be dismantled and let to strangers. I intended to travel back to Davos, and to spend the winter there. An active Graubündener would be of use to me ; and I felt sure that I could make three or four months in my family of great service to him. I asked him, therefore, whether he could leave his situation on the spot. If so, I was prepared to engage him as under-man-servant, and to put him in the way of learning English well. Of course he jumped at my proposal. How he got loose from the restaurant I never inquired. But, next evening, we were established together in my old home.

I always liked the looks of Melchior, and now I grew to like him personally, and heard many of the facts I have related in this simple history. I gave him lessons in English—he told me lately that I had given him forty, but I cannot remember the precise number. I only wish for his sake that the lessons had been more frequent ; he then would have been able to write a better letter than this, which I present as a specimen of his orthography :—

My Wörth Mr. S——,—firsly I muss beg your pardon, because I have not written to you befor and let you now that I was not going to South of France. I heret bad news from there, and Mr. M—— kam tweis asking me to kome bak to my old place. And so I though it would be better for me to be nere home. I am very well this yaehr, and I hope Mr. S—— and theaer Familie is also well, I alwais expectet you some time in X. I am hape to tell you that my boy is going on well ; he already begins to eet with us at Table.

I now not any other news, witsch would interess you.

I remen with many Salitations and the best wisches for Christmas and new Jear your

traute servant,
MELCHIOR.

Goldenen Adler. X. the 23 of xii. 86.

Melchior Ragetli

It will be seen that the English, barring orthography, is good enough : and I must add that, in the three months he passed with me in England, I was greatly struck with the man's capacity for picking up our language. He got it orally well and with a good accent. Much was left to be desired in writing, though he worked diligently at this branch in the time allotted him.

While Melchior was in my service I used more and more to wonder why he had chosen this profession of a porter. As an animal, as a man too, he seemed to me above it. There was something in him made to handle firearms rather than blacking-brushes, a nature more adapted to the field and forest than to the servants' hall. As my friend Peter said at Lady Collop's : " Que diable allait-il faire dans cette galère ?" even so I often asked myself why Melchior had thrust himself into this hole of industry. The answer to these questionings is very simple. He wanted to make money, and had the most resolute intention, after making it, to settle down at home and live the pleasant life of his forefathers in the mountains. In olden days he would have fought on any or every battle-field of Europe to get cash. But European history has turned over a new leaf. "Tempora mutantur et nos mutamur in illis," and the Swiss make more by *Fremdenindustrie* than they could do by foreign military service in this age.

When he left England with me in the November of 1881, he was twenty-one years of age, and had spent five years in acquiring experience, French and English. He is now married, as the letter I have quoted from him indicates ; and is on the way to become a substantial man in Emsenau. What happened in the interval between 1881 and 1887 remains to be described. From this part of my narrative it will appear how porters make their fortune after they have succeeded in gaining the necessary equipment.

The most interesting period of Melchior's *Wanderjahren* was now closed; but he had by no means come to the end of his wanderings. Five years had still to elapse before he settled down into anything like a continuous course of life; and this he only did at last because he had accumulated sufficient money, and had taken to himself a wife. He worked for the first year at a railway hotel in St. Gallen, which was frequented by commercial travellers. Here he discharged the whole of a head-porter's functions, engaging and paying an under-strapper, whose duty it was to carry out his orders.

I must inform my readers that a porter in Swiss hotels gets no wages. He has food and lodging provided by the establishment. But he is entirely dependent for his profits upon the tips he receives from visitors to the house, and upon the commissions he is able to exact. To this point I shall afterwards return. It is enough now to lay down the general principle, that head-porters receive no salary from the hotel. Indeed, they often pay rent for the occupation of their posts. There are some houses in large towns for the porter's place in which as much as £30 is yearly handed over. If the head-porter engages helps at his own risk, he will have to pay these at the rate of 25 to 30 francs a month. They live free of cost, and he is entitled to receive their gratuities. In first-class establishments, however, the system is different. All degrees of porters, the concierge, the omnibus-porter, and the boots, are in immediate relation to the management, upon special terms of agreement. The upper-servant is responsible for supplying brushes and blacking, the cost of which may amount to some 10 francs a week in a large house. The details of these arrangements vary

Melchior Ragetli

so much with circumstances that it is impossible to present a full view of the matter here. This much may, nevertheless, be taken for certain : porters exist mainly upon the generosity of the travelling public, and have to meet considerable expenses before they can clear a net profit. English people in general do not, I think, comprehend this system, and are not aware that the porter, upon whose efficiency their comfort largely depends, ought to be liberally rewarded by them.

It follows as a natural consequence from what I have just said that the more showy situations are not always the most remunerative. During one year, in a comparatively bad hotel at St. Gallen, Melchior cleared about £80. The next year, which he divided between an English *pension* at Davos and a little inn at Thusis, brought him considerably less. Boarding-houses, where families reside for periods of several months, are not profitable ; commercial inns, where there is a perpetual coming and going of guests, pay most. But the pace at which Melchior had to work in St. Gallen was more than he could stand. If he secured four hours of sleep he thought himself fortunate. Up late to receive arrivals by the last trains, up early to despatch outgoers upon their journey by the first trains, occupied throughout the day with the luggage of tourists and the paraphernalia of commercial travellers, responsible besides for all kinds of odd jobs about the town, he lived in one continual whirl of petty but exacting duties. It was not wonderful that he should seek a respite at the end of these twelve months.

This explains why, in the autumn of 1882, Melchior wrote to inform me that he meant to accept a situation in the South of France. His brother, Balthazar, was concierge in a good hotel at Mentone, and had the refusal

Our Life in the Swiss Highlands

of an omnibus porter's place open. The journey cost 100 francs, for Melchior travelled with companions, and they lived joyously upon the road. The back journey was not less expensive, so I think that he had not very much to show of clear gain by the move. His health, however, profited, and he greatly appreciated the delights of a southern winter on the Mediterranean. Next summer he provided himself with a similar place at Vevey, where he had to work harder, but put more money in his pocket.

The *Wanderlust*, or thirst to see the world, is, as I have stated, a strong motive passion in men who take to the porter's trade. It does not wear off rapidly ; and the conditions of their daily life are so unrestful, so exacerbating, that they always fancy they will be happier in some new situation. This causes a great waste of money, but if they have good stuff in them, as Melchior had, it adds enormously to their eventual efficiency. Other motives contribute to their frequent change of scene. Living away from home and its restraining influences, they form connections which after a while they are desirous of shaking off. Great hotels, however well managed, offer innumerable temptations to young men. These are places where people of both sexes meet upon a common ground of liberty. That awful power, the village censorship, more formidable even than Mrs. Grundy, is absent in Nice, or Cannes, or Zürich. It will easily be understood that much may happen which a man, at the end of his temporary engagement, is only too glad to forget. Here, too, the comparison I instituted between porters and sailors holds good.

Yet I have noticed that these wandering spirits, after some time spent in oscillation, usually settle down to a fixed routine. What they like best is to secure two comfortable situations, one on the Riviera for the winter, the other in some tourists' place in Switzerland for the summer. It is true that a part of their earnings goes in travelling expenses. But they have spring and autumn holidays in their own village. And the net results of their twelve months' work will amount to over £100. A three months' season in a good hotel in the Upper Engadine brings in 2,000 francs, or £80, which is as much as the pastor of a Graubünden village gets in a whole year. About as much may be expected from a winter in Cannes. I have heard of exceptionally advantageous situations where as much as £150 can be laid by. Deduct current outgoings, and the income of £100 is clear. Indeed, I believe that I am considerably understating the average of profits in first-class places. Other men solve the problem of how to secure permanence and fixity of profit by taking an appointment in an hotel which works all the year round. This must of necessity be one which depends more on commerce than on tourists for its support. The labour is monotonous and exacting, but the conditions are well understood. Nothing is lost on journeys. I am personally of opinion that a man gains most in the long run who sticks to a post of this description. If he has married, the advantages are incontestable. He establishes his home in the neighbourhood of his place of business. His life then falls into the rhythm of an ordinary citizen's existence. This, I may add, is how Melchior eventually settled down—not, indeed, without grumblings and repinings, for he long continued to feel the *Wanderlust*, but compelled thereto by the exigencies of a young wife and a little boy to be provided for. The highest prizes of this sort in the profession are concierge situations in hotels like the " Bauer in der Stadt " at Zürich, or the " Bernerhof " at Berne. I am informed that these are worth a steady £150 up to £200 a year.

Before passing to consider how head-porters make their income, I ought to add some details concerning the relation of a Swiss workman to his family. Since the application of the Code Napoléon to Switzerland, families may be regarded roughly as joint-stock companies, managed by the parents for the common benefit. It is known that when both parents die, the estate will be divided into equal portions among the children, boys and girls sharing alike. All money, therefore, which is drawn from the estate by sons or daughters for extraordinary purposes is debited against them. If a boy, for instance, elects to be a doctor, he anticipates his share in the eventual division. On the other hand, labour expended by them to the profit of the estate is reckoned to their credit. If a boy stays at home and works like a farm-servant, he acquires a future claim in proportion to his service rendered. It is for the interest of each member to pay off debts upon the property or to increase its value. Consequently, when a son goes out into the world, after his education has been completed, it is expected of him to remit a portion of his earnings to the family fund. This stands in lieu of work he might have done at home, and also as a recognition of his early rearing. The precise amount to be thus contributed by individuals is determined by feeling and instinct more than by any fixed rule. The system cannot have the exactitude of a mercantile concern ; yet it approximates to that standard. The result is that both sons and daughters in a Swiss family feel it their duty either to discharge personal functions in the home or else to send a part of their gains yearly back to the common stock.

Melchior Ragetli

Such being the case, it will be clear that considerable deductions have to be made from the earnings of a porter before he acquires anything substantial for himself. Not unfrequently he gives the father or the mother all that he has made for several years. If he has received advances from the family estate he applies his savings to the repayment of this loan. But the time comes when he thinks himself justified in founding a private estate. Then he opens an account at the bank ; and from that moment forward his expenditure is more economical, his profits sensibly increase. So important is the principle laid down by Aristotle that social institutions depend upon τὸ ἴδιον καὶ ἀγαπητὸν—the things men own and love as their particular possessions.

The relations in which Swiss people stand to their Gemeinde and to their family, on both of which I have now touched, determine their conduct in a very remarkable degree. Whithersoever they go in the world, whatever occupation they engage in, they never lose that tie of interest, as well as of sympathy, which binds them to their birthplace. It is there, if the worst comes to the worst, that they have rights of maintenance. It is there that, when the old folk die, they can reckon on some scrap or shred of the fields beloved in boyhood. Consequently, they only emigrate for a season, with the object of amassing capital. Consequently, after running adventures in all parts of Europe, they most frequently marry a woman of their own village. The Swiss rarely become colonists in our Anglo-Saxon sense of the word. They rarely build up large fortunes in foreign countries. What they want to do is to make money, and to come back better off than their neighbours who stayed at home. They are modest in their desires, for a very moderate amount of wealth places them in a superior position among their kindred. Such being their scheme of conduct, they naturally prefer to take a home-bred girl to wife. She will appreciate the goods of fortune they have won ; she will not be above the services demanded from a housekeeper. She will inherit something to be added to her husband's property. With more of ease and comfort than they enjoyed in boyhood, they look forward to renewing the old round of homely joys and duties. This abnegation of vulgar ambitions, this piety for the past, this contentment with the solid goods of life, challenge our respect. The social institutions of the commune and the family, as they are framed in Switzerland, contribute largely to the state of things I have described. We must also make allowance for the sense of personal dignity, inalienable from a Swiss burgher, who in his own place has no superior, and who is eligible to the highest political offices of his national Government. But I am fain to imagine that, over and above all these considerations, the romance of the Swiss mountains has something to do in creating this attachment of their people to its soil.

I have already observed that Swiss porters gain their living exclusively by gratuities and commissions. It is only simple and untravelled folk who imagine, when they see " service " entered as an item in their hotel bill, that their obligations toward the servants are discharged. What the item for " service " really means is idemnification to the landlord for his kitchen establishment, for the numerous *employés* who do not meet the tourist's eye. Meanwhile, the porter's claims to special remuneration are generally noted in a memorandum on the bill.

There is much to be said on both sides regarding the question of tipping servants in hotels. For my own part, I like to tip the people with whom I am brought into

Melchior Ragetli

personal contact. While it pleases me to feel that the item of " service " at so much a head exonerates me of any duty towards cooks, scullions, ostlers, cleaners-up, and hangers-on, I am not above appreciating the kind of attention which a generous gratuity secures. Moreover, I know enough of the Swiss working-classes to be sure that they prefer earning their money in this way. An equal amount paid quarterly has not the same attractions for their frugal minds. The present mixed system, commonly in vogue, meets, therefore, with my approbation. I know what can be urged against it. I know that shy or indolent travellers do not like the trouble of remembering and remunerating their personal attendants. On this point I reply that they lose a great deal of such interest as direct dealings with inferiors supply in life. I know that people who cannot afford to tip liberally are supposed to find themselves at a disadvantage. But this I positively declare to be not the case. They are faithfully served ; for all the servants in a Swiss hotel regard themselves as responsible for duties discharged, not to the visitors, but to the master of the house. Moreover, the poorer kind of travellers would find themselves very heavily taxed for " service," if the system in use at Lucerne, of making one large charge for " service " upon the bill and prohibiting gratuities, were universally adopted. I know, lastly, that tips are supposed to demoralize their recipients. I do not accept this view, though I admit that in Switzerland, as elsewhere, generous givers are better liked and more warmly remembered than the parsimonious. Tipping is so rooted in human nature that the strictest regulations will not eradicate it. We have only to remember what happens on English railway platforms, face to face with pompous prohibitory placards. Surely, then, it is better for hotel servants to expect lawful gratuities than to receive them on the sly, with a bad conscience. Finally, I will observe, as a fact of my experience, that I would far rather sacrifice a couple of expensive items on a foreign tour, a *petit diner soigné* in the Palais Royal, or a box at the Scala on a gala night in Milan, or even the sight of some picture like Giorgione's at Castelfranco, than not have cash enough to spare for the men and women who have served me.

The question of commissions offers considerations of more difficulty. It must be remembered that in Switzerland they talk openly of *Fremdenindustrie*. This industry, which we may call *l'exploitation des étrangers*, implies the distribution of foreign capital over a numerous and varied class of individuals engaged in it. The chief middle-man, who gets his living out of travellers, is the innkeeper. He takes the largest share of profits, for he has embarked upon the largest venture, and has organized the machinery by which subordinates obtain their share of gain. Drivers, guides, and shopkeepers come next in the scale; and these people are greatly dependent upon porters for recommendation to travelling families. It follows that a small percentage upon the value of articles supplied to tourists is universally conceded to the porter. If he does not duly receive it, he may boycott the offending tradesman, and transfer his patronage to a rival. With drivers the commission system is conducted on a large scale. The very considerable profits which can be made by a head-porter at some of the most fashionable mountain-places in a single season, are derived to a large extent from percentages on carriages supplied to tourists. Suppose, for example, that a family wants to take a driving tour which will cost them by the tariff 500 francs. The porter puts this opportunity up to auction among those coachmen whom he knows to have good carriages and

Melchior Ragetli

trustworthy horses. There are always more *vetturini* in
search of jobs than the demand requires. The lowest
bidder among these gets the family, and pays the difference between his offer and the tariff price to the porter.
Then the coachman is introduced, as recommended by
the hotel. If the family express their intention of not
going at the tariff rate, then the auction takes place on
a somewhat reduced scale all round. A " return-carriage"
is vamped up ; Paterfamilias thinks himself clever ; Jehu
and porter divide somewhat inferior booty. Drivers who
contrive to bargain with tourists without the intervention of the porter, run some risk of being written down
upon that functionary's black book. This is by no means
such a mere trifle as it may appear. Porters constitute
a guild which is distributed all over Europe ; and they
have their own ways of communicating information to
their colleagues and successors. I happened once to be
travelling in Italy with a courier who had been a porter
in his youth. I noticed an odd mark on one of our portmanteaus, and called his attention to it. He cried out,
" The stupid fellow !" but, being in a confidential mood,
he afterwards explained that the mark meant I was a
liberal and easy-going traveller ; only it ought not to
have been chalked up so obviously. Afterwards he showed
me other signs, of quite a different significance, which I
should have been sorry to have carried round upon my
baggage. This incident made me understand that it
would not be good for tradespeople or drivers to get into
the bad graces of an influential porter.

I confess that I dislike the commission system, and
think that it must have a deteriorating effect upon the
characters of those who gain by it. Yet at bottom it
contains nothing worse than the principle upon which all
middle-trade depends. Somebody is wanted to bring

165

Our Life in the Swiss Highlands

the producer and the consumer into *rapport*, and to settle the current price of commodities. It would, indeed, be well for both producer and consumer if this intermediary, with his large profits, could be eliminated. In many branches of industry there is good hope that he will speedily disappear. But hotels, with their complex machinery, must long subsist as legitimate and necessary middle-trade concerns. We cannot do without them in the hurry of travel. Tourists are glad to pay mine host 6 francs for a good bottle of wine which the producer could have given them for 4 francs, because they cannot get at the producer on a journey and he cannot get at them. By parity of reasoning, we pay the tariff price of 100 francs for a carriage, 10 francs of which will go into the pockets of the porter who guaranteed its serviceableness. If we had bargained with some coachman on the open street, and he had taken us for 90 francs, he would have been no better off, and we should not have had the security of a good establishment's recommendation. Tourists who dislike the commission system can always post at a somewhat higher cost than the tariff for private carriages. And I, for one, have not unfrequently had no reason to complain of men whom I engaged without introduction simply because I liked their looks.

If any one reads through this study of the "Life of a Swiss Porter," he may justly accuse me of chronicling small beer. I will not, however, plead guilty to the charge of having metaphorically suckled fools. A man like Melchior Ragetli, in whom I have tried to depict the average servant of his class, is neither a fool nor a knave, but a human being who deserves respect. It was my object to show what amount of enterprise and what versatility the first steps in his profession called into

Melchior Ragetli

play ; afterwards to deal frankly with the less attractive side of his money-making career. He is the same sort of man as those ancestors of his who fought at Marignano and governed the Valtellina. They returned to Switzerland with the plunder of Lombardy, and built the old houses which we see. Those old houses bear pious inscriptions on their fronts ; and the war-beaten soldiers who aged beneath their roofs were honest un-Italianated citizens. So it is with the porters of the present epoch. By careful toil and the conscientious discharge of responsible duties, they acquire their right to carve a large slice out of the *Fremdenindustrie*. Then they retire to Emsenau, build or improve their homestead, hew their forest and manure their fields, rear children, and live as though a foreigner in Switzerland was never dreamed of.

J. A. S.

SWISS ATHLETIC SPORTS

I

THE Federal Athletic sports of Switzerland, which are celebrated triennially, under the name of *Turnfest*, or *Fête de Gymnastique*, or *Festa Ginnastica* (for this Republic always has to use three languages), may be called the Olympic Games of the Helvetian Fatherland. Great towns compete for the expensive honour of holding them in turns, regarding this in the light of what the Greeks would have termed a Leitourgia. In July, 1891, it fell to the lot of Geneva to perform the patriotic duty. No city of the Confederation can vie with Geneva in local and material advantages, whereby a spectacle of national importance may be presented on an adequate scale.

Fagged out by writing six successive chapters of a *Life of Michelangelo*, I resolved to take the opportunity of brain-rest offered by this festival. So I joined a group of five contending athletes from the Gymnastic Club which I have helped to found and house at Davos. In the company of these good fellows, who never even heard the name of Michelangelo, I knew that I should pass six days without the tyrannous preoccupation of my subject.

The journey from Davos to Geneva carries one right across Switzerland, from the extreme frontier of Tyrol

Swiss Athletic Sports

to the verge of French territory. It can only be done with great difficulty in one day. We broke it into two days, sleeping the first night at Baden.

Early next morning our little band joined a special train for gymnasts, composed entirely of third-class carriages, and freighted with about six hundred men. We found ourselves in the midst of a club from Basel, who had on board three drums, upon which they drummed the whole day through, one fellow taking up the sticks when his neighbour put them down. What with this drumming, and the singing of patriotic songs (" O, mein Heimathland ; O, mein Vaterland," etc.), and occasional interludes of bally-ragging, the journey proved lively enough. I could not, however, in spite of the noise, refrain from admiring the conduct of these hundreds of young men out for a holiday, without guide or governor to curb their spirits, yet all behaving well. No unseemly action did I notice, and no word was heard which might have brought a blush to a boy's cheek. Then they were so comradely, so brotherly, so ready to make friends ; albeit some spoke French and others German, and both found it difficult to fraternize, except by the exchange of tobacco, wine, and so forth. The Swiss people are, in a true sense of the term, a law to themselves. This their centuries of freedom, equal political rights, and gradually enlarged democracy have wrought, establishing a liberty which is not license, and fostering republican tendencies which remain conservative. Much, too, may be ascribed to that mild form of compulsory service in the army, which stamps habits of discipline upon the youth without destroying domestic or industrial virtues.

Among a mass of Swiss gymnasts you cannot say what social elements compose each club. The nation is so radically democratic that the same section may contain

Our Life in the Swiss Highlands

sons of bankers and landowners of ancient blood, mixing on an equal footing with clerks and artisans. Such a club would belong to one of the great towns. At festivals they compete with other clubs composed of peasants and Alpine herdsmen, or with lads from the Cantonal schools, or undergraduates at the universities studying to be doctors, clergymen, professors, lawyers. When they come together it is only strength, courage, dexterity, personal beauty, pleasant manners, or some other quality peculiar to the individual, which gives superiority to one man over the other. Even the undistinguished and the stupid are kindly accepted by their brotherhood. Of wealth, birth, position in the world, there is no question. What brings them together as athletes is love of sport, just as what brings them together in the barrack is duty to the country.

There were gymnasts of all sorts, sizes, and ages in our special train, from Verlaine's Pierrot—

> " Corps fluet et non pas maigre,
> Voix de fille et non pas aigre—"

up to bruisers like Milo of Croton, brawny, thick-set men, of bone and muscle, able to fell oxen with a fist-blow on the forehead. Most people think the Swiss an ugly, ill-developed race. They have not travelled with 600 of these men on a summer day, as lightly, tightly clad as decency and comfort allow. It is true that one rarely sees a perfectly handsome face, and that the Swiss complexion is apt to be muddy. But the men are never deficient in character ; and when denuded of the ill-made clothes they usually wear, they offer singular varieties of strength, agility, and grace. The nation is so mixed of Celtic, Teutonic, and Latin elements—Helvetian, Burgundian, Alemannic, Italian, Rhaetian—and these elements have been so little fused and worn down by inter-marriage, owing to the maintenance of the Canton and the Commune, that when some thousands congregate on these occasions, strongly contrasted types of physique are presented upon every hand. The artist's glance may range from the willowy, white-skinned, grey-eyed dwellers on the Bodensee to the wiry, swarthy herdsmen of Ticino ; from the tall gaunt peasant of the Vorder Rheinthal to the lithe and mobile Vaudois ; from the bulls of Uri and the bears of Berne to the roe of Jura and the steinbock of the Upper Engadine. Of course, a train full of gym-nasts, picked young men from all the Cantons, highly developed by athletics and airily attired in the costume suited to their sports, offered particularly favourable opportunities for this study of types.

It was a placid day of July sunlight between nights of storm. Our train, with its freight of drumming, singing, sportive comrades, swept through that luminous, sweet landscape of lower Switzerland, all deep in hay, and ready for the harvest. When we passed mowers on the meadows they stood, presented scythes, and waved their hats in the air. On we swept, by gliding Limmat and stormy Aar, past Olten with its furnaces, romantic Aarburg, Burgdorf like an Albert Dürer etching on its wooded hill. The silver vision of the Jungfrau soared from fleecy clouds into pale light above the town of Berne. Then Fribourg, with her bridges and brown Gothic towers. Onward, through lawns and homesteads deep-embowered in groves of pine and beech. At Palezieux the descent becomes rapid ; and soon we glided into that azure of the Leman Lake, which Byron called " beautiful as a dream." A symphony of blues : the amethystine hills, the fiery sapphire of the upper sky, the clear, pure breadth of sleeping water. At Nyon all Mont Blanc hove into

Our Life in the Swiss Highlands

sight, deploying pinnacle and snow-field in a mighty pyramid. The gymnasts gathered to the windows, clung upon the steps outside, saluting the monarch of mountains with three volleyed cheers, that rolled above the drums along the ringing rails. It was a triumphal progress through scenes " which neither man nor boy, nor all that is at enmity with joy," could spoil. Indeed, our boys and men were made to spoil nothing that is beautiful in Nature. They added to those spreading landscape lines, to that aerial colouration, the subtler, keener accents of man's living form divine.

II

At last we reached Geneva. The young men marched off to the barracks provided for them by the town, while I retired to my inn-room overlooking the swift outflowing of the Rhone. We were not separated for long, however. I came as a member of a Swiss gymnastic club, and enjoyed the privileges appertaining to that quality. That is to say, I was free to go whither I liked upon the exercising grounds, to mingle with the athletes at their sports, to sit in the circles formed by men around the wrestling spaces, and to eat and drink at their tables. Every club had its own ribband, metal clasp, and other distinguishing points of costume. Wearing these, one ceased to be an individual from the common herd ; and there were men with greyer heads than mine who appeared upon the field in a like capacity. The clubs carry banners also, which are set up above the common boards in the dining-hall ; and round their flag the members gather, as a rallying-point in the enormous crowd. Four thousand active gymnasts are said to have been present

MONSTEIN.

Swiss Athletic Sports

at Geneva. To these must be added their friends, and the public of spectators.

We arrived in good time for the procession which opened the Festival. It was a fine sight to see those thousands, marching under their banners, with their different costumes and colours. Bands of music broke their ranks at intervals, and golden sunlight poured upon the scene, as the men debouched upon the Place du Rhone and crossed the Pont des Bergues. Beyond their ranks that great new fountain sprang from the jetty 200 feet into the air, and fell back to the lake in foamy fleeces of rainbow-coloured spray. Beside the numerous Swiss clubs there came two sections of Italians from Milan, several from France, and one from Germany. A few Englishmen also put in their appearance.

The *cortége* returned by the Rue de la Corraterie to the Place Neuve, where all the athletes, clustering round the bronze equestrian statue of General Dufour, intoned the Swiss National Hymn. By this time the sun was sinking, and a rosy light began to flush the broken precipices of the Salève ridge. I strolled into the precincts allotted to the sports. The whole of that level piece of ground, which is known as La Plaine, had been divided into three unequal parts. The first, which formed a kind of vestibule, presented the aspect of a village fair. It was covered with booths, panoramas, acrobats, fat ladies, monsters, dwarfs, shooting galleries, shops, etc. On the outskirts a score of merry-go-rounds, with ships, swans, horses, and careering cars, whirled in sickening gyrations to the clangour of their Barbary organs, while a perilous switchback railway ran along a line of boundary trees. The second, and by far the largest, portion was railed off for the exercises of the next two days. I do not know how many acres the space covered; but it would have

173

sufficed an English University, with all the colleges, for cricket-ground and football-ground combined. Beyond that came the third part, upon which a vast wooden building had been erected, largely opened at both ends, high in the rafters, easily accommodating some five thousand persons at the tables set for food. One side was occupied by a raised stage, the other by a music-gallery, and the whole shone brilliantly illuminated with electric light. In these precincts, then, our days were spent, from dawn till dewy eve. The scene at nightfall in the Festival Hall was exceedingly animated : 4,000 men at supper, with a military band playing ; the " Marseillaise," the " National Anthem," and other well-known songs, chanted by all those robust voices ; the clinking of hundreds of glasses, the rolling cheers, the keen bluish light falling upon eager faces and broad shoulders and arms naked to the elbows. At each end of the shed appeared a superb back-scene, painted by no hand of man. Southward rose the Salève, with a bouquet of solemn trees and a church spire, bathed in moonlight ; northward stretched a distant reach of Jura and a faintly-coloured after-sunset sky. Viewed through the steady glare of the electric light these large, simple compositions wore exactly the aspect and the colour-quality of scenes in an opera, proving how true to Nature, under certain conditions, the art of the stage-painter can be.

III

I do not propose to attempt a detailed account of the athletic sports. They include, of course, those general exercises in which every gymnast is bound to qualify, and for special excellence in which prizes may be won

Swiss Athletic Sports

by the competing sections. After these the gymnastics divide themselves in Switzerland into two distinct branches. The one, called "National," embraces stone-lifting and stone-putting, wrestling of two kinds, and leaping. The other, called "Artistic," has principally to do with the parallel bars, the trapeze, and the suspended rings. Specialities, like running, boxing, fencing, swimming, etc., are provided for; individuals present feats of strength or agility, studied apart from the customary course; whole sections exhibit elaborate dances, exercises with clubs or iron bars or balls, pyramids bringing masses of men into strangest combinations. Most of these latter shows, being eminently scenic, were given after supper while the band was playing. Under the electric light the effect was something superb, and the vociferous applause elicited seemed well deserved. It will be readily conceived, with so many men in competition, and such a variety of sports, that a little army of umpires were required and kept in almost continual activity.

For my own part I took the greatest interest in the wrestling. In Switzerland wrestling is of two kinds. The one which is called "Ringen" does not differ in any essential respect from that practised by us English. The point about the other is that the combatants wear loosely-fitting drawers of canvas over their ordinary breeches, with a powerful clasped leather belt. Grip is got by each man grasping the girdle behind his antagonist's back with the left hand, while the other takes firm hold of the loose end of the canvas drawers above the left knee. This is called "Schwingen," because it often happens, with the grip described, that one of the wrestlers lifts the other in the air and whirls him round. In the course of the struggle the grip changes, and every con-

Our Life in the Swiss Highlands

ceivable form of clasp or grasp may be observed. When two vigorous fellows of equal build and strength are paired, say a couple of herdsmen from the Bernese Emmen-Thal or rustic Appenzell, wrestling of both sorts is extremely exciting and not without an element of danger. It is in some respects even more interesting when a young giant, without much practice in the sport, happens to be mated with a dexterous opponent—brute force and weight matched against nimbleness and science. Victory not unfrequently crowns him who looked but mean and contemptible beside the heroic form of his rival. Though very rough handling has to be expected in the wrestling-ring, nothing like bad blood or resentment ever came beneath my notice. The victor and vanquished shake hands and drink a cup of wine together ; and after a desperate encounter, in which blood has been drawn and each lies panting on the ground for minutes, you will see the two men rise together, link arms round waists, and walk across the field to take their rest. I asked a friend of mine—a staglike youth from Graubünden, tall and sinewy, like young Achilles on a fresco at Pompeii—how all the gymnasts in this country came to be so brotherly. " Oh," he replied, " that is because we come into physical contact with one another. You only learn to love men whose bodies you have touched and handled." True as I believe this remark to be, and wide-reaching in its possibilities of application, I somehow did not expect it from the lips of an Alpine peasant.

As this young fellow is a good specimen of the Swiss gymnast, I will try to describe him. Twenty-one years of age, he stands six feet two in his stockings. He has the legs of the Apoxyomenos, the breast and arms of an Apollo. Poised above his strong full throat and broad square shoulders rises a head which might be carved upon a gem or stamped upon a medal. It is a head of noticeable beauty; small in proportion to the stature of the man, crisped over with dark massive curls, the features finely cut in profile down from a low white forehead to the firm round chin and full curved lips. It would be a head for a sculptor, were it not that it owes much of its grace to an ever-laughing light of gladness in the black eyes, a smile in the friendly mouth, and a warmth of colour which only Giorgione could do justice to. His clothing was a pair of tight-fitting flannel drawers, black woollen stockings clasping the calves, a thin jersey leaving the arms bare, and a girdle of broad red silk wound firmly about the loins. Thus clad, the young Achilles moved unconscious of his charm across the stage, against the screen of distant trees, under the flooding sunlight; detaching his triumphant manhood from the atmosphere and breadth and verdure of the plain, which seemed to fall into their proper place as framework for the noble form and godlike presence of the youth.

IV

Saturated with Michelangelo, I roamed these fields in search of his characteristic type. I wished to detect in some forms there—not David; that was sufficiently rendered for me by the young Achilles—but those Genii of the Sistine and that bound Captive of the Louvre: the peculiar shape of male, in short, which stands for seal and signature of Buonarroti's sense of beauty, and yields the keynote of his temperament. This type I did not discover in the brawny Bernese wrestlers, with their gently-sloping shoulders and bossy muscles on the thorax, fore and aft. I did not find it in iron-thewed, uncouth

Our Life in the Swiss Highlands

herdsmen from Glarus and Uri ; nor in supple Italians, where hip and thigh outbalanced the masses of the torso ; nor yet again in those dying-gladiator kind of men, who come from Thurgau, flexible and dreamy, like captives on the Arch of Constantine. Everywhere I sought ; and in the search I became aware how singular and beautiful the type must be. At last I ran it down in one young fellow from the Jura. There was the small head, rising from a thick and sinewy neck, extending into ample shoulders ; the lines of the body giving wide girth for chest and flexible back, descending to narrow flanks, extending into length of thigh-bone, and contracting to fine articulations in the knees and ankles. Large hands and powerful feet for the extremities. Here, then, I caught my master's scheme of the male form, the note preferred by him from all the symphony of living human beings. Then I compared nature with the uses to which my master's art turned what nature gave him, for the production of vast decorative architectural effects : Titanic forms, suspended for ever as symbols of human energy and loveliness upon aerial ceilings or in works of sculptured marble. The young man from the Jura seemed more simply beautiful ; and I thought how Raphael would have seized the vigorous grace of him, just as he lounged there. At the same time the conviction pressed upon my brain that, so seized, so taken *au vif*, this model might have passed almost unnoticed in the crowd of Saints and Popes, Sibyls and Prophets. It was necessary to accentuate the broader aspects of the type. This Michelangelo did by adding weight to the shoulders and the thorax, increasing the volume of the arms and thighs, exaggerating the leg in its proportion to the torso, while keeping the relations of head, throat, hands, and feet. The beauty of life, alive there in a man, was felt by him acutely. But when it came to decorative work, he enforced the rhythm of that beauty, and maintaining relative form-values, converted them to monumental and abiding visions of the truth he had perceived.

Thus comparing the living men before me with Michelangelo's superhuman race of Titans, I began to learn much which has an important bearing on his preference for complicated attitudes. It is not probable that he would have derived instruction from the Turnfest at Geneva. He knew everything which nature has to teach and science to discover in the region of design. But his disciple learned, by watching all those models in vehement action or in indolent repose (especially the straining wrestlers and the ring of recumbent athletes round them), how truly the boldest violences of Michelangelo are justified as possibilities of transitional or momentary pose. Whether we ought to regard them as justified, when translated into the stationary fact of marble, is another matter. Nevertheless I am certain there is not one of his most questionable postures that could not have been verified upon the wrestling-ground. For arriving at this critical conclusion it was an immense advantage to have so many hundreds of unconscious models always posing together in groups, and without premeditation. From the habit I acquired of fixing on my mental retina some movement which illustrated a corresponding problem of the master's design, I became sure that he possessed an eye as rapid and a memory as retentive as the lens and film of a detective camera for arresting and recording transitory phases of corporeal action. It might be argued that he worked out these strained attitudes schematically, from his knowledge of bony and muscular structure in the human frame. But, even if he did so, it is certain that in many most difficult cases he could only have verified the product of his science by referring to the model in a posture lasting but a fraction of a second.

The crowning event of the Festival, for an æsthetical spectator, was when the thousands of the gymnasts stood drawn up in ranks and sections to perform their general exercises. These consist of various movements, bringing each limb by turns into activity, and displaying the whole muscular resources of the body. The wide field was covered with men, every one of whom moved in concert with the mighty mass, rhythmically, to the sound of music. The show lasted for half an hour, and finer drill was never seen. It had not the overwhelming effect produced by the marching past of an army, or the wheeling of columns and forming of squares on a review day. But for plastic beauty, for variety of posture, for melodic cadence in the lithely swaying figures, it surpassed anything which I have known. A German, who had come from Munich for the Festival, happened to stand beside me on the platform, whence we surveyed the spectacle. He burst into tears, exclaiming : " Ach, wie rührend !" I confess to having shared his sentiment ; and when the whole elastic multitude dispersed, a shadowy vision of the life of men swept through my soul, obscuring thought. " Creatures of a day ; what is a man, and what is a man not ?" The mysteries of the universe and the eternities are prisoned in a single man ; and here there were men by thousands rejoicing in their health and strength. Yet man is but a dream about a shadow, a flower that perisheth, a blade of grass that falls beneath the scythe. And all those thousands with their souls mysterious, their bodies beautiful and vigorous, must pass away. After but half a century, how few of them, decrepit greybeards, will be crawling on the earth they now so lightly spurn with heels like those of feathered Hermes ?   J. A. S.

TOBOGGANING ON A GLACIER

THE Silvretta glacier, which is a very large one, descending at various points into the upper valleys of Vorärlberg, the valley of the Landquart, and the Upper Engadine, lies about 10,000 feet above the level of the sea. It stretches its enormous back for nearly twenty miles across the mountains; and for the most part it is smooth and void of those dangers which we connect with the thought of a glacier. From its billowy snow-fields start great pyramids of rock—the Rothflüh, Silvrettahorn, and Pitz Buin to eastward; to the west the jagged Verstanklahörner and gigantic Pitz Linard. Standing at the highest point of the ridge which forms the watershed between the Prättigau and Lower Engadine, one commands one of the strangest and most fascinating views in Switzerland. It is the enormous foreground of glacier which produces this perhaps unique effect. For one's eyes are carried over the great white snow-fields on the one hand down to the vegetation of Prättigau, and thence up again to the lower ranges of Casanna, Calanda, and Weissflüh, on to Tödi and the mighty giants of the Bernese Oberland—the Jungfrau, Mönch, and Eiger. Then, turning towards the Engadine, one surveys, through a frame formed by the rocks of Buin and Mittelhorn, the huge domed mass of the Ortler, and, farther to the left, the ranges of Bernina, with Pitz Palü and Morteratsch.

Our Life in the Swiss Highlands

I had never been in these regions, and their largeness
and beauty were a revelation to me when, in the late
October afternoon, I, with our guide, Herr Leonhard
Guler, his boy Christian, and a girl friend of mine, reached
the club-huts. We had left Davos in the morning and
driven up through the Vereina Thal to Sardasca—a
summer alp—where we ate our lunch sitting on the low
roof of the now deserted cow-stables. At 2.30 we started
upon our walk, and ascended the steep track, which wound
through rocks, scarce tufts of grass, and withering bil-
berry-bushes, into the barren domains of ice and stone
above. Our march was a very slow and laborious one,
for this reason : Herr Guler, who knows these parts well,
being a native of them, and a guide and hunter over
them, had for a long time past entertained the brilliant
and adventurous plan of tobogganing down over a large
portion of the Silvretta glacier. As the autumn advanced the surface grew ever smoother and more fit, and
he urgently entreated me to join his expedition. I
willingly went, rejoicing at the thought of such a novel
experience in my favourite sport. Four toboggans had,
therefore, to be carried up the 4,000 feet. Christian
Guler, being a taciturn youth of great determination,
shouldered three and started on in front, producing, as
he ascended through the alder-bushes, a very uncouth
effect. His father carried a fourth, and as few provisions
as four strong people could subsist upon for twenty-four
hours. The day was hot, and the earth extremely dry
after a period of three weeks' brilliant weather. We only
halted once ; and, for a small diversion, set the hillside
on fire. Innumerable little flames ran swiftly over the
ground, leaving black tracks behind them. At 4.30 we
reached the club-hut. It is a tiny stone edifice—square,
with two little rooms, a table, some hay to sleep on, and

Tobogganing on a Glacier

a most superior iron stove. On this stove we cooked some coffee. We had no milk. The weight of the toboggans had forbidden any needless luxuries. After our coffee we hurried out with a rope and an ice-axe to make a hasty survey of the ice-fall which breaks over the cliffs above Sardasca. The glacier was already in shadow then, and a faint reflected glow from the sunset cast strange grey-green lights down through the deep crevasses, where the unseen waters gurgled on mysteriously. All the upper peaks, however, glowed still for many minutes with an intense crimson hue. Darkness fell very suddenly, and we were forced to turn in early to the huts. An old white hare bustled likewise home among the boulders. A tin of mock turtle soup, added to the guide's Mehlsuppe, formed our evening meal. An ancient pack of cards was then produced, and the evening was spent in the thrilling pursuit of " Schwarzer Peter." A shrill wind whistled down over the glacier against the outside walls, but we were warm within, and the light of a single candle cast our shadows round the room. It was a wonderful world of snow and stars upon which we gazed before we went to sleep.

At 3 a.m. we were aroused. The aspect of the sky had greatly changed. The Great Bear had disappeared, but the brilliant belt of Orion stood directly opposite, and very near the Pleiades. The whole sky shimmered with innumerable lights, and the thin wind blew through the unclouded air, down over the snow, as it had blown all night. Weak black coffee and butterless bread is not an appetizing meal whereof to partake at 3.30 a.m. At least, those who have not won their night's rest on a truss of hay might quarrel with it. I know that I was willing enough to devour the meagre meal. At 4.30 we left the huts, and, by the light of a single lantern, we commenced

Our Life in the Swiss Highlands

our march.   We were preceded by the lounging form of the imperturbable Christian, who, with his back bowed beneath the weight of three toboggans, and carrying a bundle of sticks under his arm, might, as he walked against the stars, have laid the foundation for many mountain myths.   We soon reached the glacier, and there welcomed the faint light of dawn, which now became visible above the sharp black ridge of the Rothflüh.   One by one the stars vanished, but the bitter night wind still struggled with the smile of morn and cut against our faces.   About half an hour up the glacier we left our lantern and put down the toboggans, for it was now easier to draw them over the snow than to carry them.   We then continued our steady march for fully an hour and a half up over the snow-fields, stopping about every forty yards to place a stick in the snow, which should guide us on our downward tobogganing course.   There was a sprinkling of freshly fallen snow, from two to six inches deep in places, and we trod through this rather sorrowfully, fearing less it should interfere with our tobogganing projects.

One by one the great peaks rose behind us—one by one the crimson rays of the rising sun caressed their glittering summits.   First Tödi shone, then Eiger, Mönch, Verstanklahorn, Ortler, and Palü.   We were walking towards the dawn, and the dawn was chasing back the earth-shadow— which produced a line of purple lights, fringed with tawny orange, in the pallid western sky.

At 7.30 we reached the top of the glacier, and there we left our toboggans, intending to ascend the Pitz Buin. But an unfortunate incident occurred which greatly frightened and delayed us.   My friend, unused to such high altitudes and early rising, complained of feeling faint from cold, and, upon examination, Herr Guler found that her right hand was badly frost-bitten.   This entailed fully

Tobogganing on a Glacier

an hour and a half of continuous rubbing ; but, thanks to the sustained exertions of Guler, life was restored to the frozen fingers, and we were able to return to the glacier and to our toboggans. Christian and I took our seats at once, and started slowly forward over the first gentle incline. Guler followed in the rear, towing my scarcely recovered friend at a pace which he made as moderate as the steepness of the descent allowed. It was my privilege to ride a very superior racehorse ; but I soon saw to my sorrow that Christian's progress was much faster than my own, owing to the fact that he carried two alpenstocks, with the help of which he propelled himself successfully forward. So I hastened back to the starting-point, picked up two of our remaining markers, and with these sticks to push me on I rode in pursuit of the fast-disappearing Christian upon that immense expanse of virgin snow.

I can now only relate my own experiences of that memorable ride. Smooth and very slowly at first ; then, on a sudden, the runners of my toboggan glided easier—then bounded forward. I realised that I was on the verge of the great Kegel, or rounded summit, of the Silvretta pass. Below me lay the billowy sea of unending white ; beyond that again broken bits of moraine ; then glimpses of the verdurous Prättigau, surmounted by innumerable ranges ending in Tödi and the whole Bernese Oberland. I could not fully realise the superb immensity of that Alpine view. I merely tore off my hat, leant back, lifted my feet, and felt my toboggan springing forward into space. Then followed the most breathless flight I have ever known. Up dashed the fresh snow into my face, filling my ears, my eyelids, my mouth and nostrils, and plastering itself in upon my chest. All power of controlling my headlong course had vanished. I believed I invoked the Deity and myself to stop at once this mad career. Then for a second all consciousness of danger forsook me. I was seized with the intoxication of movement, and hurled forward with closed eyes and lungs choked by the driving snow, which rose in a cloud before me. When I recovered my senses it was to find myself launched forth upon a gentler slope, and many metres to the left of the assigned course. A few feet in front of me I became aware of an old scar of a crevasse. It was neck or nothing, and I had no energy to stop. I shot across it, and steered out upon the even plain of glacier. I had descended, through the sunlight, in the space of five minutes, a tract of snow-field which it had taken us over an hour to climb at dawn.

Thus ended my ride. Gladly would I repeat it. My companions followed. The tandem was not a speedy affair, and wobbled heavily over the snow. Christian had steered a longer course. His breath, too, was gone. He let his toboggan slip as he dismounted, and it dashed off riderless down to a small frozen lake by the moraine. So he got up behind my sledge, and we went in pursuit.

We returned to the huts to pick up some small possessions, and at five in the afternoon of that same day we reached Davos. We had had a unique experience, and it had been acted on a stage worthy of its charm.

M. S.

HAY HAULING ON THE ALPINE SNOW

AT the end of summer, when all the hay of the lower valleys has been gathered and housed, the peasants proceed to the higher pastures, and there they mow and carefully scrape together in the wildest and steepest places, and also in the pleasantest oases, those short and strongly-scented grasses which grow so slowly and blossom so late upon the higher mountains. This hay has a peculiar and very refined quality. It is chiefly composed of strong herbs, such as arnica and gentian, and is greatly prized by the peasants. The making of it is a process much enjoyed, and families will sleep out upon the heights above their homes for days together, till they have mown, dried, and stacked the Berg-heu in those tiny huts which are built low and firm on mountain-ridges. These huts are then shut up and abandoned till winter snows have fallen and the valley-hay has been consumed. Then comes a novel form of tobogganing, where the peasants' hard labour is salted with a pinch of exquisite excitement and a dangerous joy. The men climb up through the deep snow, dig out their huts, tie the hay into bundles, and ride down upon it into the valley. This process is a difficult and often a very perilous one; for to steer such heavy and unwieldy burdens over the sheer and perpendicular descents is no light matter. A smooth track is soon formed, and each day increases the speed of progression down it.

Our Life in the Swiss Highlands

Two nights ago a young peasant came to my father and said he was bringing his hay from the Alps on the Dörfliberg, and that we three girls might go with him, which invitation we gladly accepted. We had clamoured for it more loudly than ordinary young ladies clamour for ball-cards. The thing was novel and very exciting, owing to the element of risk which certainly attends it. Accordingly, at ten yesterday morning we started and drove to the foot of the mountain. There we left our sledge, and began the ascent of such a track as I have described above. There was not a cloud in the whole sky, and although in the shade it was freezing hard, the sun-heat was tremendous. We had never been on the path before, and had some difficulty in disentangling it from other wood-tracks. But we followed the scent, so to speak, by noting the remnants of hay which lay here and there upon the snow, and we steered a straight course up the indescribably steep ascent. At first we passed over meadows, then struck into scattered forest. The trees stood out almost black against a sky so solid in its sapphire that it rivalled the pines in depth of tone. The road was very rough at first where wood-hauling and horse-traffic had broken into the lighter crust formed by the descent of hay-bundles. But as we mounted higher the path became a smooth, unbroken surface, so shiny, steep, and even, that it was no longer possible to gain a footing on its icy banks, and we had to turn off as the men who had gone before us did, and climb the mountain-side by a series of short deep steps which they had cut into the snow. This was a most laborious task ; but up and over the slopes we clambered, and whenever we got to the top of a ridge we beheld another ridge beyond it, with the thin greened hay-track going up it straight as a dart, the foot-steps by its side, and above the great white moun-

HAY HAULING ON THE ALPINE SNOW.

Hay Hauling on the Alpine Snow

tains, blazing, unbroken by any rock or shadow, under the mid-day sun.

We were very hot and very anxious to push forward, and we pulled ourselves up with scant intervals for breathing, till at length we came in sight of some men, with haypacks ready for the downward leap, upon the hill-crest over us. To them we waved with frantic joy, and proceeded with renewed energy. But they were not *our* men or *our* hay, and, seeing us, they came rushing over the hills on their bundles with such a vast amount of " side " on that they lost control and fell. So we came up with them, inquired our way, and told them of our projects. Whereat they pointed out our distant destination, and informed us that they considered ours a rash and dangerous proceeding, and then we parted. We were well above the forest now, and on the broad slopes of the mountain. Great winds of winter had swept the snow from ledges and silted it into gullies ; and there was something intensely clean and smooth and large, away from men and their ways, in that white landscape.

We stood 2,000 feet or more above the valley, in regions wellnigh untrodden ; and here a light wind blew across the snow-fields full of the scent of summer hay, for the châlet doors were open wide, and some men were working amongst the hay like moles where the great white tracts of virgin snow were humped up on the edge of the hill, and three châlets nestled all buried to their roofs in drift. The men had dug a narrow track to the doors, which are formed of boards placed lengthways and easily removed. These were pulled away and a wealth of withered flowers and grasses lay within in heaps upon the floors. The pent-up scent of all these summer flowers rushed out upon the winter air, and burdened it with aromatic fragrance.

At last we reached our châlet—the highest one of all.

Our Life in the Swiss Highlands

Johannes and his cousin were taking out the hay in little bundles, and building them up into layers of straw and rope, to bind them into those firm packs on which we were to travel down into the valley in the afternoon. It is worth observing that the straw which serves to keep the packs together has to be brought up on the backs of men to these high regions. They seemed a trifle surprised to see that we had really kept our promise to come so far. But they had long ago been warned of our approach, as we carried with us a newly-acquired syren, into which we blew incessantly when breath was attainable. There was a small square place cut out around the door of the hut. On all sides of this the snow rode in dense walls above our shoulders. The houses and the big hotels looked very small and mean down there, and the train, which crawled along, seemed but a trivial thing, all huddled, too, as these objects were, in wreaths of smoke, whilst we—oh! we were up 2,000 feet above it all, in the heart of a mountain winter-world, with a dream of summer at our backs.

However, I do honestly think that we realised at first the entire pleasures of the situation. We had clambered up the snow slopes, "escalading, escalading those interminable stairs" for an hour and more, with the unclouded glare of the mid-day sun upon our winter clothing. So when we reached our destination it was to sink down with an untold satisfaction under the shadow of the eaves and partake of some refreshment in the shape of fig-jam sandwiches. Then after that we looked around us. Johannes and his cousin were slowly and surely making up their bundles by binding them around with strong rope. Their grey homespun coats fitted in with their surroundings, and their strong, graceful movements were pleasing to watch in idleness. The boy found that teeth. as well as hands and feet, were helpful in his endeavours

Hay Hauling on the Alpine Snow

to secure a nice fat bundle. We crept through the door
of the tiny barn, and lay down in the shaft of sunlight on
the hay, picking among the grasses for familiar flowers.
So dry is the air at these heights that the blossoms retain
their colours in death, and we made up charming posies
of purple onions, daisies shining white, geums, forget-me-
nots, and primulas. Routing about in that grass, too,
the pollen dust arose as it would from a field in August,
and half-choked us, yet all around lay the snows of an
Alpine winter, making the contrast strange. The bundles
were now made up, and we prepared to leave this pleasant
point upon the surface of the globe. One of the party
was heard to murmur that she " funked it like jingo."
This was but a passing sentiment, of which I assumed
entire ignorance. The remainder of the hay was raked
tidily back into the barns, the doors closed—and we
started.

There were six large packs of hay, each about 6 feet
long, 3 broad, and 4 high. These were divided in half,
and each three tied tightly together. My cousin and I
mounted upon the three first, my sister followed in solitary glory upon the last, with the boy to guide her.
Johannes went in front with his shoulders supporting the
foremost bundle, and guiding with his legs. We were
advised to combine a firm with a light hold upon the cord
which surrounded the hay. I inclined, I believe, to the
former hint, for, whatever happened to my steed during
that memorable ride, I always found myself firmly attached to its back, whether for better or worse I know not.
We started with a slow writhing movement which was
wholly pleasant. We slid and glided over the first snow-
field with enormous ease. Looking behind me I saw my
companions sitting as it were on the backs of nice green
snakes which wriggled noiselessly through sunlight and

through shade. But then we came to the end of gentle
meadow lands, and slowed off on the brink of a sheer
descent of some 300 feet, at the end of which the track
disappeared in the pine forest. For awhile we rested in
the sunlight on the plateau, and during that breathing
space an awful fear possessed me. But before I could
indulge my cowardice by flight we were off. The sluggish
snake now suddenly bounded forward, then bounced and
leapt along for a terrific minute, during which I realised
that the young man who guided it had lost all control, and
that we were sliding over his prostrate form. Then the
writhing subsided into the quiet of a snow-drift. Johannes emerged from under the hay unharmed. We
breathed once more, and turned to watch my sister descending triumphant on a load which she gloried in
guiding.

The descent recommenced. A yell from the front
warned us to duck under, as we shot through the first
skirts of forest, the branches breaking against our heads,
and out again down another shoot, steeper than the
first, but smooth, and ending in a flat meadow. There
was another pause, and then we plunged sheer into the
pinewood. The track was very narrow, and evidently
carried over the roughest ground, for it rose and fell in
mighty curves like the waves of the sea. (I might better
compare it to a switchback, only such pinchbeck con-
trivances seem very far from the simplicity of mountain-
ways.) On either hand the solid trunks of fir-trees
stood to bruise the dangling and unwary toe. In the
middle of the wood another halt was called, and some
of the hay left behind to be fetched at a future period.
We were now requested to sit tight and look about us,
and it was grimly borne in upon our minds that a nasty
thing lay in front, as Johannes muttered that we were

Hay Hauling on the Alpine Snow

likely to find the way " *komisch*." But we had passed
through so much in such safety that I could not now feel
alarmed, and sat up very superior on my soft saddle.
Moreover, ignorance is bliss, and we could see nothing
ahead : the road seemed suddenly to disappear. The
cause of this disappearance was only too manifest the
next minute, for, after a lull, a lurch much more tremendous than any before experienced warned us of a
real danger. We were shot forward down a narrow
gully between high trees, and precipitated at an angle
which seemed absolutely perpendicular. To increase the
terror of that minute the hay-snake seemed to have
assumed a diabolical personality. It hit Johannes about
the head, jumped over him, still bearing us powerless
upon its back, and then it literally ramped forward into
an abyss, darkened by the depth of forest. We obeyed
orders, my cousin and I—we sat tight, with our hearts
anywhere but in the right position. Then we were
thrown to the ground.

The next thing I was aware of was a dead halt, with
the hay on the top of me, and my fingers still tightly
holding the rope, my cousin in the same position, and the
figure of our driver emerging from a drift far above in
the wood. No one was hurt, and the trees surveyed the
havoc with profound serenity. The descent had been in
all ways up to our expectations. Its dangers added to
its excitement, and its excitement to its charm. We
shook ourselves together, and plunged for some minutes
along a deep track of level woodland, then out of the
trees at last, and down more meadows into the open
valley.   M. S.

A FOUR DAYS' SLEIGH-DRIVE

THERE is a great monotony in a mountain winter. A desire for change must inevitably be bred in the minds of those who have lived, week after week, month after month, within the limits of one narrow valley, with nothing but white and black to mark the well-known mountains and equally familiar meadows, dear though they be. Just a slight variation, even of outline in the hills, is all that the restless soul requires ; and a small local journey in a sledge has a great charm and fascination.

Such a journey had, in the winter of 1888, been much talked about by my father and me. We proposed to leave Davos one day, and, going by Wiesen to Chur, reach Thusis, see the Via Mala under its winter aspect, then return home by the Schyn Pass and Tiefenkasten. But the weather had kept us back—the severe winter weather and heavy snow which so mercilessly visited the High Alps that season.

As soon as the weather seemed settled, and the roads were in passable condition, we started. At nine o'clock we left Davos, packed tightly and warmly into our open sledge, with the driver and two portmanteaus up behind. The valley lay smiling placidly—an interminable stretch of white, with the water-mists slowly rising and vanishing from the river under the rays of the newly-risen sun.

A Four Days' Sleigh-Drive

The road to Wiesen had only been open two days since the heavy snows. This road, or that part of it which is called the Züge (in English, " Tracks of Avalanches "), is one of the most dangerous passes in the Canton. Numerous avalanches had fallen, both in the narrow gorge and higher up at Glaris, occasioning in two cases loss of life, and stopping all traffic. Very few would go there for pleasure, unless, perhaps, such pleasure as is born of curiosity. The Züge, even in the softness of summer-time, is, at its best, grand and terrific ; but on that morning, as we drove through, it was ugly in its terror, wicked in grandeur. The largest avalanche had fallen just below the village of Glaris. I believe that an Englishman who ventured down to inspect it returned crestfallen, declaring himself disappointed by the sight, for he could, he said, see no more in this snow than in any other snows. Perhaps it was well for him that he could not. The avalanche swept through a narrow *couloir*, having gathered in its furious descent all the snows from the mountain-sides. When it came to rest at last in the flat of the valley, it heaped itself out in a fan shape, crossing the river, and swinging up the opposite mountain. Wherever its mighty wind passed it mowed off the tops of the tough larch and pine-trees as though they were blades of grass. So the post-road was suddenly lifted to an altitude of from 50 to 60 feet above its usual level. We drove very stealthily over the snow mountain, and as we descended the other side we came upon a scattered crowd of peasants digging still in search of a comrade who had been swept away six days before. They had been digging, these fifty men, for five days, and had not found his corpse. After this we plunged into the gorge below Hoffnungsau. Here every curve of snow was a miracle, as it clung about the stern

N 2

Our Life in the Swiss Highlands

precipitous rocks. But something in the cold wicked-
ness of this seemingly soft substance fills one with
horror when one has learnt its force. I could not forget
its cruel violence as we drove across innumerable
avalanches, fallen so close upon each other that the road
had taken the form of some hard frozen sea of billows ;
nor, as we galloped through the dark rock-tunnels draped
with weird icicles, did I forget ; no, it was impossible to
forget the look of dismal despair upon the faces of those
fifty hard-working men digging for the comrade they had
lost, and whose body only the warmth of summer suns
would return to them.

I think that my father and I were both well pleased
when Wiesen was reached—sunny, hospitable Wiesen,
perched smilingly upon its steep hillside. Sitting on
the balcony after lunch, with the great snow-sweeps of
Pitz Michel and the Tinzenhorn stretching out before us,
we could converse with our host at ease upon the dangers
of our morning drive, and listen to his account of the
serious perils of the Züge road.

At three o'clock we prepared to take a short walk, but
other and unexpected pleasures awaited us. As we
strolled down the village street we found that the whole
place was in a state of great excitement. " Heute wird
Theater gespielt in Schmitten," we were informed by
some eager young ladies who were busily packing themselves into their sledges. " Let us go, too, and see this
play in Schmitten," I cried ; and accordingly we went.
Our sledge was soon ready, and I in it, hastening after
the merry band in front. Hans *jodled* loudly and joy-
fully on the board behind, and cracked his whip over
Ruedi, our horse's ears, who, much elevated also, plunged
down the steep road snorting vigorously, and kicking the
snow in balls upon my face, as though he shared the

THE TINZENHORN.

A Four Days' Sleigh-Drive

general rejoicing. The pleasure of that sunny drive was short, and soon the doll-church of Schmitten was seen, perched on its high hillside. We drew up before the door of the village inn, whose hospitable landlord came out to meet us. "Alas, you are late, meine Herren," he cried. "The play has already begun. Go in, go in." So in we went, having paid the modest entrance fee of 50 centimes apiece.

Such an atmosphere! But then the outdoor air was cold, and the contrast naturally striking. A prevailing sense of tobacco smoke, old Sunday clothes, and hot working people—that was all. We crowded on to a narrow bench, the audience, with most polished courtesy, squeezing itself to give us room ; and then we entered as best we could into the spirit of the performance. Previous to our arrival the great *coup* of the piece had already taken place, and all the actors were to the fore. (I noticed throughout that when once an actor had come upon the boards he never again left them till the curtain fell. He stayed to the last, even as a sort of mute encumbrance.) The stage was a miracle of peasant artifice. Footlights there were none ; but a paraffin lamp, swinging from the ceiling, cast a grim and fitful glare over the faces of the performers. The platform was very slightly raised above the audience, and portioned off by airily-hung sheets. The drop-curtain consisted of a yellow bed-cover, and the stage decorations of two stunted geraniums grown in potted-meat tins. The ball-room of a village inn at Schmitten is, of course, not large, but the inhabitants of Schmitten *are* large and well-grown men. The tall bodies of the actors seemed at times to overwhelm the tiny theatre, while their heads were not seldom hidden by the front boarding. Their costumes were varied and grotesque. The earnestness of their expres-

Our Life in the Swiss Highlands

sion and the stolid repetition of their gestures struck one with a sense of the marvellous. No art could have made them act their parts to the life as these men did, simply because the "Hausknecht," the Swiss soldier, the "Notar," the "Polizei," all were by nature and profession what they represented histrionically ; and they *were* it admirably. Such simplicity is surely to be admired ; for it cannot long continue, even in Schmitten. Perhaps the great want of all dramatic action in the people might have been lamented by some spectators ; but this very want, combining as it did with the total void of plot in either of the pieces chosen, seemed to me to constitute the chief comic element of the performance. For instance : a tall gentleman in a chimney-pot hat, upon finding his long-lost son and wife, betrayed no greater signs of pleasure or astonishment than by drawing his hand pensively across his brow and sighing. Another, upon being accused of theft and murder, merely smiled placidly across the trembling bayonets pointed at his person, limply raising his arm as a token of mild protest. One young and ardent lover in white gloves, it is true, rose to a pitch of poetic admiration when he compared the mistress of his affections to a "pyramid." I think the supreme consciousness of those white gloves lent him something like the polish of an artist.

When the performance was over we packed ourselves into the sledge again, and were soon crawling up the hill down which we had come so gaily two hours before. The sun had set and a grey mist crept over the blue sky. The long winter night was closing in quickly, touching the distance with shadowy vapours, and making both mind and body sleepy. The stillness of the way was only broken faintly by the thin shrill voices of the girls behind us, who were singing their songs into the winter twilight.

A Four Days' Sleigh-Drive

Perhaps those who keep high holiday in the lowlands during carnival time do not imagine that their more sober mountain brethren keep it too, and do so heartily.

Wiesen was reached at last, and after a comfortable little supper-party in the parlour of our host and his wife, we all repaired to the ball-room. It was a small room—very full of tobacco and steam—steam produced by the snow brought in on the hobnailed boots of the men. The scene, when once we had become accustomed to the murky light and thick air, was a most entertaining one. When Bündners dance, they usually become a little animated ; but when Bündners put on fancy-dress, the effect produced is startling and supreme. Of all those present, the most imposing figure was a tall washer-woman who, for the occasion, had stepped into her great-grandfather's shoes, swallow-tail coat, knee-breeches, and white night-cap. She was dancing vigorously in a very determined manner, stamping the buckled shoes, and tossing the tassled night-cap. But if her costume appeared grotesque, there were others again which were extremely *chic*, which, in fact, possessed a something of Parisian freshness, forming a strange contrast to the rusticity of their surroundings. For instance, a young lady dressed to personate an Italian contadina, with dainty white arms and quite coquettish mien ; a fairy-like damsel, too, in airy blue tulle skirts and velvet bodice —these two were the belles of the ball, and, be it forgiven to their souls, they knew it. Those who had neither time nor money to provide costumes were quite content to appear with corked faces. Smiling benignly, I watched them pass, mightily pleased, as it appeared, with the economy-combining effect of their appearance. A nigger in white linen performed the buffoon of the evening, rolling on the floor with the intention of, if possible, tripping up the couples as they turned. All in that ball-room seemed highly pleased with their performance, but I, after such an eventful day, was very willing to retire early to rest.

We awoke to a dull sunrise. Much knowledge of mountain weather made us aware that the smoky flakes of cloud creeping so stealthily around the mountain-tops boded no good for the coming day. At nine o'clock we left Wiesen in the covered post-sledge. My father got a seat on the box with the postillion, but I was forced to resign myself to the " Kasten " (closed box), as the people of the country call the vehicle. At Crapaneira, however, I parted company with the Kasten, vowing that thither I would not return unless upon the strongest compulsion. "Where, then, will you go ?" inquired our affable conductor (guard of the post-carriage), smiling blandly upon the imbecility of my talk. "Why, upon the luggage," I answered promptly ; and upon the luggage we accordingly went—my father and I. The luggage is always conveyed in a low sledge, which is attached to the post-sledge by a long pole and a hook. It was a warm dull morning. Our two portmanteaus made an admirable perch, and with our legs swinging airily just off the ground and much good talk, we lurched and bumped cheerfully on to Lenz, pretending to think that we had found the spring, because a tuft or two of heather was in bloom on the rocks round the ruins of Belfort. These, alas, were vain dreams, for a driving wind was hurrying the scattered sleet across the Lenzer Heide, and the outside air no longer spoke of spring. By this time, too, we had been forced to resume our places in the Kasten. While my father engaged a local magnate, our companion, in conversation on parochial topics, I tried, by dint of flattening my nose against the

A Four Days' Sleigh-Drive

window, to see something of the outside world. But the Lenzer Heide is not a cheerful corner of the world even in summer-time. Dreary and desolate then, it was now only one great bare wilderness of snow. Snow fallen, snow falling, snow blown by the wind in wreaths and fitful eddies. At times the walls of snow through which our road was dug rose to a level of two feet above the roof of the carriage, and then I could, of course, see nothing at all. At Parpan a fat old Landammann got into the Kasten. He was a portentous person, with polished manners ; and the general sense of squeeze and heat was now complete. He informed us with glee and importance that we might expect to find a very gay state of affairs in Chur, where carnival festivities were at their highest. " Yes," he added, consulting his watch, " you may even arrive in time to see the procession." All my attention was therefore directed to catch the first glimpse of Chur.

Chur appeared at last. From the post-road one looks down into it with all its little old houses neatly packed together under their big mountains. I realized that its streets were crowded with people. The carnival procession had just arrived upon the bridge we had to cross, and we were forced, by the throng of people, to draw up before it. " Come with me. Get on to the box," shrieked our conductor in my ear ; then seizing my arm in his enthusiasm he pulled me up to the high perch, where I sat jammed in between himself and the postillion, seeing all that was to be seen, and mightily pleased with the show. The metropolis of Graubünden had been to me always the sleepy little old Swiss town, such as my readers also probably remember it. Now it was wide-awake and full of bustle. The procession consisted of a troop of Chinamen, a set of gaudily-attired gentlemen

on foot and horseback, with a confused crowd of masks
and dressed-up respectabilities—the whole enveloped in
a snow-storm.

Having seen all I could, I was preparing to get off the
box and complete my journey in the Kasten. I knew
by hearsay how refined and aristocratic are the ladies of
Chur, and did not wish to be perceived by them driving
on the box of the coach in the train of King Carnival. In
an awful moment, however, the postillion drew himself
together, and cracked his long whip loudly. Away we
started. The dense crowd broke, laughing and shouting,
before the post and its four horses. Over the bridge and
under the triumphal arches we plunged, greeted with
yells, and besieged with missiles from the masqueraders.
I felt the feather tremble on my hat, and the crowd
swam in a sea below me, when, suddenly casting my eyes
up along the rows of windows which lined the street, I
awoke to the ghastly consciousness that close to their
panes were glued the faces of pyramids of ladies of Chur
watching me. There was no consolation. The very
sky showered a watery snow upon me. But help was at
hand. A masked gentleman in plumes, velvet, and
tights, dashed his bladder (they all carried these instruments of torture, and used them freely on the faces and
backs of spectators) into the nose of our off leader. The
situation threatened to become tragic. The insulted
steed kicked and plunged. The postillion, who had
checked all former insolences with the unreserved use of
his whip, now cursed all his surroundings. The crowd
pushed back. The masqueraders became alarmed. The
inhabitants of a car of aborigines cowered down in their
straw. But this diversion had cleared the way; and,
gathering our forces together, we tore forth into the open
road and reached the post-house in safety. Here we were

A Four Days' Sleigh-Drive

met by the landlord of the "Weisse Kreuz," and having taken up our quarters in his old-fashioned inn, we again went forth into the streets.

This time we were introduced into the drawing-room of a very aristocratic mansion, whose owners had invited us to witness the procession from its windows. The maskers made a fine picture as they passed slowly under the massive towered gateway, a dim reflected snow-light shimmering on the gilded hands of the clock, and across the winged helmets of the soldiers. The silent snow which fell so steadily upon the green velvet jerkins and hose of these men had fallen upon the same clothes many years before, when they were worn by the knights of Graubünden ; therefore the falling flakes rather heightened than spoilt the effect of their slow march through the narrow street. The Chinamen, it is true, looked out of place, and their stiff print costumes had become limp and sordid. When the show was over, we returned to our inn. The evening had set in, and it was pleasant to rest quietly after our long day.

With a crackling fire and a good book I could sit down in my arm-chair and think calmly over my afternoon entrance into Chur. And considering it, I became glad. "For," I thought, "if ever I live to see the day when Chur has indeed developed into a metropolis, when her streets are broadened, her ladies become too numerous to be critical, when the old Kasten is abolished and steam-trams and steam-engines convey the inquisitive tourist to her hotels, and sully with their soot her quiet snow— then I shall recall the day with pride and joy on which I entered her streets at carnival time upon the box of the old stage-coach." Thus thinking, I opened my window and looked out over the sloping roofs into the still night. The stars were shining brilliantly up there in the deep black of the winter sky. Faint sounds of carnival revelry broke the air. "That time must be a long way off," I thought ; and closing my window I went to bed.

The next morning was cold and fine. Everything bore a new sharp aspect in the early light ; the very gutters were turned to silver runnels of pure ice. Only the sun was missing—the sun which never rises upon Chur during three months of winter, so high are the mountains which surround this tiny city. Still, there is a curious charm about the calm tranquillity of the sunless winter days. We were to leave Chur at nine, but not, I entreated, without first going up to the cathedral. So we breakfasted early, and were out in the sleepy streets soon after eight, climbing the steep hill, down which the boys of the Cantonal-Schule were hastening to class in their blue coats. One has to climb a long way up by the city walls before one reaches the open square in front of the Münster. We found the great doors of the cathedral closed. The Lombard lions which guard the gates seemed frozen and asleep. The rough-hewn stones of the façade seemed frozen too. I had only seen the cathedral in summer-time. In winter it has a more majestic beauty, when its block of black buildings stands forth in strange relief against the snow of distant mountains. We went into the churchyard, which lies along a narrow plateau behind the cathedral, and under the vineyards. The sun was just tipping its high wall ; only the tops of the black crosses with their trailing crape bands appeared above the tranquil sea of snow. Beyond, across the Rhine, the mountains of the Oberland—Tödi and his comrades—were shining in a blaze of the morning sun. Below, again, was the sleepy town buried deep in its winter shadow.

A Four Days' Sleigh-Drive

I was very anxious to enter the cathedral before leaving. Still more anxious was I to talk with its old sacristan, whose language, manners, and appearance have always fascinated me. So we went to his house, and he came out, carrying his big keys, and took us into the Münster. It was very cold in there, and grim with the rugged irregular architecture and the smell of frozen incense, but beautiful. " Schön ist sie nicht, aber uralt," cried the old man, singing his eternal note of praise, always the same, and always apologetically pathetic. He lighted a long wax taper, which he took off the altar, and led us down into the crypt to see the bits of carving on the pillars, left there by the Romans 1,700 years ago. These pillars are still unchanged, though times and religions have changed. The place is no longer a temple dedicated to Mars, the God of War, where Roman matrons witnessed sacrifice, but has become a Christian seat of worship, where the good ladies of Chur can tell their beads on Sundays and on feast-days, sitting comfortably in their wooden pews, and criticising their neighbours' skirts and bonnets.

When we left the crypt, my old friend the sacristan led us to a favourable point, commanding a full view of the new organ. It is indeed a hideous object, erected, " regardless of taste, by some architects of Vienna," the old man explained. " Schön ist es nicht, it is not even alt," he cried. " They do not comprehend the Beautiful, and they are going the right way to turn my Münster into a bedchamber. I cannot endure to see this place, which I have lived in and loved for forty years, spoilt by ignorant men, and I am glad that my time is nearly up—I am glad to die." After this burst of indignation the venerable man went on to explain, in the suave and altered tones of a court-gentleman, that it was the day of St. Valentine.

Our Life in the Swiss Highlands

Mass had been said very early, and he had been up on the roofs scraping away the ice and snow—hence his "négligé!" He need not thus have excused himself. The "négligé" only heightened the picturesque in his appearance.

We were obliged to quit the cathedral and the sacristan and to return to our inn. The sledge was ready—an open one this time, with a jolly little black horse—and we were soon swinging away at a brisk trot over the frozen roads to Thusis. It was a delightful little bit of journey, though the cold was intense, and a tearing wind, sweeping down the Rheinthal, bit through all our furs and wraps. But the sun shone with unusual brilliancy, and all the country smiled back under its dazzling glow. Grim as it ever is, the castle of Rhäzuns, with its blank yellow walls rising from the mound above the moat, its towers and melancholy poplar trees, caught the sunlight gladly, and shone back like a jewel over the grey yawning chasm of the Rhine.

We reached Thusis at twelve, and were received by our host at the Rhätia with his usual hospitality. We were glad to thaw a little, and to eat a good lunch in the pleasant warmth of the Stube. After our meal we started in an open sledge up the Via Mala. Herr Lamalta drove his small black horse at a great rate, whilst his fat black dog came puffing behind. The wind had died away, and a feeling of coming spring was in the air. I could see, with joy, the creeping ivy plants round the stems of silver pines, and the hepatica leaves darting, heart-shaped, through the melting snow. A balmy scent of newly-felled trees was abroad in the air, and the woodmen were carting down great yellow trunks through precipitous tracks on to the post-road. Yet those who watched the primrose budding in green English lanes, and the new

A Four Days' Sleigh-Drive

grass covering the meadows, would have laughed at my spring-dreams and called them mad.

Perhaps you may know the Via Mala only in summer-time ; and perhaps when first you saw it you had just crossed the Splügen, your mind full of the delicious warmth of spreading chestnut groves away across the pass in Italy. Then, the eternal majesty of these grey rocks struck you with horror, while the dust on that winding road half-choked you. Now, you would indeed, as I did, have found things changed. Driving noise-lessly over the snow-road between the solemn pines, and gazing up those chasms and impending precipices, you would have felt yourselves in quite another world. There was not much snow within the gorge, but every drop of water which could freeze had frozen into solid ice and hung suspended—huge pendants of airy colour, like the bluest blue of an Italian sky and the green of a summer sea—upon sheer rugged cliffs, from the woods above down to the dark abyss below, through which one heard, but could not see, the Rhine. They took away the harsh-ness of the cliffs—those great ice-pillars—and added something inexpressibly beautiful, strange, and weird. Andersen, I thought, would have loved to lay the scene here of one of his fairy stories. It is easy, indeed, to picture to oneself ice-maidens and ideal airy forms sport-ing through the winter days in and out of those blue caves and frozen streams, so far apart from anything we know on earth, and never touched by hand or foot of mortal man. Not an unclean speck enters or can ever enter into the stillness of those crystal waters ; only the blue light of heaven plays through them, and the sunbeams kiss them softly. They cannot be spoiled by any touch of change, for before the summer suns and dust are come, their every trace will have melted away. But my

memory of them can never melt away. I only wish that
I could describe their beauty better to my readers, that
something of the glory of those ice-fabrics might
remain with them too, and be to them as near a revelation of ideal beauty in the mind as they will ever be
with me.

We left our sledge at the point where the second bridge
spans the chasm. The snow lay so deep upon the narrow
bridge that the parapet had almost disappeared. We
could stand here, and make huge snowballs and toss them
down the 300 feet into the water which boiled below ;
and it was a wild joy to me to see them disappearing in
the angry clutches of the Rhine.

We rested for a short time at Zillis ; and there, in the
inn, we discussed various topics with the handsome half-
Italian landlady. We talked of rice-fields, Indian corn,
and the dangers arising from scorpion stings. " A curious
contrast," I thought, as I sat in the broad panelled win-
dow-seat, looking out over the white far-stretching snow-
fields of the Hinter Rheinthal.

Then we drove home quickly by the way we had come.
Ice, snow, rocks, and trees, were melting into the grey
harmony of coming darkness. One great ice-pillar
thrown out from the lip of a precipice, 60 or 70 feet in
height, and standing quite free from the wall of rock,
loomed like a great blue never-to-be-forgotten dream
into the winter twilight. It was the finest icicle that we
had seen—so strong, so firm, and yet so ethereally fragile.
I was sorry when we drew up in the dusk before our inn
at Thusis—sorry to know that the mysteries of the Via
Mala lay behind, and that this was the last of our journey.

The next day we rose before it was light, since we were
to take the early post *via* the Schyn to Davos. When

dressed, a despairing cry from my father's room bade me look out upon the weather. This I did, and the sight which welcomed me, though beautiful, was by no means a pleasing one. Through the shimmering light of a grey dawn the snow was falling steadily with that still persistency which, to eyes accustomed to the sight, bodes no good. One foot of snow had already fallen during the hours of night. The village street was an unbroken sea of white. The little tree-twigs in the garden opposite were laden heavily, save where a disconsolate and ruffled sparrow shook the snow off them with his drooping wings. It was not a difficult matter to decide that this was no day for the Schyn Pass and the Züge, but that our way lay back by Chur and Landquart. Thirteen hours of continuous driving in a snow-storm may not appear an enlivening prospect to those who have not tried it, but they need not dread it if they ever have to face it. I myself have found it very pleasant.

We took extra post, dawdled away some time, and at 9.30 A.M. we left Thusis. The road was like a ploughed field. Our horses plunged up to their knees. The driving snow beat against our windows and penetrated every crack of the old covered sledge. It was a quite horrid old sledge, I regret to say, and a tom-cat had evidently made it his headquarters during the winter months, also some spiders with decorative ideas, for the roof was hung with airy webs. I opened my window, with the result that the snow drove in and covered me ; not that I cared, provided I could see the world outside. It was a beautiful world of snow—very different to what we are accustomed to in our more bleak and rugged home. Through the falling flakes I could see, as in a dream, the banks and fields through which we crawled along. Every twig in the shadowy beech-woods and copses was a

Our Life in the Swiss Highlands

miracle, so closely and so lightly did the fresh snow cling and weave into wonderful forms. Then the orchards in the far-spreading snow-fields! Four years ago I saw fruit growing for the first time in Switzerland on these same trees—large red-faced apples and delicious golden pears, all aglow in the warmth of an autumnal sky. Now they were scarcely recognisable. Pears and apples had changed to snow-like things in a fairy tale. To believe that seven months hence that same glory would reappear was an impossibility.

No sun fell on the walls of Rhäzuns to-day as we passed it by. The high poplar-trees round the castle raised their heads, very still, like shadows, into the thick air. The mysterious sloping roofs and turrets were white. The grimness of the river-bed and the greyness of those ancient walls were now in harmony with one another. The river sent up a filmy mist to creep about the turrets, and over all fell the quiet flakes of snow-like sleep.

Carnival time was over in Chur as we drove through to the station, and her streets presented the deserted untidiness of past gaieties. The short piece of railway to Landquart was made even longer and slower than it usually is—if that were possible—by the heavy snow which clogged the line. At Landquart we took our places in the post, and settled down peacefully for the seven hours' drive before us. The snow had fallen slowly and ceaselessly ever since six o'clock in the morning, when first we looked from our windows at Thusis. It was falling with the same slow persistency when, at half-past nine that night, we reached home.[1]

Such a journey as this produces no fatigue, no sense of

[1] This was written in 1888, before the railway had been made from Landquart up to Davos.

A Four Days' Sleigh-Drive

weariness. It is monotonous, but not disagreeable. One falls into a sort of mental lethargy, and the scenes through which one passes leave but half-realised pictures, dreamy and very pleasant, on the brain—pictures where everything is like one vast billowy sea of never-ending snow, out of which the muffled objects start like shadows, or as the sinking waves upon a slumbrous ocean.

M. S.

A PAGE OF MY LIFE[1]

How am I to fulfil the promise I have made of writing
" A Page of My Life "? My life is so monotonous
among those mountains of Graubünden—the snow-
landscape around me spreads so uniform beneath the
burning sun or roof of frozen cloud, that a month, a week,
a day, detached from this calm background, can have
but little interest for actors on the wide stage of the
world.

Twelve years ago I came to Davos, broken down in

[1] This article was written at the request of the editor of the *Fortnightly Review*. He wished me to give some notion of the conditions
under which my life and work had been conducted since I was obliged
to settle at Davos. I selected what may very truly be called a few
" specimen days." Still it must not be imagined that the whole of
my time is spent in this manner. Were that the case, I could not
have produced so much literature as I have done in the space of the
last fourteen years : to wit, two volumes of Italian Sketches, four
volumes of *Renaissance in Italy*, four volumes of original verse, two
volumes of translated verse, three volumes of English biography
(*Shelley, Sidney, Ben Jonson*), one volume on the *Early English Drama*,
translations of two lengthy Italian autobiographies, two volumes of
Essays Speculative and Suggestive, two volumes on the *Life of Michelangelo Buonarroti*, the present volume, and a considerable amount of
work for the *Encyclopædia Britannica* and other publications. In
truth, I have been able to labour hard at my chosen craft, while the
open-air life in a mountain country, of which so much is recorded in
this book, has been very serviceable to me as a student.

J. A. S. (*February*, 1892).

A Page of My Life

health, and with a poor prospect of being able to prolong
my days upon this earth. I did not mean to abide here,
but having regained a little strength, I hoped to pass the
winter in a Nile boat. The cure of lung disease by Alpine
air and sun and cold was hardly known in England at that
time. When I found my health improve beyond all
expectation, the desire to remain where I was, to let well
alone, and to avoid that fatiguing journey to Cairo, came
over me. Slung in my hammock among the fir-trees of
the forest, watching the August sunlight slant athwart
the branches, the squirrels leap from bough to bough
above my head, it seemed to me that life itself would not
be worth living at the price of perpetual travelling in
search of health. I was thirty-six years of age ; and,
reviewing the twenty-three years which had elapsed since
I went to Harrow as a boy of thirteen, I found that I had
never spent more than three months in one place. At all
hazards I resolved to put an end to these peregrinations,
looked the future calmly in the face, and wrote twenty-
two sonnets on "The Thought of Death." Then I informed my good and famous physician in London that
I meant to disobey his orders and to shut myself up for
the next seven months in this snow-bound valley. He
replied that " if I liked to leave my vile body to the
Davos doctors, that was my affair ; he had warned me."
In the following spring I composed an article on my experience, which was printed in a number of the *Fortnightly Review*, and which contributed something, perhaps, to the foundation of the English colony at Davos-
Platz.[1]

Since then, Davos has been my principal place of
residence. I have worked incessantly at literature—
publishing more than twenty volumes, besides writing a

---

[1] See the first essay printed in this volume.

Our Life in the Swiss Highlands

large amount of miscellaneous matter, and three volumes which still remain inedited. The conditions under which these tasks have been performed were not altogether favourable. Every book I needed for study and reference had to be dragged to the height of 5,400 feet above the sea. A renowned Oxford scholar was paying me a visit once, when, looking round my modest shelves, he exclaimed, with the sardonic grin peculiar to him: " Nobody can write a book here !" I knew that it was very difficult to write a good book in Davos ; that I could not hope to attain perfection or fullness of erudition in the absence from great libraries, in the deprivation of that intellectual stimulus which comes from the clash of mind with mind. But my desire has always been to make the best of a bad business, and to turn drawbacks, so far as in me lay, into advantages. Therefore I would not allow myself to be discouraged at the outset. I reflected that the long leisure afforded by Davos, my seclusion from the petty affairs of society and business, and the marvellous brain-tonic of the mountain air, would be in themselves some compensation for the loss of privileges enjoyed by more fortunately situated students. Moreover, I have never been able to take literature very seriously. Life seems so much graver, more important, more permanently interesting than books. Literature is what Aristotle called διαγωγή—an honest, healthful, harmless pastime. Then, too, as Sir Thomas Browne remarked, " it is too late to be ambitious." Occupation, that indispensable condition of mental and physical health, was ready to my hand in literary work ; and I determined to write for my own satisfaction, without scrupulous anxiety regarding the result.

The inhabitants of the valley soon attracted my atten-

A Page of My Life

tion. I resolved to throw myself as far as possible into their friendship and their life. These people of Graubünden are in many ways remarkable and different from the other Swiss. It is not generally known that they first joined the Confederation in the year 1803, having previously, for nearly four centuries, constituted a separate and independent State—highly democratic in the forms of government, but aristocratic in feeling and social customs, proud of their ancient nobility, accustomed to rule subject Italian territories and to deal with sovereigns as ambassadors or generals. These peculiarities in the past history of the Canton have left their traces on the present generation. Good breeding, a high average of intelligence, active political instincts, manliness and sense of personal freedom, are conspicuous even among the poorest peasants. Nowhere, I take it. upon the face of the earth, have republican institutions and republican virtues developed more favourably. Nowhere is the social atmosphere of a democracy more agreeable at the present moment. What I have learned from my Graubünden comrades, and what I owe to them, cannot be here described in full. But their companionship has become an essential ingredient in my life—a healthy and refreshing relief from solitary studies and incessant quill-driving.

So much about my existence as a man of letters at Davos had to be premised in order that the " Page of My Life " which I have promised should be made intelligible. And now I really do not know what page to tear out and present here. Chance must decide. My desk-diary for this year (1889) happens to lie open at the date February 28. That page will do as well as any other.

Friends are kind enough to come and stay with us

Our Life in the Swiss Highlands

sometimes, even in the winter. We had been enjoying visits from one of the British Museum librarians, from an eminent English man of letters and his more than beautiful wife, and also from a Secretary of Legation to one of the German Courts. During the first two months of the year sleighing-parties, toboggan-races, and the other amusements of the season had been going forward. I was further occupied with founding a gymnasium for the young men of Davos, which occasioned endless colloquies at night in the dusky rooms of the old Rathhaus, followed by homeward walks across the noiseless snow, beneath the sharp and scintillating stars. All this while I had been correcting the proofs of my book on *Carlo Gozzi*, and composing four laborious essays on that puzzling phenomenon which we call "Style." I was fairly tired, and wanted a change of scene. So I proposed to one of my daughters that we should pay a long-contemplated visit to some Swiss friends living at Ilanz in the Vorder-Rheinthal, or, as it is also called, the Bündner Oberland.

Behold us starting, then, for our thirteen hours' sleighing journey, wrapped from head to foot in furs ! It is about half-past six on a cold grey morning, the thermometer standing at 3° Fahr., a sombre canopy of mist threatening snow, and the blue-nosed servants of the watering-place torpidly shivering back to their daily labours like congealed snakes. Davos-Platz does not look attractive at this hour of a winter morning, when the chimneys of the big hotels and bakehouses are pouring forth spirals of tawny smoke, which the frozen air repels and forces back to blend with vapours lying low along the stream. Tearing through the main street on such occasions, I always wonder how long what boasts to be a "Luft kur-ort," or health resort, depending on the

216

purity of air for its existence, will bear the strain of popularity and rapid increase.

As we break away into the open country these gloomy thoughts are dispelled. For now the sun, rising behind the mountains of Sertig in gold and crimson, scatters the mist and gives the promise of a glorious day. Spires and pinnacles of burnished silver smite the flawless blue of heaven. The vapour clinging to their flanks and forests melts imperceptibly into amber haze; and here and there broad stripes of dazzling sunlight turn the undulating snowfields round our path to sheets of argent mail, thickly studded with diamonds—crystals of the night. Every leafless larch or alder by the stream-bed is encrusted with sparkling frost-jewels, and the torrents, hurrying to the Rhine, chafe and foam against gigantic masses of grey-green ice, lipped with fantastically curving snow-wreaths. We are launched on the intoxication of a day-long sledge-drive. Hour after hour passes with no change but the change of postillions and horses, occasional halts at wayside inns, and the every-varying pageant of the frozen landscape unrolled around us.

Ravines and gorges, to which the sunlight never pierces, but walks with feet of fire along the cliffs above, turning those bristling pines against the sky-line into burning bushes, and sleeping for miles upon white ridges whence the avalanche descends. Slow climbings up warm slopes between the red trunks of larches, where squirrels flirt upon the russet needles shed through unstirred air. Break-neck gallopings down steep snow-covered hills, through sleepy villages, past waggons laden with enormous tree-stems, under the awful icicles suspended like shining swords of Damocles from cliffs 100 feet above our heads. How so many tons of ice, apparently defying the law of gravitation, keep their place upon those precipices through

Our Life in the Swiss Highlands

a winter, increasing imperceptibly in volume, yet never altering their shape, nor showing the least sign of moisture at their extremities, has always been a mystery to me. The phenomenon of the growth of ice cataracts from little springs hidden in the crannies of black drizzling rocks ought to be investigated by a competent scientific authority. It is a standing wonder to the layman.

I have said that there is a kind of intoxication in such a journey. But a better word for the effect would perhaps be hypnotism. You resent any disturbance or alteration of the main conditions. Except to eat or drink at intervals, you do not want to stop. You are annoyed to think that it will ever end. And all the while you go on dreaming, meditating inconsecutively, smoking, exchanging somnolent remarks with your companion or your driver, turning over in your mind the work which you have quitted or the work you have begun. This day my thoughts were occupied with the national hero of Graubünden, Georg Jenatsch—a personage like some one in the Book of Judges—the Samson who delivered his oppressed tribesmen from the hands of their Amalekites, Moabites, and Philistines (French and Spanish and Austrian armies), during the Thirty Years' War. Georg Jenatsch accompanied me through the hypnotism of that drive. We passed some of the scenes of his great exploits —the frightful cliffs of the Schyn Pass, over which he brought his Engadine troops one winter night by a forced march, losing many heavy-armed men among their murderous ravines—the meadows of Valendàs, where he defeated the population of the Oberland in a pitched battle at night, fighting up to the waist in snow and staining it with blood—the castle of Riedberg, where he murdered Pompey Planta with his own hands among the tyrant's armed allies one Sunday morning—the church of Scharàns, where, to use his own words, he "lied so much," before he exchanged the pastor's gown and ruff for casque of steel and harquebuss—the village of Thusis, in which he held his Reign of Terror, torturing and beheading the partisans of the Spanish Crown.[1]

It would be tedious to relate all the details of this journey. Following the Landwasser and the Albula, we reached the Rhine at Thusis, and drove along its banks to the point where the solitary castle of Rhäzuns frowns above melancholy precipices, crested with enormous Scotch firs, surveying the gloomy eddies of the river. Then we turned suddenly aside, and began to ascend the valley of the Vorder-Rhein, among the weird earth-chasms of Versàmm. This is a really hideous place, unlike anything but the sinister *Balze*, which break away below Volterra. But here, 600 feet beneath the road, the inaccessible Rhine chafes, throttled in its stony gorge ; and the earth-slopes above, for ever crumbling away and shooting stones down on the traveller, rise to an equal height, dismal, forlorn, abandoned by the beautifying veil of snow, which slides away from them in avalanches ; rent and ploughed into ravines as by the malice of some evil spirit. Day was wellnigh spent when we emerged from these dangerous chasms into the woods which close the entrance to the Safien Thal. The unearthly ethereal lucidity which winter skies assume at sunset in our mountains, shed soft lights of amber and of rose upon the distant range of Tödi, and bathed the ridges of Calanda and the alps of Flims in violet glory. Our horses toiled slowly upward through the forest, whose sombre trunks and sable plumage made the distant glow

---

[1] I hope to write a book on Georg Jenatsch and his part in the Thirty Years' War. The book still remains to be written, if life permits.

Our Life in the Swiss Highlands

more luminous—crunching with their hoofs a snow-path hard as Carrara marble, and grinding the runners of the sleigh into the track, which shrieked at every turning. That is the only noise—this short, sharp shriek of the frozen snow ; that, and the driver's whip, and the jingling bells upon the harness—you hear upon a sledge-drive. And these noises have much to do with its hypnotism.

It was nearly dark when we left the wood, and broke away again at a full gallop for Ilanz. In a broad, golden space of sky hung the young moon and the planet Venus, lustrous as pearl illuminated by some inner fire, and the whole open valley lay still and white beneath the heavens.

Ilanz is a little walled town—proud of its right to be called *Stadt* and not *Dorf*, in spite of the paucity of its inhabitants. It is almost wholly composed of large houses, built in the seventeenth century by noble families with wealth acquired in foreign service. Their steep gabled roofs, towers, and portals, charged with heraldic emblazonry, cluster together in a labyrinth of alleys. Orchards stretch on every side around the town-walls, which are pierced with old gateways, where the arms of Schmid von Grüneck, Salis, Planta, and Capoul shine out in ancient carvings, richly-gilt and highly-coloured. The sleepy little town is picturesque in every detail, and rapidly falling into decay. From being a nest of swash-bucklers and captains of adventure, it has become the centre of an agricultural district, where Swiss provincial industry is languidly carried on by the descendants of the aristocratic folk who built the brave old mansions. One narrow and tortuous street runs through the town from main gate to gate. On the farther side, among the orchards, stands the house of our Swiss friends, under whose hospitable roof I left my daughter. At the other side is the principal inn, close to the covered wooden

A Page of My Life

bridge across the Rhine ; and here I took up my own quarters. The street between offered a variety of dangers during the night-hours. It was innocent of lamps, and traffic had turned it into a glassy sheet of treacherous, discoloured ice.

There was a concert and a ball in the hotel that evening. A singing-club for male voices, renowned throughout the Canton under its name of "Ligia Grischa," assembles once a year at Ilanz, gives a musical entertainment, sups in state, dances till dawn, and disperses in the morning to homes among the hills. I always wished to be present at one of this club's meetings, and had timed my visit to Ilanz accordingly. I ought to say that the old State of Graubünden was composed of three Leagues, the eldest of which was called, *par excellence*, the Grey League ; and the folk who formed it for their freedom in the first years of the fifteenth century had their hold in Ilanz and the neighbourhood. They spoke then, and the people still speak, a dialect of rustic Latin, which we call Romanisch. In this dialect the Grey League is *Ligia Grischa*. Hence the designation of the singing-club.

It was a splendid opportunity for seeing the natives of the Bündner Oberland. Not only were the rank and fashion of Ilanz present in full force, but men and women from remote valleys hidden in the folds of the surrounding hills—the hills whose glaciers roll down the fountains of the Rhine—had trooped into the town. The concert-room was crammed to overflowing. Its low roof did but little justice to those masculine and ringing voices, which throbbed and vibrated and beat against the walls above the densely-packed heads of the audience. What a striking sea of faces and of forms ! I wished that my good friend, Dr. John Beddoe, the illustrious ethnologist,

221

had been there to note them ; for the people reckon, I believe, among the purest aboriginals of Central Europe. They are for the most part dark-complexioned, with very black hair and eyebrows ; a long, narrow, rounded forehead, curving upwards to a small oval skull ; deep-set brilliant eyes, placed close together, blazing sometimes like coals. The face is narrow, like the forehead, with a great length of nose and firmly-formed prominent jaws. Set upon shoulders of athletic breadth and a sinewy throat, this small head, with its packed and prominent features, gives the impression of colossal and plastic strength. In old men and women the type is wonderfully picturesque, when the wrinkles and experience of a lifetime have ploughed their record deep. But, as is usual with Swiss mountaineers, the young women are deficient in comeliness, not to say in grace and beauty ; and the young men, though more attractive, from their limber muscularity and free disdainful carriage, do themselves no credit by their dress. They wear the coarsest, ill-made homespun. It is only when their superb forms are stripped for athletic exercise that you discern in them models fit for Donatello and Michel Angelo—those lovers of long-limbed, ponderous-shouldered, firmly-articulated, large-handed specimens of humanity, with powerful necks and small heads.

The faces of these young men make me pause and wonder. They are less like human faces than masks. Sometimes boldly carved, with ardent eyes, lips red as blood, and a transparent olive skin, these faces yield no index to the character within by any changes of expression. The speech that comes from them is simple, well-bred, unimaginative, destitute of ideas and emotions. And yet I know that these same men are capable of the most tenacious passions, the suddenest self-abandonment to overmastering impulse. It seems as though their concentrated life in village homes had made them all of one piece, which, when it breaks or yields, splits irretrievably to fragments.

I will tell some stories which prove that the Graubünden peasants, though they look so stolid, have in them the stuff of tragedy. There was a lad in a valley called Schanfigg, not long ago, who loved and was betrothed to a girl in the Hinter-Rheinthal, below Splügen. She jilted him, having transferred her affections to another ; and he went to take a formal farewell of his sweetheart in her home. Everything passed decorously ; so much so, that the girl's brother put his horse into the cart and drove the rejected lover with his own sister down to Thusis. The three had reached that passage of the Via Mala where the Rhine loses itself in a very deep, narrow gorge. It is called the " Verlorene Loch," and is spanned by a slender bridge thrown at right angles over the river. Here, as they were spinning merrily down-hill, the lad stood up in the cart, sprang to the parapet of the bridge, and dashed himself at one bound into the grim death of jagged rocks and churning waves below them. It was a stroke of imaginative fancy to commit suicide for love just at this spot. And now a second tale of desperate passion. A rich man in the Prättigau had two children, a daughter and a son. The daughter wheedled him into allowing her to marry some peasant, who was poor and an unequal match in social station. Then his son set his affections upon a girl equally ineligible. The father stormed ; but the youth was true to his plighted troth. During a temporary absence of the son, his father contrived to send the girl off to America with a round sum of money. On his return, after hearing what had happened, the lad said nothing, but went down to the Land-

Our Life in the Swiss Highlands

quart water in the evening and drowned himself there. And now a third tale. Last spring, in a village not three hours distant from Davos, lived a young man who was an orphan. He had inherited a considerable estate, and expected more from two uncles. Life, could he have managed it prudently, would probably have made him the wealthiest farmer in the neighbourhood ; and he was, to boot, a stalwart fellow on whom Nature had lavished all her gifts of health and comeliness. Unluckily, he loved a girl of whom his uncles disapproved as the mate for such a youth of consequence. One Saturday evening, as the custom is here, he went to pay his addresses by stealth to this maiden of his choice, and returning early next morning, he was upbraided by his interfering uncles. I do not know what he replied, but certainly he made no scene to speak of. When the uncles left him, he un-hooked his gun from the wooden panelling of the house-room, strolled out alone into the copse hard by, and put a bullet through his brain.

That is the sort of things of which these youngsters, with their heavy gait and scornful carriage, are capable of doing. The masks they wear for faces are no index to the life that throbs within.

Well, I am digressing from Ilanz and the Ligia Grischa. After the concert there came the banquet, and after the banquet came the ball. About three in the morning, having smoked many pipes with friends in homespun, I retired to my well-earned rest and slept soundly, although the whole inn was resonant with fifes and violins, and stamping, shouting Burschen. You should have seen the last dregs of the orgy, the *petits crevés* of Ilanz, when I came down to breakfast at eight. Some of them were still dancing.

Next day we took a sleigh and drove up the valley of

THE RHINE AT LANDQUART.

A Page of My Life

Lungnez. Such a silent snow-scene under the steady flooding sunshine! The track between wood and precipice was just broad enough for our runners till we came close to Villa. There the valley expands, yielding a vast prospect over the mountain-passes which lead to Splügen and to Olivone—a wilderness of craggy peaks and billowy snowfields, all smoothed and softened with clear sunshine and blue shadows. No one can paint, no words can describe, that landscape. It must be seen; and then it will never be forgotten. A baronial family, De Mont, were lords of Villa in old days, and now they keep an inn there in one of their ancestral houses. Portraits of generals and ladies look down upon the casual guest, among emblazoned scutcheons with famous quarterings—Schauenstein, Castelberg, Toggenburg—discernible by specialists who (like myself) love to trace a nation's history in its heraldries. Photographs of more recent De Monts, abroad in the world, occupy a modest place beneath these canvases upon the planks of cembra-pine which form the panelling. It is by no means uncommon in this country to find the homes of people whose ancestors were counts or barons of the Empire, nobles of Spain and France, and whose descendants could bear such titles if they chose, turned into hostelries. I sometimes wonder what they think of American and English tourists. When I make inquiries about their former state, and show some knowledge of their family, it is always appreciated in the grave, dignified way these people of Graubünden have with them.

The chief attraction of Villa—letting alone the annals of Lungnez, of which I have not here the time to speak—is an old church, at Pleif, built on a buttress of the hills far up above the torrent. It occupies a station which would be singular in any land; and it commands a view of peaks, passes, snow-fields, and precipices, which even in Switzerland is rare. Once it was the only church in the vast upland region it surveys. The tolling of its bell brought stalwart Catholics from far and near, trooping under arms to join their forces with the men of Ilanz, Trons, and Dissentis, and then to march with flying flags on Chur. That was in the times when Graubünden struggled in religious strife between Catholics and Protestants, partisans of the French and Spanish sides. The building is large and of venerable antiquity. On its walls hangs a huge oil painting—surprising to find in such a place—a picture, clearly by some Venetian artist, of the battle at Lepanto ; just such a canvas as one sees in the Ducal Palace on the Lagoons. The history of this picture, and why it came to Pleif, seems to be forgotten ; but we know that the Grisons in the sixteenth century were stout allies and servants of St. Mark's.

It was not the inside of the church at Pleif which attracted my notice, but the graveyard round it, irregularly shaped to suit the rocky station, girt with fern-plumed walls, within which were planted ancient ash-trees. A circuit of gnarled, bent, twisted, broken ash-trees. In Westmoreland or Yorkshire they would not have had the same significance ; but here, where all deciduous trees are scarce, where the very pine woods have been swept away by avalanches and the violence of armies, each massive bole told a peculiar story. I thought of the young men whose athletic forms and faces like masks impressed my fancy, and something breathing from the leafless ashes spoke to me about them. Here was the source of their life's poetry ; a poetry collected from deep daily communings with Nature in her shyest, most impressive moods ; a poetry infused into their sense unconsciously ; brought to a point and carried into some supreme emotion by meetings with a girl in such a place as this—the hours of summer twilight, when the ash-trees are laden with leaves, and the mountains shrink away before the rising moon, and the torrent clamours in the gorge below, and the vast divine world expresses its meaning in one simple ineffaceable word of love. I seemed, as I sat upon the wall there in the snowy, sunny silence, to understand a little more about the force of passion and the external impassiveness of this folk, whom I dearly love. I felt why those three lads of whom I spoke had thrown their lives away for an emotion, breaking to pieces because the mainspring of their life was broken—that which moved them, for which they had grown up to manhood, through which the dominant influences of Nature on their sensitive humanity had become manifest in an outburst of irreversible passion. Then I remembered how a friend of mine from Trins talked to me once about the first thoughts of love evoked in him, just in a place like this. It was on the top of a hill called Canaschàl, where there is a ruined castle and a prospect over both the valleys of the Rhine, and the blending of that mighty river's fountains as it flows towards Chur. He was a boy of fifteen, my friend, when he saw the simple thing of which he told me at the age of twenty-three. A pair of lovers were seated on the cliffs of Canaschàl—the lad and the girl both known to him—and he was lying in the bushes. It was the sight of their kisses which informed him what love was ; and the way in which my carpenter friend spoke of the experience seven years afterwards, made me conceive how the sublime scenery and solitudes of these mountains may enter into the soul of Burschen who have nothing to show the world but masks for faces.

I give this here for what it is worth. We have heard much of the Swiss in foreign service dying of home-

Our Life in the Swiss Highlands

sickness at the sound of the " Ranz des Vaches." We have also learned the proverb, " Pas d'argent, pas de Suisse." I think that the education of young men in these Siren mountains—far more Siren than the mermaids of Sorrento or Baiae, to any one who once has felt the spirit of the Alps—combined with their poverty, their need of making money to set up house with, accounts for the peculiar impression which they make on town-bred foreigners, and for their otherwise inexplicable habit of wedding the uncomely daughters of the land.

I will not linger over our drive back from Ilanz. One sleigh-journey is like another, except for the places one stops at, the postillions one talks to, the old wooden rooms one drinks in, the friends one visits on the way, and the varieties of the grand scenery one sweeps through.

It has been my constant habit for many years to do a considerable amount of hard study while travelling. It would be difficult to say how many heavy German and Italian books on history, biography, and criticism, how many volumes of Greek poets, and what a library of French and English authors, have been slowly perused by me in railway stations, trains, steamers, wayside inns, and Alpine châlets. I enjoy nothing more than to sit in a bar-room among peasants, carters, and grooms, smoking, with a glass of wine beside me, and a stiff work on one of the subjects I am bound to get up. The contrast between the surroundings and the study adds zest to the latter ; and when I am tired of reading, I can lay my book down and chat with folk whom I have been half-consciously observing.

On this short trip I had taken a remarkable essay, entitled *La Critique scientifique*, by a young and promising French author—now, alas ! no more—M. Emile Hennequin. The writer tries to establish a new method

A Page of My Life

of criticism upon a scientific basis, distinguished from the æsthetical and literary methods. He does not aim at appreciating the merit of works of art, or of the means employed in their production, or of the work itself in its essence, but always in its relations. He regards art as the index to the psychological characteristics of those who produce it, and of those whom it interests and attracts. His method of criticism may be defined as the science of the work of art regarded as a sign. The development of these ideas in a lengthy and patient analytical investigation taxes the reader's attention pretty severely ; for some of Hennequin's views are decidedly audacious, and require to be examined with caution. Well, I had reached Chur on my homeward route, and was spending the evening in the little hotel I frequent there. It has a long, low, narrow room, with five latticed windows and an old stove of green tiles for its *Stube*, or place of public resort. Here I went to smoke and read M. Hennequin's book on criticism. Three diligence conductors and a postillion, excellent people and my very good friends, were in a corner by the stove, playing a game of Yass ; and after exchanging the usual questions with these acquaintances, I took my seat near them and began to study. About ten o'clock they left, and I was alone. I had reached the point in Hennequin's exposition of what he somewhat awkwardly termed *esthopsychologie*, which is concerned with the theory of national literature taken as a sign of national character. This absorbed my attention, and nearly an hour must have passed when I was suddenly disturbed by the noisy entrance of seven hulking fellows in heavy greatcoats, with, strange to say, eight bright green crowns upon their heads instead of hats. I write eight advisedly, for one of them wore two wreaths, of oak and bay respectively.

Our Life in the Swiss Highlands

In a moment I perceived that a gymnastic performance, or *Turnfest*, must have taken place ; for I recognised two of the men, whom I knew to be famous athletes. They came up, shook hands, introduced to me their comrades, and invited me to drink a double-litre of Valtelline wine. I accepted with alacrity, shut up my treatise upon criticism, and sat down to the long central table. Meanwhile the gymnasts had thrown off their greatcoats, and stood displayed in a costume not very far removed from nudity. They had gained their crowns, they told me, that evening at an extraordinary meeting of the associated *Turnvereins*, or gymnastic clubs of the Canton. It was the oddest thing in the world to sit smoking in a dimly-lighted, panelled tap-room with seven such companions. They were all of them strapping bachelors between twenty and twenty-five years of age ; colossally broad in the chest and shoulders, tight in the reins, set massively upon huge thighs and swelling calves ; wrestlers, boxers, stone-lifters, and quoit-throwers. Their short bull-throats supported small heads, closely clipped, with bruised ears and great big-featured faces, over which the wreaths of bright green artificial foliage bristled. I have said that the most striking thing, to my mind, about the majority of young faces in Graubünden is that they resemble masks, upon which character and experience have delved no lines, and which stare out in stolid inscrutability. These men illustrated the observation. Two of them had masks of wax, smooth, freshly-coloured, joining on to dark, cropped hair. The masks of three seemed to be moulded out of grey putty, which had hardened without cracking. The sixth mask was of sculptured sandstone, and the seventh of exquisitely chiselled alabaster. I seemed to be sitting in a dream among vitalised statues of the later emperors, executed

A Page of My Life

in the decadence of art, with no grasp on individual character, but with a certain reminiscence of the grand style of portraiture. Commodus, Caracalla, Alexander Severus, the three Gordians, and Pertinax might have been drinking there beside me in the pothouse. The attitudes assumed by these big fellows, stripped to their sleeveless jerseys and tight-fitting flannel breeches, strengthened the illusion. I felt as though we were waiting there for slaves, who should anoint their hair with unguents, gild their wreaths, enwrap them in the paludament, and attend them to receive the shouts of "Ave Imperator" from a band of gladiators or the legionaries of the Gallic army. When they rose to seek another tavern I turned, half-asleep, into my bed. There the anarchy of dreams continued that impression of resuscitated statues—vivified effigies of emperors, who long ago perished by the dagger or in battle, and whose lineaments the craft of a declining civilisation has preserved for us in forms which caricature the grace and strength of classic sculpture.

Next day I found myself at Davos-Platz, beginning my work again upon accumulated proofs of Gozzi and the impossible problem of style.   J. A. S.

BACCHUS IN GRAUBUNDEN

I

LONG residence in this Canton made me familiar with all
sorts of Valtelline wine : with rough Inferno, generous
Forzato, delicate Sassella, harsher Montagner, the raspberry flavour of Grumello, the sharp invigorating twang
of Villa. The colour, ranging from garnet to almandine
or ruby, told me the age and quality of the vintage ; and
I had learned many secrets about the proper way of
handling it. I furthermore arrived at the conclusion,
which is certainly a just one, that good Valtelline can only
be tasted at a very considerable height above the sea ;
for this wine matures slowly in the cold of a mountain
climate, and acquires a bouquet here unknown at lower
levels. In a word, it amused my leisure to make or
think myself a connoisseur. My literary taste was
tickled by the praise bestowed in the Augustan age on
Rhætic grapes by Virgil—

> " Et quo te carmine dicam
> Rhætica ? nec cellis ideo contende Falernis."

I piqued myself on thinking that, could the poet but
have drunk one bottle of old Grumello at Samaden—
where Stilicho, by the way, in his famous recruiting
expedition, described so eloquently by the poet Claudian,

Bacchus in Graubünden

may perhaps have drunk it—he would have been less chary in his panegyric. For the point of inferiority on which he seems to insist—namely, that Valtelline wine does not ripen well in the cellar—is only proper to this vintage in Italian climate. Here it attains its maximum of excellence after it has been kept a quarter of a century in wood ; and certainly no Falernian manufactured at the present day can compete with it.

Such meditations led my fancy on the path of history. Is there truth, then, in the dim tradition that this mountain-land was colonized by Etruscans ? Is *Ras* the root of Rhætia ? The Etruscans were accomplished wine-growers, we know. It was their Montepulciano which drew the Gauls to Rome, if Livy can be trusted. Perhaps they first planted the vine in Valtelline. Perhaps its superior culture in that district may be due to ancient use surviving in a secluded Alpine valley. One thing is certain, that the peasants of Sondrio and Tirano understand viticulture better than the Italians of Lombardy.

Then my thoughts ran on to the period of modern history, when the Grisons seized the Valtelline in lieu of war-pay from the Dukes of Milan. For some three centuries they held it as a subject province. From the Rathhaus at Davos or Chur they sent their nobles—Von Salis and Buol, Planta and Sprecher von Bernegg—across the hills as governors or podestàs to Poschiavo, Sondrio, Tirano, and Morbegno. In those old days the Valtelline wines came duly every winter over snow-deep passes to fill the cellars of the Signori Grigioni. That quaint traveller, Tom Coryat, in his so-called *Crudities*, notes the custom early in the seventeenth century. And as that custom then obtained, it still subsists with little alteration. The wine-carriers—Wein-führer, as they are called —first scaled the Bernina Pass, halting then as now, per-

Our Life in the Swiss Highlands

haps, at Poschiavo and Pontresina. Afterwards, in order
to reach Davos, the pass of the Scaletta rose before them
—a wilderness of untracked snow-drifts. The country-
folk still point to narrow, light hand-sledges, on which
the casks were charged before the last pitch of the pass.
Some wine came, no doubt, on pack-saddles. A meadow
in front of the Dischma Thal, where the pass ends, still
bears the name of the Ross-Weid, or horse-pasture. It
was here that the beasts of burden used for this wine
service rested after their long labours. In favourable
weather the whole journey from Tirano would have
occupied at least four days, with scanty halts at night.

The Valtelline slipped from the hands of the Grisons
early in this century. It is rumoured that one of the
Von Salis family negotiated matters with Napoleon more
for his private benefit than for the interests of the State.
However this may have been, when the Graubünden
became a Swiss Canton, after four centuries of sovereign
independence, the whole Valtelline passed to Austria,
and so eventually to Italy. According to modern and
just notions of nationality this was right. In their period
of power the Grisons masters had treated their Italian
dependencies with harshness. The Valtelline is an Italian
valley, connected with the rest of the peninsula by ties
of race and language. It is, moreover, geographically
linked to Italy by the great stream of the Adda, which
takes its rise upon the Stelvio, and after passing through
the Lake of Como, swells the volume of the Po.

But, though politically severed from the Valtelline,
the Engadiners and Davosers have not dropped their old
habit of importing its best produce. What they formerly
levied as masters they now acquire by purchase. The
Italian revenue derives a large profit from the frontier
dues paid at the gate between Tirano and Poschiavo on

Bacchus in Graubünden

the Bernina road. Much of the same wine enters Switzerland by another route, travelling from Sondrio to Chiavenna and across the Splügen. But until quite recently, the wine itself could scarcely be found outside the Canton. It was indeed quoted upon Lombard wine lists. Yet no one drank it ; and when I tasted it at Milan I found it quite unrecognisable. The fact seems to be that the Graubündeners alone know how to deal with it ; and, as I have hinted, the wine requires a mountain climate for its full development.

II

The district where the wine of Valtellina is grown extends, roughly speaking, from Tirano to Morbegno, a distance of some fifty-four miles. The best sorts come from the middle of this region. High up in the valley soil and climate are alike less favourable. Low down a coarser, earthier quality springs from fat land where the valley broadens. The northern hillsides to a very considerable height above the river are covered with vineyards. The southern slopes on the left bank of the Adda, lying more in shade, yield but little. Inferno, Grumello, and Perla di Sassella are the names of famous vineyards. Sassella is the general name for a large tract. Buying an Inferno, Grumello, or Perla di Sassella wine, it would be absurd to suppose that one obtained it precisely from the eponymous estate. But as each of these vineyards yields a marked quality of wine, which is taken as standard-giving, the produce of the whole district may be broadly classified as approaching more or less nearly to one of these accepted types. The Inferno, Grumello, and Perla di Sassella of commerce are, therefore, three sorts of good Valtelline, ticketed with famous names to indicate certain differences of quality. Montagner, as the name implies, is a somewhat lighter wine, grown higher up in the hill vineyards. And of this class there are many species, some approximating to Sassella in delicacy of flavour, others approaching the tart lightness of the Villa vintage. This last takes its title from a village in the neighbourhood of Tirano, where a table wine is chiefly grown.

Forzato is the strongest, dearest, longest-lived of this whole family of wines. It is manufactured chiefly at Tirano ; and, as will be understood from its name, does not profess to belong to any one of the famous localities. Forzato, or Sforzato, forced or enforced, is in fact a wine which has undergone a more artificial process. In German the people call it Stroh-wein, which also points to the method of its preparation. The finest grapes are selected and dried in the sun (hence the *Stroh*) for a period of eight or nine weeks. When they have almost become raisins, they are pressed. The must is heavily charged with sugar, and ferments powerfully. Wine thus made requires several years to ripen. Sweet at first, it takes at last a very fine quality and flavour, and is rough, almost acid, on the tongue. Its colour, too, turns from a deep rich crimson to the tone of tawny port, which indeed it much resembles.

Old Forzato which has been long in cask, and then perhaps three years in bottle, will fetch at least 6 francs, or may rise to even 10 francs a flask. The best Sassella rarely reaches more than 5 francs. Good Montagner and Grumello can be had perhaps for 4 francs ; and Inferno of a special quality for 6 francs. Thus the average price of old Valtelline wine may be taken as 5 francs a bottle. These, I should observe, are hotel prices.

Valtelline wines bought in the wood vary, of course,

according to their age and year of vintage. I have found that from 2.50 francs to 3.50 francs per litre is a fair price for sorts fit to bottle. The new wine of 1881 sold in the following winter at prices varying from 1.05 francs to 1.80 francs per litre.

It is customary for the Graubünden wine merchants to buy up the whole produce of a vineyard from the peasants at the end of the vintage. They go in person, or depute their agents, to inspect the wine, make their bargains, and seal the cellars where the wine is stored. Then, when the snow has fallen, their own horses, with sleighs and trusted servants, go across the passes to bring it home. Generally they have some local man of confidence at Tirano, the starting-point for the homeward journey, who takes the casks up to that place and sees them duly charged. Merchants of old standing maintain relations with the same peasants, taking their wine regularly ; so that from Lorenz Gredig at Pontresina or Andreas Gredig at Davos-Dörfli, from Fanconi at Samaden or from Giacomi at Chiavenna, special qualities of wine, the produce of certain vineyards, are to be obtained. Up to the present time this wine-trade has been conducted with simplicity and honesty by both the dealers and the growers. One chief merit of Valtelline wine is that it is pure. How long so desirable a state of things will survive the slow but steady development of an export business may be questioned.

III

With so much practical and theoretical interest in the produce of the Valtelline to stimulate my curiosity, I determined to visit the district at the season when the

Our Life in the Swiss Highlands

wine was leaving it. It was the winter of 1881-82, a winter of unparalleled beauty in the high Alps. Day succeeded day without a cloud. Night followed night with steady stars, gliding across clear mountain ranges and forests of dark pines unstirred by wind. I could not hope for a more prosperous season; and indeed I made such use of it, that between the months of January and March I crossed six passes of the Alps in open sleighs—the Fluela, Bernina, Splügen, Julier, Maloja, and Albula—with less difficulty and discomfort in mid-winter than the traveller may often find on them in June.

At the end of January my friend Christian and I left Davos long before the sun was up, and ascended for four hours through the interminable snow-drifts of the Fluela in a cold grey shadow. The sun's light seemed to elude us. It ran along the ravine through which we toiled; dipped down to touch the topmost pines above our heads; rested in golden calm upon the Schiahorn at our back; capriciously played here and there across the Weisshorn on our left, and made the precipices of the Schwartzhorn glitter on our right. But athwart our path it never fell until we reached the very summit of the pass. Then we passed quietly into the full glory of the winter morning—a tranquil flood of sunbeams pouring through air of crystalline purity, frozen and motionless. White peaks and dark brown rocks soared up, cutting a sky of almost purple blueness. A stillness that might be felt brooded over the whole world; but in that stillness there was nothing sad, no suggestion of suspended vitality. It was the stillness rather of untroubled health, of strength omnipotent but unexerted.

From the Hospiz of the Fluela the track plunges at one bound into the valley of the Inn, following a narrow

THE SCHIAHORN.

cornice carved from the smooth bank of snow, and hung, without break or barrier, a thousand feet or more above the torrent. The summer road is lost in snow-drifts. The galleries built as a protection from avalanches, which sweep in rivers from those grim, bare fells above, are blocked with snow. Their useless arches yawn, as we glide over or outside them, by paths which instinct in our horse and driver traces. As a fly may creep along a house-roof, slanting downwards we descend. One whisk from the swinged tail of an avalanche would hurl us, like a fly, into the ruin of the gaping gorge. But this season little snow has fallen on the higher hills ; and what still lies there is hard frozen. Therefore we have no fear as we whirl fast and faster from the snow-fields into the black forests of gnarled cembras and wind-wearied pines. Then Süss is reached, where the Inn hurries its shallow waters, clogged with ice-floes, through a sleepy hamlet. The stream is pure and green, for the fountains of the glaciers are locked by winter frosts, and only clear rills from perennial sources swell its tide. At Süss we lost the sun, and toiled in garish gloom and silence, nipped by the ever-deepening cold of evening, upwards for four hours to Samaden.

The next day was spent in visiting the winter colony at San Moritz, where the Kulm Hotel, tenanted by some twenty guests, presented in its vastness the appearance of a country-house. One of the prettiest spots in the world is the ice-rink, fashioned by the skill of Herr Caspar Badrutt on a high raised terrace, commanding the valley of the Inn and the ponderous bulwarks of Bernina. The silhouettes of skaters, defined against that landscape of pure white, passed to and fro beneath a cloudless sky. Ladies sat and worked or read on seats upon the ice. Not a breath of wind was astir, and warm beneficent sun-

Our Life in the Swiss Highlands

light flooded the immeasurable air. Only, as the day declined, some iridescent films overspread the west ; and just above Maloja the apparition of a mock sun—a well-defined circle of opaline light, broken at regular intervals by four globes—seemed to portend a change of weather. This forecast fortunately proved delusive. We drove back to Samaden across the silent snow, enjoying those delicate tints of rose and violet and saffron which shed enchantment for one hour over the white monotony of Alpine winter.

At half-past eight next morning the sun was rising from behind Pitz Languard as we crossed the Inn and drove through Pontresina in the glorious light, with all its huge hotels quite empty, and none but a few country-folk abroad. Those who only know the Engadine in summer have little conception of its beauty. Winter softens the hard details of bare rock, and rounds the melancholy grassless mountain flanks, suspending icicles to every ledge and spangling the curved surfaces of snow with crystals. The landscape gains in purity, and, what sounds unbelievable, in tenderness. Nor does it lose in grandeur. Looking up the valley of the Morteratsch that morning, the glaciers were distinguishable in hues of green and sapphire through their veil of snow ; and the highest peaks soared in a transparency of amethystine light beneath a blue sky traced with filaments of windy cloud. Some storm must have disturbed the atmosphere in Italy, for fan-shaped mists frothed out around the sun, and curled themselves above the mountains in fine feathery wreaths, melting imperceptibly into air, until, when we had risen above the cembras, the sky was one deep solid blue.

All that upland wilderness is lovelier now than in the summer ; and on the morning of which I write, the air

Bacchus in Graubünden

itself was far more summery than I have ever known it
in the Engadine in August. We could scarcely bear to
place our hands upon the woodwork of the sleigh because
of the sun's fierce heat. And yet the atmosphere was
crystalline with windless frost. As though to increase
the strangeness of these contrasts, the pavement of beaten
snow was stained with red drops spilt from wine-casks
which pass over it.

The chief feature of the Bernina—what makes it a
dreary pass enough in summer, but infinitely beautiful
in winter—is its breadth ; illimitable undulations of
snow-drifts ; immensity of open sky ; unbroken lines of
white, descending in smooth curves from glittering ice-
peaks.

A glacier hangs in air above the frozen lakes, with all
its green-blue ice-cliffs glistening in intensest light. Pitz
Palü shoots aloft like sculptured marble, delicately veined
with soft aerial shadows of translucent blue. At the
summit of the pass all Italy seems to burst upon the eyes
in those steep serried ranges, with their craggy crests,
violet-hued in noonday sunshine, as though a bloom of
plum or grape had been shed over them, enamelling their
jagged precipices. The top of the Bernina is not always
thus in winter. It has a bad reputation for the fury of
invading storms, when falling snow hurtles together with
snow scooped from the drifts in eddies, and the weltering
white sea shifts at the will of whirlwinds. The Hospice
then may be tenanted for days together by weather-
bound wayfarers ; and a line drawn close beneath its
roof shows how two years ago the whole building was
buried in one snow-shroud. This morning we lounged
about the door, while our horses rested and postillions
and carters pledged one another in cups of new Veltliner.

The road takes an awful and sudden dive downwards,

quite irrespective of the carefully engineered post-track. At this season the path is badly broken into ruts and chasms by the wine traffic. In some places it was indubitably perilous : a narrow ledge of mere ice skirting thinly-clad hard-frozen banks of snow, which fell precipitately sideways for hundreds of sheer feet. We did not slip over this parapet, though we were often within an inch of doing so. Had our horse stumbled, it is not probable that I should have been writing this.

When we came to the galleries which defend the road from avalanches, we saw ahead of us a train of over forty sledges ascending, all charged with Valtelline wine. Our postillions drew up at the inner side of the gallery, between massive columns of the purest ice dependent from the rough-hewn roof and walls of rock. A sort of open *loggia* on the farther side framed vignettes of the Valtelline mountains in their hard cerulean shadows and keen sunlight. Between us and the view defiled the wine-sledges ; and as each went by, the men made us drink out of their *trinketti*. These are oblong, hexagonal wooden kegs, holding about fourteen litres, which the carter fills with wine before he leaves the Valtelline, to cheer him on the homeward journey. You raise it in both hands, and when the bung has been removed, allow the liquor to flow stream-wise down your throat. It was a most extraordinary Bacchic procession—a pomp which, though undreamed of on the banks of the Ilissus, proclaimed the deity of Dionysos in authentic fashion. Struggling horses, grappling at the ice-bound floor with sharp-spiked shoes ; huge, hoarse drivers, some clad in sheepskins from Italian valleys, some brown as bears in rough Graubünden homespun ; casks, dropping their spilth of red wine on the snow ; greetings, embracings ; patois of Bergamo, Romansch, and German roaring

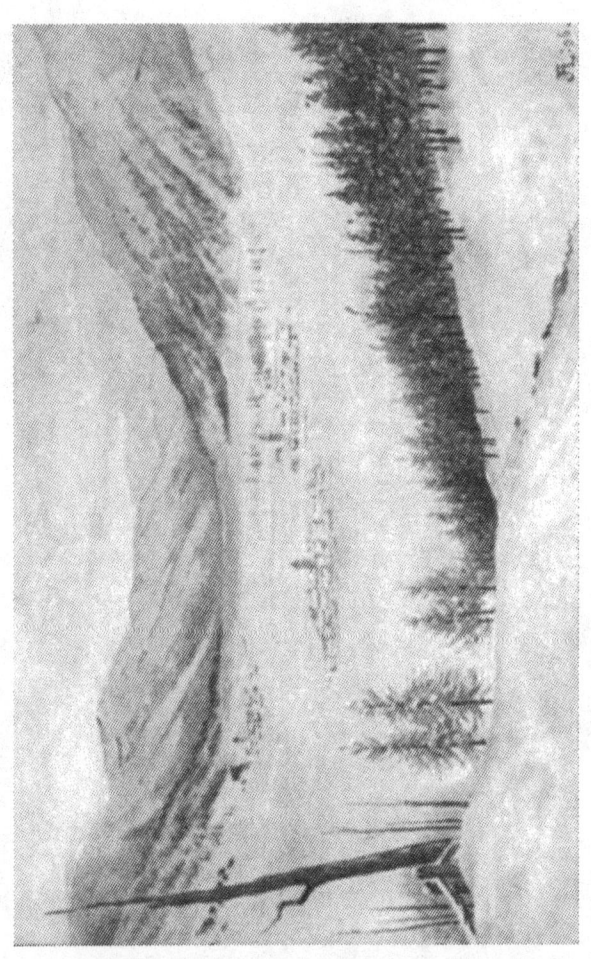

WINTER SUNRISE ON CRESTA, CELERINA,
AND SAMADEN.

around the low-browed vaults and tingling ice pillars ;
pourings forth of libations of the new strong Valtelline
on breasts and beards ;—the whole made up a scene of
stalwart jollity and manful labour such as I have nowhere
else in such wild circumstances witnessed. Many
Davosers were there, the men of Andreas Gredig, Valär,
and so forth ; and all of these, on greeting Christian,
forced us to drain a *Schluck* from their unmanageable
cruses. Then on they went, crying, creaking, struggling,
straining through the corridor, which echoed deafeningly,
the gleaming crystals of those hard Italian mountains in
their winter raiment building a background of still
beauty to the savage Bacchanalian riot of the team.

How little visitors who drink Valtelline wine at San
Moritz or Davos reflect by what strange ways it reaches
them. A sledge can scarcely be laden with more than
one cask of 300 litres on the ascent ; and this cask, according to the state of the road, has many times to be shifted
from wheels to runners and back again before the journey
is accomplished. One carter will take charge of two
horses, and consequently of two sledges and two casks,
driving them both by voice and gesture rather than by
rein. When they leave the Valtelline, the carters en-
deavour, as far as possible, to take the pass in gangs, lest
bad weather or an accident upon the road should over-
take them singly. At night they hardly rest three hours,
and rarely think of sleeping, but spend the time in drinking and conversation. The horses are fed and littered ;
but for them, too, the night-halt is little better than a
baiting-time. In fair weather the passage of the mountain is not difficult, though tiring. But woe to men and
beasts alike if they encounter storms ! Not a few perish
in the passes ; and it frequently happens that their only
chance is to unyoke the horses and leave the sledges in

a snow-wreath, seeking for themselves such shelter as may possibly be gained, frost-bitten, after hours of battling with impermeable drifts. The wine is frozen into one solid mass of rosy ice before it reaches Pontresina. This does not hurt the young vintage, but it is highly injurious to wine of some years' standing. The perils of the journey are aggravated by the savage temper of the drivers. Jealousies between the natives of rival districts spring up ; and there are men alive who have fought the whole way down from Fluela Hospice to Davos-Platz with knives and stones, hammers and hatchets, wooden staves and splintered cart-wheels, staining the snow with blood, and bringing broken pates, bruised limbs, and senseless comrades home to their women to be tended.

Bacchus Alpinus shepherded his train away from us to northward, and we passed forth into noonday from the gallery. It then seemed clear that both conductor and postillion were sufficiently merry. The plunge they took us down those frozen parapets, with shriek and *jauchzen* and cracked whips, was more than ever dangerous. Yet we reached La Rosa safely. This is a lovely solitary spot, beside a rushing stream, among grey granite boulders grown with spruce and rhododendron : a veritable rose of Sharon blooming in the desert. The wastes of the Bernina stretch above, and round about are leaguered some of the most forbidding sharp-toothed peaks I ever saw. Onwards, across the silent snow, we glided in immitigable sunshine, through opening valleys and pinewoods, past the robber-huts of Pisciadella, until at evenfall we rested in the roadside inn at Poschiavo.

Bacchus in Graubünden

IV

The snow-path ended at Poschiavo ; and when, as usual, we started on our journey next day at sunrise, it was in a carriage upon wheels. Yet even here we were in full mid-winter. Beyond Le Prese the lake presented one sheet of smooth black ice, reflecting every peak and chasm of the mountains, and showing the rocks and water-weeds in the clear green depths below. The glittering floor stretched away for acres of untenanted expanse, with not a skater to explore those dark mysterious coves, or strike across the slanting sunlight poured from clefts in the impendent hills. Inshore the substance of the ice sparkled here and there with iridescence like the plumelets of a butterfly's wing under the microscope, wherever light happened to catch the jagged or oblique flaws that veined its solid crystal.

From the lake the road descends suddenly for a considerable distance through a narrow gorge, following a torrent which rushes among granite boulders. Chestnut trees begin to replace the pines. The sunnier terraces are planted with tobacco, and at a lower level vines appear at intervals in patches. One comes at length to a great red gate across the road, which separates Switzerland from Italy, and where the export dues on wines are paid. The Italian custom-house is romantically perched above the torrent. Two courteous and elegant *finanzieri*, mere boys, were sitting wrapped in their military cloaks and reading novels in the sun as we drove up. Though they made some pretence of examining the luggage, they excused themselves with sweet smiles and apologetic eyes— it was a disagreeable duty !

A short time brought us to the first village in the Valtelline, where the road bifurcates northward to Bormio and the Stelvio Pass, southward to Sondrio and Lombardy. It is a little hamlet, known by the name of La Madonna di Tirano, having grown up round a pilgrimage church of great beauty, with tall Lombard bell-tower, pierced with many tiers of pilastered windows, ending in a whimsical spire, and dominating a fantastic cupola-building of the earlier Renaissance. Taken altogether, this is a charming bit of architecture, picturesquely set beneath the granite snow-peaks of the Valtelline. The church, they say, was raised at Madonna's own command to stay the tide of heresy descending from the Engadine ; and in the year 1620, the bronze statue of St. Michael, which still spreads wide its wings above the cupola, looked down upon the massacre of 600 Protestants and foreigners, commanded by the patriot Jacopo Robustelli.

From Madonna the road leads up the valley through a narrow avenue of poplar trees to the town of Tirano. We were now in the district where Forzato is made, and every vineyard had a name and history. In Tirano we betook ourselves to the house of an old acquaintance of the Buol family, Bernardo da Campo, or, as the Graubündeners call him, Bernard Campbèll. We found him at dinner with his son and grandchildren in a vast, dark, bare Italian chamber. It would be difficult to find a more typical old Scotchman of the Lowlands than he looked, with his clean close-shaven face, bright brown eyes, and snow-white hair escaping from a broad-brimmed hat. He might have sat to a painter for some Covenanter's portrait, except that there was nothing dour about him, or for an illustration to Burns's " Cotter's Saturday Night." The air of probity and canniness, combined with a twinkle of dry humour, was completely Scotch ; and when he tapped his snuff-box, telling stories of old days,

Bacchus in Graubünden

I could not refrain from asking him about his pedigree. It should be said that there is a considerable family of Campèlls or Campbèlls in the Graubünden, who are fabled to deduce their stock from a Scotch Protestant of Zwingli's time ; and this made it irresistible to imagine that in our friend Bernardo I had chanced upon a notable specimen of atavism. All he knew, however, was that his first ancestor had been a foreigner, who came across the mountains to Tirano two centuries ago.[1]

This old gentleman is a considerable wine-dealer. He sent us with his son, Giacomo, on a long journey underground through his cellars, where we tasted several sorts of Valtelline, especially the new Forzato, made a few weeks since, which singularly combines sweetness with strength, and both with a slight effervescence. It is certainly the sort of wine wherewith to tempt a Polyphemus, and not unapt to turn a giant's head.

Leaving Tirano, and one more passing through the poplars by Madonna, we descended the valley all along the vineyards of Villa and the vast district of Sassella. Here and there, at wayside inns, we stopped to drink a glass of some particular vintage ; and everywhere it seemed as though god Bacchus were at home. The whole valley on the right side of the Adda is one gigantic vineyard, climbing the hills in tiers and terraces, which justify its Italian epithet of *Teatro di Bacco*. The rock is a greyish granite, assuming sullen brown and orange tints where exposed to sun and weather. The vines are grown on stakes, not trellised over trees or carried across boulders, as is the fashion at Chiavenna or Terlan. Yet

[1] The Grisons surname Campèll may derive from the Romansch Campo Bello. The founder of the house was one Kasper Campèll, who in the first half of the sixteenth century preached the Reformed religion in the Engadine.

every advantage of the mountain is adroitly used ; nooks and crannies being especially preferred, where the sun's rays are deflected from hanging cliffs. The soil seems deep, and is of a dull yellow tone. When the vines end, brushwood takes up the growth, which expires at last in crag and snow. Some alps and châlets, dimly traced against the sky, are evidences that a pastoral life prevails above the vineyards. Pan there stretches the pine thyrsus down to vine-garlanded Dionysos.

The Adda flows majestically among willows in the midst, and the valley is nearly straight. The prettiest spot, perhaps, is at Tresenda or San Giacomo, where a pass from Edolo and Brescia descends from the southern hills. But the Valtelline has no great claim to beauty of scenery. Its chief town, Sondrio, where we supped and drank some special wine called *il vino de' Signori Grigioni*, has been modernised in dull Italian fashion.

V

The hotel at Sondrio, La Maddalena, was in carnival uproar of maskers, topers, and musicians all night through. It was as much as we could do to rouse the sleepy servants and get a cup of coffee ere we started in the frozen dawn. "Verfluchte Maddalena!" grumbled Christian as he shouldered our portmanteaus and bore them in hot haste to the post. Long experience only confirms the first impression, that, of all cold, the cold of an Italian winter is most penetrating. As we lumbered out of Sondrio in a heavy diligence, I could have fancied myself back once again at Radicofani or among the Ciminian hills. The frost was penetrating. Fur coats would not keep it out ; and we longed to be once more in open sledges on Bernina rather than enclosed in that cold coupé. Now we passed Grumello, the second largest of the renowned vine districts ; and always keeping the white mass of Monte di Disgrazia in sight, rolled at last into Morbengo. Here the Valtelline vintage properly ends, though much of the ordinary wine is probably supplied from the inferior produce of these fields. It was past noon when we reached Colico, and saw the Lake of Como glittering in sunlight, dazzling cloaks of snow on all the mountains, which look as dry and brown as dead beach leaves at this season. Our Bacchic journey had reached its close ; and it boots not here to tell in detail how we made our way across the Splügen, piercing its avalanches by low-arched galleries scooped from the solid snow, and careering in our sledges down perpendicular snow-fields, which no one who has crossed that pass from the Italian side in winter will forget. We left the refuge station at the top together with a train of wine-sledges, and passed them in the midst of the wild descent. Looking back, I saw two of their horses stumble in the plunge and roll headlong over. Unluckily, in one of these somersaults a man was injured. Flung ahead into the snow by the first lurch, the sledge and wine-cask crossed him like a garden roller. Had his bed not been of snow, he must have been crushed to death ; and as it was, he presented a woeful appearance when he afterwards arrived at Splügen.

VI

Though not strictly connected with the subject of this paper, I shall conclude these notes of winter wanderings in the high Alps with an episode which illustrates their curious vicissitudes.

It was late in the month of March, and nearly all the

Our Life in the Swiss Highlands

mountain roads were open for wheeled vehicles. A carriage and four horses came to meet us at the termination of a railway journey at Ragatz. We spent one day in visiting old houses of the Grisons aristocracy at Mayenfeld and Zizers, rejoicing in the early sunshine, which had spread the fields with spring flowers—primroses and oxlips, violets, anemones, and bright blue squills. At Chur we slept, and early next morning started for our homeward drive to Davos. Bad weather had declared itself in the night. It blew violently, and the rain soon changed to snow, frozen by a bitter north blast. Crossing the dreary heath of Lenz was both magnificent and dreadful. By the time we reached Wiesen, all the forests were laden with snow, the roads deep in snow-drifts, the whole scene wintrier than it had been the winter through.

At Wiesen we should have stayed, for evening was fast setting in. But in ordinary weather it is only a two hours' drive from Wiesen to Davos. Our coachman made no objections to resuming the journey, and our four horses had but a light load to drag. So we telegraphed for supper to be prepared, and started between five and six.

A deep gorge has to be traversed, where the torrent cleaves its way between jaws of limestone precipices. The road is carried along ledges and through tunnels in the rock. Avalanches, which sweep this passage annually from the hills above, give it the name of Züge, or the Snow-Paths. As we entered the gorge darkness fell, the horses dragged more heavily, and it soon became evident that our Tyrolese driver was hopelessly drunk. He nearly upset us twice by taking sharp turns in the road, banged the carriage against telegraph-posts and jutting rocks, shaved the very verge of the torrent in places where there was no parapet, and, what was worst of all, refused to leave his box without a fight. The darkness by this time was all

250

SARGANS CASTLE, NEAR RAGATZ.

but total, and a blinding snow-storm swept howling through the ravine. At length we got the carriage to a dead stop, and floundered out in deep wet snow toward some wooden huts where miners in old days made their habitation. The place, by a curious, perhaps unconscious irony, is called Hoffnungsau, or the Meadow of Hope. Indeed, it is not ill named ; for many wanderers, escaping, as we did, from the dreadful gorge of avalanches on a stormy night, may have felt, as we now felt, their hope reviving when they reached this shelter.

There was no light ; nothing above, beneath, around, on any side, but tearing tempest and snow whirled through the ravine. The horses were taken out of the carriage ; on their way to the stable, which fortunately in these mountains regions will be always found beside the poorest habitation, one of them fell back across a wall and nearly broke his spine. Hoffnungsau is inhabited all through the year. In its dismal, dark kitchen we found a knot of workmen gathered together, and heard there were two horses on the premises besides our own. It then occurred to us that we might accomplish the rest of the journey with such sledges as they bring the wood on from the hills in winter, if coal-boxes or boxes of any sort could be provided. These should be lashed to the sledges and filled with hay. We were only four persons ; my wife and a friend should go in one, myself and my little girl in the other. No sooner thought of than put into practice. These original conveyances were improvised, and after two hours' halt on the Meadow of Hope, we all set forth again at half-past eight.

I have rarely felt anything more piercing than the grim cold of that journey. We crawled at a foot's pace through changeful snow-drifts. The road was obliterated, and it was my duty to keep a petroleum stable-lamp swinging

Our Life in the Swiss Highlands

to illuminate the untracked wilderness. My little girl was snugly nested in the hay, and sound asleep with a deep white covering of snow above her. Meanwhile, the drift clave in frozen masses to our faces, lashed by a wind so fierce and keen that it was difficult to breathe it. My forehead bone ached, as though with neuralgia from the mere mask of icy snow upon it, plastered on with frost. Nothing could be seen but millions of white specks, whirled at us in eddying concentric circles. Not far from the entrance to the village we met our housefolk out with lanterns to look for us. It was past eleven at night when at last we entered warm rooms, and refreshed ourselves for the tiring day with a jovial champagne supper. Horses, carriage, and drunken driver reached home next morning.   J. A. S.

WINTER NIGHTS AT DAVOS

I

LIGHT, marvellously soft yet penetrating, everywhere diffused, everywhere reflected without radiance, poured from the moon high above our heads in a sky tinted through all shades and modulations of blue, from turquoise on the horizon to opaque sapphire at the zenith— *dolce color*. (It is difficult to use the world *colour* for the scene without suggesting an exaggeration. The blue is almost indefinable, yet felt. But if possible, the total effect of the night landscape should be rendered by careful exclusion of tints from the word-palette. The art of the etcher is more needed than that of the painter.) Heaven overhead is set with stars, shooting intensely, smouldering with dull red in Aldeboran, sparkling diamond-like in Sirius, changing from orange to crimson and green in the swart fire of yonder double star. On the snow this moonlight falls tenderly, not in hard white light and strong black shadow, but in tones of cream and ivory, rounding the curves of drift. The mountain peaks alone glistened as though they were built of silver burnished by an agate. Far away they rise diminished in stature by the all-pervading dimness of bright light, that erases the distinctions of daytime. On the path before our feet lie crystals of many hues, the splinters of a thousand gems. In the

253

wood there are caverns of darkness, alternating with spaces of star-twinkled sky, or windows opened between russet stems and solid branches for the moony sheen. The green of the pines is felt, although invisible, so soft in substance that it seems less like velvet than some materialized depth of dark green shadow.

II

Snow falling noiseless and unseen. One only knows that it is falling by the blinking of our eyes as the flakes settle on their lids and melt. The cottage windows shine red, and moving lanterns of belated wayfarers define the void around them. Yet the night is far from dark. The forests and the mountain bulk beyond the valley loom softly large and just distinguishable through a pearly haze. The path is purest trackless whiteness, almost dazzling though it has no light. This was what Dante felt when he reached the lunar sphere—

> " Pareva a me, che nube ne coprisse
> Lucida, spessa, solida e pulita."

Walking silent, with insensible footfall, slowly, for the snow is deep above our ankles, we wonder what the world would be like if this were all. Could the human race be acclimatised to this monotony (we say) perhaps emotion would be rarer, yet more poignant, suspended brooding on itself, and wakening by flashes to a quintessential moon. Then fancy changes, and the thought occurs that even so must be a planet, not yet wholly made, nor called to take her place among the sisterhood of light and song.

Winter Nights at Davos

III

Sunset was fading out upon the Rhætikon and still reflected from the Seehorn on the lake, when we entered the gorge of the Fluela—dense pines on either hand, a mounting drift of snow in front, and faint peaks, paling from rose to saffron, far above, beyond. There was no sound but a tinkling stream and the continual jingle of our sledge-bells. We drove at a foot's face, our horse finding his own path. When we left the forest, the light had all gone except for some almost imperceptible touches of primrose on the eastern horns. It was a moonless night, but the sky was alive with stars, and now and then one fell. The last house in the valley was soon passed, and we entered those bleak gorges where the wind, fine, noiseless, penetrating like an edge of steel, poured slantwise on us from the north. As we rose, the stars to west seemed far beneath us, and the Great Bear sprawled upon the ridges of the lower hills outspread. We kept slowly moving onward, upward, into what seemed like a thin impalpable mist, but was immeasurable tracts of snow. The last cembras were left behind, immovable upon dark granite boulders on our right. We entered a formless and unbillowed sea of greyness, from which there rose dim mountain flanks that lost themselves in air. Up, ever up, and still below us westward sank the stars. We were now 7,500 feet above sea-level, and the December night was rigid with intensity of frost. The cold, and movement, and solemnity of space, drowsed every sense.

Our Life in the Swiss Highlands

IV

The memory of things seen and done in moonlight is
like the memory of dreams. It is as a dream that I recall
the night of our tobogganing to Klosters, though it was
full enough of active energy. The moon was in her
second quarter, slightly filmed with very high thin clouds,
that disappeared as night advanced, leaving the sky and
stars in all their lustre. A sharp frost, sinking to three
degrees above zero Fahrenheit, with a fine pure wind, such
wind as here they call " the mountain breath." We drove
to Wolfgang in a two-horse sledge, four of us inside, and
our two Christians on the box. Up there, where the Alps
of Death descend to join the Lakehorn Alps, above the
Wolfswalk, there is a world of whiteness—frozen ridges,
engraved like cameos of aerial onyx upon the dark, star-
tremulous sky ; sculptured buttresses of snow, enclosing
hollows filled with diaphanous shadows, and sweeping aloft
into the uplands field of pure clear drift. Then came the
swift descent, the plunge into the pines, moon-silvered on
their frosted tops. The battalions of spruce that climb
those hills defined the dazzling snow from which they
sprang, like the black tufts upon an ermine robe. At the
proper moment we left our sledge, and the big Christian
took his reins in hand to follow us. Furs and greatcoats
were abandoned. Each stood forth tightly accoutred,
with short coat, and clinging cap, and gaitered legs for
the toboggan. Off we started in line, with but brief
interval between, at first slowly, then glidingly, and when
the impetus was gained, with darting, bounding, almost
savage swiftness—sweeping round corners, cutting the
hard snow-path with keen runners, avoiding the deep
ruts, trusting to chance, taking advantage of smooth

places, till the rush and swing and downward swoop
became mechanical. Space was devoured. Into the
massy shadows of the forest, where the pines joined overhead, we pierced without a sound, and felt far more than
saw the great rocks with their icicles ; and out again,
emerging into moonlight, met the valley spread beneath
our feet, the mighty peaks of the Silvretta and the vast
blue sky. On, on, hurrying, delaying not, the woods and
hills rushed by. Crystals upon the snow-banks glittered
to the stars. Our souls would fain have stayed to drink
these marvels of the moon-world, but our limbs refused.
The magic of movement was upon us, and seven minutes
swallowed the varying impressions of two musical miles.
The village lights drew near and nearer, then the sombre
village huts, and soon the speed grew less, and soon we
glided to our rest into the sleeping village street.

V

It was just past midnight. The moon had fallen to the
western horns. Orion's belt lay bar-like on the opening
of the pass, and Sirius shot flame on the Seehorn. A
more crystalline light, more full of fulgent stars, was never
seen, stars everywhere, but mostly scattered in large
sparkles on the snow. Big Christian went in front,
tugging toboggans by their strings, as Gulliver, in some
old woodcut, drew the fleets of Lilliput. Through the
brown wood châlets of Selfrangr, up to the undulating
meadows, where the snow slept pure and crisp, he led us.
There we sat a while, and drank the clear air, cooled to
zero, but innocent and mild as mother Nature's milk.
Then in an instant, down, down through the hamlet, with
its châlets, stables, pumps, and logs, the slumbrous hamlet,

where one dog barked, and darkness dwelt upon the path of ice, down with the tempest of a dreadful speed, that shot each rider upward in the air, and made the frame of the toboggan tremble—down over hillocks of hard frozen snow, dashing and bounding, to the river and the bridge. No bones were broken, though the race was thrice renewed, and men were spilt upon the roadside by some furious plunge. This amusement has the charm of peril and the unforeseen. In nowise else can colder, keener air be drunken at such furious speed. The joy, too, of the engine-driver and the steeplechaser is upon us. Alas, that it should be so short ! If only roads were better made for the purpose, there would be no end to it ; for the toboggan cannot lose his wind. But the good thing fails at last, and from the silence of the moon we pass into the silence of the fields of sleep.

VI

The new stable is a huge wooden building, with raftered lofts to stow the hay, and stalls for many cows and horses. It stands snugly in an angle of the pine-wood, bordering upon the great horse meadow. Here at night the air is warm and tepid with the breath of kine. Returning from my forest walk, I spy one window yellow in the moonlight with a lamp. I lift the latch. The hound knows me, and does not bark. I enter the stable, where six horses are munching their last meal. Upon the corn-bin sits a knecht. We light our pipes and talk. He tells me of the valley of Arosa (a hawk's flight westward over yonder hills), how deep in grass its summer lawns, how crystal-clear its stream, how blue its little lakes, how pure, without a taint of mist, " too beautiful to paint," its sky in

Winter Nights at Davos

winter ! This knecht is an Ardüser, and the valley of
Arosa lifts itself to heaven above his Langwies home. It
is his duty now to harness a sleigh for some night work.
We shake hands and part—I to sleep, he for the snow.

VII

´ The lake has frozen late this year, and there are places
in it where the ice is not yet firm. Little snow has fallen
since it froze—about three inches at the deepest, driven
by winds and wrinkled like the ribbed sea-sand. Here
and there the ice-floor is quite black and clear, reflecting
stars, and dark as heaven's own depths. Elsewhere it is
of a suspicious whiteness, blurred in surface, with jagged
cracks and chasms, treacherously mended by the hand of
frost. Moving slowly, the snow cries beneath our feet,
and the big crystals tinkle. These are shaped like fern-
fronds, growing fan-wise from a point, and set at various
angles, so that the moonlight takes them with capricious
touch. They flash, and are quenched, and flash again,
light darting to light along the level surface, while the
sailing planets and the stars look down complacent at this
mimicry of heaven. Everything above, around, beneath,
is very beautiful—the slumbrous woods, the snowy fells,
and the far distance painted in faint blue upon the tender
background of the sky. Everything is placid and beautiful ; and yet the place is terrible. For, as we walk, the
lake groans, with throttled sobs, and sudden cracklings of
its joints, and sighs that shiver, undulating from afar, and
pass beneath our feet, and die away in distance when they
reach the shore. And now and then an upper crust of ice
gives way ; and will the gulfs then drag us down ? We
are in the very centre of the lake. There is no use in

thinking or in taking heed. Enjoy the moment, then, and march. Enjoy the contrast between this circumambient serenity and sweetness, and the dreadful sense of insecurity beneath. Is not, indeed, our whole life of this nature ? A passage over perilous deeps, roofed by infinity and sempiternal things, surrounded, too, with evanescent forms, that, like these crystals, trodden underfoot, or melted by the Föhn-wind into dew, flash, in some lucky moment, with a light that mimics stars ! But to allegorise and sermonise is out of place here. It is but the expedient of those who cannot etch sensation by the burin of their art of words.

VIII

It is ten o'clock upon Sylvester Abend, or New Year's Eve. Herr Buol sits with his wife at the head of his long table. His family and serving-folk are around him. There is his mother, with little Ursula, his child, upon her knee. The old lady is the mother of four comely daughters and nine stalwart sons, the eldest of whom is now a grizzled man. Besides our host, four of the brothers are here to-night ; the handsome melancholy Georg, who is so gentle in his speech ; Simeon, with his diplomatic face ; Florian, the student of medicine ; and my friend, colossal-breasted Christian. Palmy came a little later, worried with many cares, but happy to his heart's core. No optimist was ever more convinced of his philosophy than Palmy. After them, below the salt, were ranged the knechts and porters, the marmiton from the kitchen, and innumerable maids. The board was tesselated with plates of birnen-brod and eier-brod, küchli and cheese and butter ; and Georg stirred grampampuli in a mighty metal bowl. For the uninitiated, it may be needful to explain these Davos delicacies. Birnen-brod is what the Scotch would call a "bun," or massive cake, composed of sliced pears, almonds, spices, and a little flour. Eier-brod is a saffron-coloured sweet bread, made with eggs ; and küchli is a kind of pastry, crisp and flimsy, fashioned into various devices of cross, star, and scroll. Grampampuli is simply brandy burnt with sugar, the most unsophisticated punch I ever drank from tumblers. The frugal people of Davos, who live on bread and cheese and dried meat all the year, indulge themselves but once with these unwonted dainties in the winter.

The occasion was cheerful, and yet a little solemn. The scene was feudal. For these Buols are the scions of a warrior race :

> " A race illustrious for heroic deeds ;
> Humbled, but not degraded."

During the six centuries through which they have lived nobles in Davos, they have sent forth scores of fighting men to foreign lands, ambassadors to France and Venice and the Milanese, governors to Chiavenna and Bregaglia and the much-contested Valtelline. Members of their house are Counts of Buol-Schauenstein in Austria, Freiherrs of Muhlingen and Berenberg in the now German Empire. They keep the patent of nobility conferred on them by Henri IV. Their ancient coat—parted per pale azure and argent, with a dame of the fourteenth century bearing in her hand a rose, all counterchanged—is carved in wood and monumental marble on the churches and old houses hereabouts. And from immemorial antiquity the Buol of Davos has sat thus on Sylvester Abend with family and folk around him, summoned from alp and snowy field to drink grampampuli and break the birnen-brod.

Our Life in the Swiss Highlands

These rites performed, the men and maids began to sing—brown arms lounging on the table, and red hands folded in white aprons—serious at first in hymn-like cadences, then breaking into wilder measures with a *jodel* at the close. There is a measured solemnity in the performance, which strikes the stranger as somewhat comic. But the singing was good ; the voices strong and clear in tone, no hesitation and no shirking of the melody. It was clear that the singers enjoyed the music for its own sake, with half-shut eyes, as they take dancing, solidly, with deep-drawn breath, sustained and indefatigable. But eleven struck ; and the two Christians, my old friend and Palmy, said we should be late for church. They had promised to take me with them to see bell-ringing in the tower. All the young men of the village meet, and draw lots in the Stube of the Rathhaus. One party tolls the old year out, the other rings the new year in. He who comes last is sconced three litres of Veltliner for the company. This jovial fine was ours to pay to-night.

When we came into the air we found a bitter frost ; the whole sky clouded over ; a north wind whirling snow from alp and forest through the murky gloom. The benches and broad walnut tables of the Rathhaus were crowded with men in shaggy homespun of brown and grey frieze. Its low wooden roof and walls enclosed an atmosphere of smoke, denser than the external snow-drift. But our welcome was hearty, and we found a score of friends. Titanic Fopp, whose limbs are Michelangelesque in length ; spectacled Morosani ; the little tailor Kramer, with a French horn on his knees ; the puckered forehead of the Baumeister ; the Troll-shaped postman ; peasants and woodmen, known on far excursions upon pass and upland valley. Not one but carried on his face the memory of winter strife with avalanche and snow-drift,

FRAUENKIRCH.

Winter Nights at Davos

of horses struggling through Fluela whirlwinds, and wine-casks tugged across Bernina, and haystacks guided down precipitous gullies at thundering speed 'twixt pine and pine, and larches felled in distant glens beside the frozen watercourses. Here we were, all met together for one hour from our several homes and occupations, to welcome in the year with clinked glasses and cries of *Prosit Neujahr !*

The tolling bells above us stopped. Our turn had come. Out into the snowy air we tumbled, beneath the row of wolves' heads that adorn the pent-house roof. A few steps brought us to the still God's acre, where the snow lay deep and cold upon high-mounded graves of many generations. We crossed it silently, bent our heads to the low Gothic arch, and stood within the tower. It was thick darkness there. But far above, the bells began again to clash and jangle confusedly, with volleys of demoniac joy. Successive flights of ladders, each ending in a giddy platform hung across the gloom, climb to the height of some hundred and fifty feet ; and all their rungs were crusted with frozen snow, deposited by trampling boots. For up and down these stairs, ascending and descending, moved other than angels—the frieze-jacketed Burschen, Grisons bears, rejoicing in their exercise, exhilarated with the tingling noise of beaten metal. We reached the first room safely, guided by firm-footed Christian, whose one candle just defined the rough walls and the slippery steps. There we found a band of boys pulling ropes that set the bells in motion. But our destination was not reached. One more aerial ladder, perpendicular in darkness, brought us swiftly to the home of sound. It is a small square chamber, where the bells are hung, filled with the interlacement of enormous beams, and pierced to north and south by open windows, from whose parapets

Our Life in the Swiss Highlands

I saw the village and the valley spread beneath. The fierce wind hurried through it, charged with snow, and its narrow space was thronged with men. Men on the platform, men on the window-sills, men grappling the bells with iron arms, men brushing by to reach the stairs, crossing, re-crossing, shouldering their mates, drinking red wine from gigantic beakers, exploding crackers, firing squibs, shouting and yelling in corybantic chorus. They yelled and shouted, one could see it by their open mouths and glittering eyes ; but not a sound from human lungs could reach our ears. The overwhelming incessant thunder of the bells drowned all. It thrilled the tympanum, ran through the marrow of the spine, vibrated in the inmost entrails. Yet the brain was only steadied and excited by this sea of brazen noise. After a few moments I knew the place and felt at home in it. Then I enjoyed a spectacle which sculptors might have envied. For they ring the bells in Davos after this fashion :—The lads below set them going with ropes. The men above climb in pairs on ladders to the beams from which they are suspended. Two mighty pine-trees, roughly squared and built into the walls, extend from side to side across the belfry. Another, from which the bells hang, connects these massive trunks at right angles. Just where the central beam is wedged into the two parallel supports, the ladders reach them from each side of the belfry, so that, bending from the higher rung of the ladder, and leaning over, stayed upon the lateral beam, each pair of men can keep one bell in movement with their hands. Each comrade plants one leg upon the ladder, and sets the other knee firmly athwart the horizontal pine. Then round each other's waist they twine left arm and right. The two have thus become one man. Right arm and left are free to grasp the bell's horns, sprouting at its crest beneath the beam. With a grave rhythmic motion, bending sideward in a close embrace, swaying and returning to their centre from the well-knit loins, they drive the force of each strong muscle into the vexed bell. The impact is earnest at first, but soon it becomes frantic. The men take something from each other of exalted enthusiasm. This efflux of their combined energies inspires them and exasperates the mighty resonance of metal which they rule. They are lost in a trance of what approximates to dervish passion—so thrilling is the surge of sound, so potent are the rhythms they obey. Men come and tug them by the heels. One grasps the starting thews upon their calves. Another is impatient for their place. But they strain still, locked together, and forgetful of the world. At length they have enough : then slowly, clingingly, unclasp, turn round with gazing eyes, and are resumed, sedately, into the diurnal round of common life. Another pair is in their room upon the beam.

The Englishman who saw those things stood looking up, enveloped in his ulster with the grey cowl thrust upon his forehead, like a monk. One candle cast a grotesque shadow of him on the plastered wall. And when his chance came, though he was but a weakling, he too climbed and for some moments hugged the beam, and felt the madness of the swinging bell. Descending, he wondered long and strangely whether he ascribed too much of feeling to the men he watched. But no, that was impossible. There are emotions deeply seated in the joy of exercise, when the body is brought into play, and masses move in concert, of which the subject is but half conscious. Music and dance, and the delirium of the battle or the chase, act thus upon spontaneous natures. The mystery of rhythm and associated energy and blood tingling in sympathy is here. It lies at the root of man's most tyrannous instinctive impulses.

It was past one when we reached home, and now a meditative man might well have gone to bed. But no one thinks of sleeping on Sylvester Abend. So there followed bowls of punch in one friend's room, where English, French, and German blent together in convivial Babel; and flasks of old Montagner in another. Palmy, at this period, wore an archdeacon's hat, and smoked a churchwarden's pipe; and neither were his own, nor did he derive anything ecclesiastical or Anglican from the association. Late in the morning we must sally forth, they said, and roam the town. For it is the custom here on New Year's night to greet acquaintances, and ask for hospitality, and no one may deny these self-invited guests. We turned out again into the grey snow-swept gloom, a curious Comus—not at all like Greeks, for we had neither torches in our hands nor rose-wreaths to suspend upon a lady's door-posts. And yet I could not refrain, at this supreme moment of jollity, in the zero temperature, amid my Grisons friends, from humming to myself verses from the Greek Anthology—

> " The die is cast! Nay, light the torch!
> I'll take the road! Up, courage, ho!
> Why linger pondering in the porch?
> Upon Love's revel we will go!
>
> " Shake off those fumes of wine! Hang care
> And caution! What has Love to do
> With prudence? Let the torches flare!
> Quick, drown the doubts that hampered you!
>
> " Cast weary wisdom to the wind!
> One thing, but one alone, I know:
> Love bent e'en Jove and made him blind!
> Upon Love's revel we will go!"

Winter Nights at Davos

And then again—

> " I've drunk sheer madness !   Not with wine,
>   But old fantastic tales, I'll arm
> My heart in heedlessness divine,
>   And dare the road, nor dream of harm !
>
> " I'll join Love's rout !   Let thunder break,
>   Let lightning blast me by the way !
> Invulnerable Love shall shake
>   His ægis o'er my head to-day."

This last epigram was not inappropriate to an invalid about to begin the fifth act in a roystering night's adventure.   And still once more—

> " Cold blows the winter wind ; 'tis Love,
>   Whose sweet eyes swim with honeyed tears,
> That bears me to thy doors, my love,
>   Tossed by the storm of hopes and fears.
>
> " Cold blows the blast of aching Love ;
>   But be thou for my wandering sail,
> Adrift upon these waves of love,
>   Safe harbour from the whistling gale !

However, upon this occasion, though we had winter wind enough, and cold enough, there was not much love in the business.   My arm was firmly clenched in Christian Buol's, and Christian Palmy came behind, trolling out songs in Italian dialect, with still recurring *canaille* choruses, of which the facile rhymes seemed mostly made on a prolonged *amu-u-u-r*.   It is noticeable that Italian ditties are specially designed for fellows shouting in the streets at night.   They seem in keeping there, and nowhere else that I could ever see.   And these Davosers took to them naturally when the time for Comus came. It was between four and five in the morning, and nearly all the houses in the place were dark.   The tall church-tower and spire loomed up above us in grey twilight. The tireless wind still swept thin snow from fell and forest. But the frenzied bells had sunk into their twelve-month's slumber, which shall be broken only by decorous tollings at less festive times. I wondered whether they were tingling still with the heart-throbs and with the pressure of those many arms ? Was their old age warmed, as mine was, with that gust of life—the young men who had clung to them like bees to lily-bells, and shaken all their locked-up tone and shrillness into the wild winter air ? Alas ! how many generations of the young have handled them ; and they are still there, frozen in their belfry ; and the young grow middle-aged, and old, and die at last ; and the bells they grappled in their lust of manhood toll them to their graves, on which the tireless wind will, winter after winter, sprinkle snow from alps and forests which they knew.

"There is a light," cried Christian, "up in Anna's window !" "A light ! a light !" the Comus shouted. But how to get at the window, which is pretty high above the ground, and out of reach of the most ardent revellers ? We search a neighbouring shed, extract a stable ladder, and in two seconds Palmy has climbed to the topmost rung, while Christian and Georg hold it firm upon the snow beneath. Then begins a passage from some comic opera of Mozart's or Cimarosa's—an escapade familiar to Spanish or Italian students, which recalls the stage. It is an episode from *Don Giovanni*, translated to this dark-etched scene of snowy hills, and Gothic tower, and mullioned windows deep-embayed beneath their eaves and icicles. *Deh vieni alla finestra !* sings Palmy-Leporello ; the chorus answers : *Deh vieni !* *Perchè non vieni ancora ?* pleads Leporello ; the chorus shouts : *Perchè ? Mio amu-u-u-r*, sighs Leporello ; and

Winter Nights at Davos

Echo cries, *amu-u-u-r !* All the wooing, be it noticed, is conducted in Italian. But the actors murmur to each other in Davoser Deutsch, "She won't come, Palmy! It is far too late ; she is gone to bed. Come down ; you'll wake the village with your caterwauling !" But Leporello waves his broad archdeacon's hat, and resumes a flood of flexible Bregaglian. He has a shrewd suspicion that the girl is peeping from behind the window-curtain ; and tells us, bending down from the ladder, in a hoarse stage-whisper, that we must have patience : "These girls are kittle cattle, who take long to draw : but if your lungs last out, they're sure to show." And Leporello is right. Faint heart ne'er won fair lady. From the summit of his ladder, by his eloquent Italian tongue, he brings the shy bird down at last. We hear the un-barring of the house door, and a comely maiden, in her Sunday dress, welcomes us politely to her ground-floor sitting-room. The Comus enters, in grave order, with set speeches, handshakes, aad inevitable *Prosits !* It is a large low chamber, with a huge stone stove, wide benches fixed along the walls, and a great oval table. We sit how and where we can. Red wine is produced, and eier-brod and küchli. Fräulein Anna serves us sedately, holding her own with decent self-respect against the inrush of the revellers. She is quite alone ; but are not her father and mother in bed above, and within earshot ? Besides, the Comus, even at this abnormal hour and after an abnormal night, is well conducted. Things seem slipping into a decorous wine-party, when Leporello readjusts the broad-brimmed hat upon his head, and very cleverly acts a little love-scene for our benefit. Fräulein Anna takes this as a delicate com-pliment, and the thing is so prettily done, in truth, that not the sternest taste could be offended. Meanwhile another party of night-wanderers, attracted by our mirth, break in. More *Prosits* and clinked glasses follow ; and with a fair good-morning to our hostess, we retire.

It is too late to think of bed. "The quincunx of heaven," as Sir Thomas Browne phrased it on a dissimilar occasion, " runs low. . . . The huntsmen are up in America ;" and not in America only ; for the huntsmen, if there are any this night in Graubünden, have long been out upon the snow, and the stable lads are dragging the sledges from their sheds to carry down the mails to Landquart. We meet the porters from the various hotels, bringing letter-bags and luggage to the post. It is time to turn in and take a cup of black coffee against the rising sun.

IX

Some nights, even in Davos, are spent, even by an invalid, in bed. A leaflet, therefore, of " Sleep-chasings " may not inappropriately be flung, as envoy to so many wanderings on foot and sledge upon the winter snows.

The first is a confused medley of things familiar and things strange. I have been dreaming of far-away old German towns, with gabled houses deep in snow; dreaming of châlets in forgotten Alpine glens, where woodcutters come plunging into sleepy light from gloom, and sinking down beside the stove to shake the drift from their rough shoulders ; dreaming of vast veils of icicles upon the gaunt black rocks in places where no foot of man will pass, and where the snow is weaving eyebrows over the ledges of grey whirlwind-beaten precipices ; dreaming of Venice, forlorn beneath the windy drip of rain, the

Winter Nights at Davos

gas-lamps flickering on the swimming piazzetta, the barche idle, the gondolier wrapped in his threadbare cloak, alone ; dreaming of Appenines, with world-old cities, brown, above the brown sea of dead chestnut boughs ; dreaming of stormy tides, and watchers aloft in lighthouses when day is finished ; dreaming of dead men and women and dead children in the earth, far down beneath the snow-drifts, six feet deep. And then I lift my face, awaking, from my pillow ; the pallid moon is on the valley, and the room is filled with spectral light.

I sleep, and change my dreaming. This is a hospice on an unfrequented pass, between sad peaks, beside a little black lake, overdrifted with soft snow. I pass into the house-room, gliding silently. An old man and an old woman are nodding, bowed in deepest slumber, by the stove. A young man plays the zither on a table. He lifts his head, still modulating with his fingers on the strings. He looks right through me with wide anxious eyes. He does not see me, but sees Italy, I know, and some one wandering on a sandy shore.

I sleep, and change my dreaming. This is St. Stephen's Church in Wien. Inside, the lamps are burning dimly in the choir. There is fog in the aisles ; but through the sleepy air and over the red candles flies a wild soprano's voice, a boy's soul in its singing sent to heaven.

I sleep, and change my dreaming. From the mufflers in which his father, the mountebank, has wrapped the child, to carry him across the heath, a little tumbling-boy emerges in soiled tights. He is half asleep. His father scrapes the fiddle. The boy shortens his red belt, kisses his fingers to us, and ties himself into a knot among the glasses on the table.

I sleep, and change my dreaming. I am on the parapet

271

of a huge circular tower, hollow like a well, and pierced with windows at irregular intervals. The parapet is broad, and slabbed with red Verona marble. Around me are athletic men, all naked, in the strangest attitudes of studied rest, down-gazing, as I do, into the depths below. There comes a confused murmur of voices, and the tower is threaded and rethreaded with great cables. Up these there climb to us a crowd of young men, clinging to the ropes and flinging their bodies sideways on aerial trapezes. My heart trembles with keen joy and terror. For nowhere else could plastic forms be seen more beautiful, and nowhere else is peril more apparent. Leaning my chin upon the utmost verge, I wait. I watch one youth, who smiles and soars to me ; and when his face is almost touching mine, he speaks, but what he says I know not.

I sleep, and change my dreaming. The whole world rocks to its foundations. The mountain summits that I know are shaken. They bow their bristling crests. They are falling, falling on us, and the earth is riven. I wake in terror, shouting : INSOLITIS TREMUERUNT MOTIBUS ALPES ! An earthquake, slight but real, has stirred the ever-wakeful Vesta of the brain to this Virgilian quotation.

I sleep, and change my dreaming. Once more at night I sledge alone upon the Klosters road. It is the point where the woods close over it and moonlight may not pierce the boughs. There come shrill cries of many voices from behind, and rushings that pass by and vanish. Then on their sledges I behold the phantoms of the dead who died in Davos, longing for their homes ; and each flies past me, shrieking in the still cold air ; and phosphorescent like long meteors, the pageant turns the windings of the road below and disappears.

Winter Nights at Davos

I sleep, and change my dreaming. This is the top of some high mountain, where the crags are cruelly tortured and cast in enormous splinters on the ledges of cliffs grey with old-world ice. A ravine, opening at my feet, plunges down immeasurably to a dim and distant sea. Above me soars a precipice embossed with a gigantic ice-bound shape. As I gaze thereon I find the lineaments and limbs of a Titanic man chained and nailed to the rock. His beard has grown for centuries, and flowed this way and that, adown his breast and over to the stone on either side ; and the whole of him is covered with a greenish ice, ancient beyond the memory of man. "This is Prometheus," I whisper to myself, "and I am alone on Caucasus."   J. A. S.

AN EPILOGUE

As a final word for this book, which has dealt so much with snows and avalanches, it may be worth adding that, while the sheets are going through the press, we are enduring what may be termed the rigours of a mediæval winter. Thirteen feet of snow, measured by the gauge, are said to have fallen since the beginning of December. The inhabitants of the valley declare that nothing to equal it has been experienced since 1817, when Davos-Platz suffered great injuries from avalanches. The peril, indeed, has been so serious that the Feuer-Gewehr, or fire-brigade, placed itself at the disposal of the Landammann, in case of sudden wreckage by the descent of avalanches. He, accepting their offer, made a public announcement that all the able-bodied men and lads of the place should obey the orders of the staff in command. To those acquainted with the phlegmatic nature of the Swiss mountaineer, and his habitual calmness under dangers due to the climate, this fact carried a grave significance, and made us feel that the natives were preparing to face a serious peril. Fortunately, the vast accumulations of snow, which hang suspended over our heads, seem, at the date when I am writing, to be settling down, owing to the prevalence of a sharp frost, which binds, congeals, and forms a substantial crust of ice upon the surface.

An Epilogue

Up to the middle of December we had very little snow this year. An old peasant, however, remarked to me : " You will see that before New Year snow will fall, and it will go on snowing till May." His prediction has been partly justified. We have now at least seven feet of snow upon the valley. Where the wind has blown it into drifts the depth is, of course, enormous. In January a huge avalanche fell above Süss, on the Fluela road, burying a carter in Herr Hans Meisser's service. The man's body has not yet been discovered. Between the 2nd and the 9th of February it snowed almost incessantly, day and night, softly, without wind, at a comparatively high temperature. Consequently, incalculable masses of heavy wet snow accumulated on all the upper mountain-sides. The railway has been blocked for a week. The postal service and all traffic are carried on by the antique method of little one-horse open sledges ; and we do not know when the line will be opened again. All telegraphic communications ceased for two days. On Monday the 8th, between 11 and 12 A.M., a sharp storm-wind blew in gusts. This brought down several (of the so-called) Dust-Avalanches (Staub-Lawinen).[1] This name is given to the species which falls in midwinter, when the snow is loose and powdery, still capable of being lifted up and carried in the air, to distinguish it from the other kind of Ground-Avalanche (Grund-Lawine), which slides in spring along the surface of the hills, and through deeply cloven ravines. One fell above Davos-Dörfli, carrying away three hay-stables, and scattering the ruins over the post-road. The Villa Wieseli was blocked with beams and hay and débris of all sorts. In one of the stables were three cows, which

---

[1] See the third Essay above.

perished ; and a man, who was extricated alive. Another avalanche started upon the very top of the Hörnli. It detached the whole snow masses from the mountain-side, and hurled them into the valley. This immense stream of snow bifurcated at the ridge of Drusatcha. One half flowed down upon Laret, carrying hay-stables with it, and burying the post-road. The other half tore away the secular forests of the Seehorn, destroyed hundreds of trees, laid bare large spaces where flourishing woods had been, poured with all this weight of timber over the railway line, and ended at the lake. I walked up to the top of it the other day. It has the appearance of a glacier, furrowed, jagged, broken into stairs and ridges like an ice-fall. Everywhere the surface bristles with broken stems ; some of the trees are at least 300 years old, and fifteen to twenty feet in girth : cembras, spruce firs, and larches. Among them I recognised one giant, which had been carried from my own wood a thousand feet above the valley. It lay across the railway line, under some twenty feet of condensed snow-drift. A third avalanche fell from the Dörfliberg, poured through the Hell-Bach, crossed the post-road, and, spreading out upon the lake, broke in the ice, which is three feet thick now. This crossed a portion of meadow belonging to me at Meierhof. A fourth came down in the Dischma Thal, tearing away a wood of fine old trees, and utterly wrecking a stable in which there were ten cows with their owner. The man escaped, but only one cow was saved alive. Two days afterwards they found a little calf, still breathing, in the ruins, and an unfortunate ox, dead, but warm, who had wrenched off both his horns in mad efforts to save his life. I also went to see this avalanche, and found a peasant digging out his cottage. It was

An Epilogue

surrounded by accumulations of heavy snow and great broken trees. Yet, strange to say, the building remained intact. This was due to the fact that the blast of the avalanche, which is even more formidable than the snow, had taken a different line from that on which the homestead stood. The man told me that when the avalanche descended his mother was seated in the living-room, and saw the horrible thing advancing to overwhelm her. She could not move. In a few seconds both the windows of the room were enveloped in opaque snow-drifts. Left in the dark, the old woman found herself alive and safe, greatly to her own surprise. Beyond this place the Dischma Thal is blocked with two other deluges of avalanches, which crossed the stream, and devastated broad tracts of forest. At Clavadel, on the same occasion, another fell, destroying huts and cattle. Meanwhile the roads to Wiesen and Süss are choked. Upon the Fluela, all the folk who live at the Alpenrose, Tschuggen, the Hospiz, etc., have been for days imprisoned ; nothing is known of them, since the telegraph is broken. What has happened in the Züge can only be guessed, because it is impassable. When explorers venture into that awful gorge they will probably find that it is a howling wilderness of snow and wreckage. The simultaneous fall of these avalanches on Monday, February 9, illustrates one law which governs them. It was the play of fretful wind upon the ill-poised weight of snow suspended in high airy stations that dislodged the first ton or two. These drew down whole acres, and hurled the snow-torrents with a force that overcame resistance.

The temperature fell to zero through two days and nights succeeding these disasters. That froze the snow

Our Life in the Swiss Highlands

upon the heights, and saved Davos from a huge catastrophe. While I am now writing, however, the wind has again shifted to a stormy quarter, and it is snowing in gusts. The air is as thick with snow, torn up from the surface of the valley and poured upon it from above, as London air with fog.

J. A. S.

AM HOF, DAVOS-PLATZ,
February 13, 1892.

THE END